**Advance Praise for**

# We are Children of the Corn/ Somos Hija/o/xs del Maíz:

## Husks of Hope, Resistance, and Latina/o/x Educational Success

The development of critical consciousness has historically been a target of those who seek to sustain systems of oppression, with schools the primary contexts where what can be taught is met with disinformation and polarization. The ability of Latina/o/x students to contest marginalization serves as evidence of the power of educators who aim to develop critical consciousness and why *We are Children of the Corn/Somos Hija/o/xs del Maíz* is such an invaluable contribution to educators, school leaders, and community stakeholders—especially in our current moment.

*—Francesca A. López,*
*Jim and Georgia Thompson Distinguished Professor of Education,*
*at the University of Wisconsin, Madison,*
*in the Department of Educational Leadership and Policy Analysis*

This compelling volume is a powerful testament to the brilliance and resilience of Latina/o/x students navigating educational borderlands. As someone whose family migrated from Texas to Michigan to work in both the fields and the auto factories, *We are Children of the Corn/Somos Hija/o/xs del Maíz* resonates with me in a deeply personal way. Conchas, Acevedo, and DeAlba beautifully cultivate testimonios, theory, and praxis—offering an essential guide for anyone committed to justice, critical consciousness, and transformative education.

*—Julian Vasquez Heilig*
*Professor of Educational Leadership, Research,*
*and TechnologyWestern Michigan University*

*We are Children of the Corn/Somos Hija/o/xs del Maíz* is at the leading-edge of student success theory, practice, and philosophy—just what is needed during an unjust, even brutally inhuman time in the nation's educational arena. Readers learn that to overcome oppressive structures it is necessary to work not only with resistance, but also with action, healing and courageous, transformative frameworks. The authors draw from Conchas and Acevedo's groundbreaking *Framework of Atrevesada/o/xs Nepantleando* and reconnect educators to ancestral knowledge, Gloria Anzaldúa's visionary philosophy, and pedagogies of liberation to offer evidence-based practices to foster agency, critical consciousness and overall educational success for Latina/o/x students. These students are portrayed as children of the corn, a metaphor that reflects an Indigenous, maíz/corn-based philosophy that connects people to nature and their environment. For all who seek hope and possibility during the tumultuous assault on DEI, the time to read this book is NOW!

*—Laura I. Rendón, Professor Emerita, UTSA,*
*author of Sentipensante Pedagogy: Educating for Wholeness,*
*Social Justice and Liberation (2023, 2nd Edition)*

*We are Children of the Corn/Somos Hija/o/xs del Maíz* is a timely anthology that highlights the resiliencies of Latina/o/x and Chicana/o/x students and provides numerous examples of ways to help them thrive and succeed academically. This book contributes to and complicates the widely used phrase, 'They tried to bury us, but forgot we were seeds.' In utilizing the metaphor about *maíz, We are Children of the Corn/Somos Hija/o/xs del Maíz* reminds us that although seeds (Latina/o/x and Chicana/o/x students) are more than capable, they should not be forced to grow on their own and instead we need to carefully attend to them. Thus, Conchas, Acevedo, and DeAlba underscore the importance of planting, cultivating, and harvesting the seeds via our unwavering advocacy, support, and mentorship. It provides an important and necessary analysis of the many wonders that can be accomplished when there is intentional structural support available to Latina/o/x and Chicana/o/x students. *We are Children of the Corn/Somos Hija/o/xs del Maíz* is a useful tool for educators, educational leaders, community-based advocates, and researchers to critically reflect on their own educational approaches and practices by exposing us to the continued harsh realities of Latina/o/x and Chicana/o/x students as demonstrated in this book, but also by prompting us to recognize these interventions as inspiring and a call-to-action.

—Martín Alberto Gonzalez, Ph.D.,
Assistant Professor at Portland State University and award-winning of
*Why You Always so Political?: The Experiences and Resiliencies of Mexican/ Mexican American/Xicanx Students in Higher Education*

While grounded in ethnic studies, *We are Children of the Corn/Somos Hija/o/xs del Maíz* is deeply interdisciplinary and essential for any field committed to understanding, engaging with, and supporting Latino/a/x communities. The metaphor of maíz/corn and its husk powerfully conveys themes of community and nourishment: the maíz/corn represents Latino/a/x students and their communities, while the husks symbolize the protective systems that help them grow and thrive. I, once again, applaud Conchas, the coeditors, and the chapter authors for centering the lived experiences of Latina/o/x individuals across PreK–16 and out-of-school spaces, especially in a political climate where Latino/a/x communities are increasingly being erased, marginalized, and silenced. Bravo!

*—Cristóbal Salinas Jr., Ph.D.,*
*Professor, Florida Atlantic University's College of Education*
*and Editor in Chief of the Journal of Hispanic Higher Education*

# Ethnic Studies Revival

EDITED BY *Gilberto Q. Conchas and Mahmoud Suleiman*

The mission of the **Ethnic Studies Revival** series is to present volumes of current research and work focused on praxis and the effective implementation of critical ethnic studies educational experiences in diasporic communities of color and Indigenous communities while making connections between the local, national, and transnational settings. The book series seeks to provide an interdisciplinary intellectual space that inspires educators in schools and outside-of-schools to transform inequities based on race, ethnicity, nationality, gender, sexuality, ability, class, and the intersections among them, while advancing visions of social, political, economic justice, and decolonial understandings of the global world. In particular, the series amplifies transformative ethnic studies models that seek to affirm the intellectual, social, racial, ethnic, and cultural being of ALL diverse groups [such as, but not limited to Pan African Americans, Pan Asian Americans, Indigenous Americans, Latinas/o/xs, and Muslim Americans]. The book series draws attention to these groups' intersectional identities, histories, plights, and contributions and educators' dynamic roles in advancing efforts to pluralize the curriculum and instruction reflective of the diverse educational and social expectations of all learners in democratic schools and societies.

Repertoires of Racial Resistance:
Pedagogical Dreaming in Transborder Educational Spaces (2024)
*Edited by Miguel N. Abad and Gilberto Q. Conchas*

We are Children of the Corn/Somos Hija/o/xs del Maíz:
Husks of Hope, Resistance, and Latina/o/x Educational Success (2025)
*Edited by Gilberto Q. Conchas, Nancy Acevedo, and Victor DeAlba*

Transforming Education for Social Justice:
Empirical Insights from Leadership, Equity, and Research in Action (2025)
*Edited by Gilberto Q. Conchas, Mahmoud Suleiman, and Victor DeAlba*

Reclaiming Space (2026)

If you are interested in submitting a proposal for publication consideration, please send your prospectus (https://myersedpress.presswarehouse.com/publishers/stylus/myers/files/Prospectus%20Guidelines%20MEP%202023.pdf) to the series editors, Gilberto Q. Conchas (gqc5330@psu.edu) or Mahmoud Suleiman (msuleiman@csub.edu) along with your current CV.

# We are Children of the Corn/Somos Hija/o/xs del Maíz:

## Husks of Hope, Resistance, and Latina/o/x Educational Success

EDITED BY *Gilberto Q. Conchas, Nancy Acevedo, and Victor DeAlba*

Myers Education Press

*Gorham, Maine*

# Dedication

A toda/os la/os Hija/o/xs del maíz.
To all the children of the corn.
You are the pillars of hope, resistance, and success.

"Where I'm From"
August 21, 2019

**A Poem**
by Erica Grace Conchas† [July 30, 2021]

I am from a bike.
From handlebars that steer in multiple
directions and continuous tires.
I am from sunshine, warm, burning, blinding.
I am from daisies, used to build natural jewelry.

I am from tamale making and curly hair.
From Lupe and Celso Conchas.
I am from the hard-working and tenacious.
From immigrant parents and endless love.

I am from Always believe and Never forget.
I am from Ventura, tortillas and meat.
From the field workers that provided for
their family.
The devastating initiations of gang life.

A bundle of letters, pictures,
and pendants packed into a shoebox.
The physicality that reminds you when
you rode down the street called life.

Published by Myers Education Press, LLC
P.O. Box 424
Gorham, ME 04038



**Myers Education Press** is an academic publisher specializing in books, e-books, and digital content in the field of education. All of our books are subjected to a rigorous peer review process and produced in compliance with the standards of the Council on Library and Information Resources.

Library of Congress Cataloging-in-Publication Data available from Library of Congress.

13-digit ISBN 978-1-9755-0665-0 (paperback)
13-digit ISBN 978-1-9755-0666-7 (library networkable e-edition)
13-digit ISBN 978-1-9755-0667-4 (consumer e-edition)

Printed in the United States of America.

All first editions printed on acid-free paper that meets the American National Standards Institute Z39-48 standard.



*Cover design by Sophie Appel*

# Contents

SERIES FOREWORD

# Ethnic Studies Revival

In a world grappling with deep-rooted and persistent manifestations of systemic disparities, the need for insightful exploration and understanding of diverse experiences has never been more urgent (Conchas, 2024). This is particularly true in PreK-12 schools and higher education institutions whereby the wrath of extreme racism, nativism, xenophobia, sexism, classism, and homophobia in today's America is most palpable (Abad & Conchas, 2024; Conchas & Acevedo, 2020). The book you hold in your hands, *We are Children of the Corn/ Somos Hija/o/xs del Maíz: Husks of Hope, Resistance, and Latina/o/x Educational Success,* is not just a collection of chapters; it is a beacon of enlightenment, a testament to the power of knowledge in combating prejudice and fostering Latina/o/x inclusivity across the higher education pipeline.

Latina/o/x communities in the United States face significant barriers when attempting to reach the "American Dream." Education has been a means for Latina/o/x students to access power and pathways for social mobility. Despite this, Latina/o/x students have had to navigate challenging educational borderlands that are filled with racism and deficit-based stereotypes that are the residue of colonialism. In their award-winning book, *The Chicana/o/x Dream,* Conchas and Acevedo (2020) emphasized that colonialism functions to label Chicana/o/x students as *atravesada/os,* as transgressors, who are made to feel that they do not belong within these educational spaces. *The Chicana/o/x Dream* pulls from the individual perspectives and identities of first-generation Chicana/o/x college students, *atravesada/os,* who are impacted by racism, racist nativism, capitalism, and inequities in educational opportunities. Their *testimonios* show how these students enact *la facultad,* a critical consciousness, that helps them see and understand the marginalization that they face on a regular basis. Through the development and enactment of *la facultad,* they become *nepantlera/os* who actively tap into limited institutional resources, navigate the inequities that they confront, and build bridges for subsequent generations.

Conchas and Acevedo (2020) coined the critical consciousness process as the Framework of *Atravesada/o/s Nepantleando* (FAN), which acknowledges the resistance of Chicana/o/x students within the education borderlands to pave pathways for educational success for themselves and others. This groundbreaking and award-winning book has helped to highlight the hope and resistance, while reframing success for Chicana/o/x students in a rapidly changing U.S. society. A foundational element in the book includes Derrick Bell's notion of racial realism to account for the persistent racism present in U.S. society. As evidenced by the recent U.S. Supreme Court decisions, the pendulum continues to swing away from justice toward racism and other forms of inequality. *The Chicana/o/x Dream* has served as a tool for educators, educational leaders, and education researchers to operationalize their work in a way that actively intervenes in the systems that have contributed to the marginalization and oppression of all Chicana/o/x students.

*We are Children of the Corn/Somos Hija/o/xs del Maíz: Husks of Hope, Resistance, and Latina/o/x Educational Success,* builds on and is guided by *The Chicana/o/x Dream* within an era when affirmative action in higher education is outlawed, anti-immigrant state legislations persist, legislators ban critical race theory, and state leaders enact dehumanizing laws against LGBTQ+ populations. In *The Chicana/o/x Dream,* FAN was used to examine how first-generation Chicana/o/x college students understand their inequities and the steps they take to counter that marginalization in community college and other higher education spaces. While FAN continues to guide *We are Children of the Corn/Somos Hija/o/xs del Maíz: Husks of Hope, Resistance, and Latina/o/x Educational Success,* there is a need to expand the framework beyond Chicana/o/x college student identities and perspectives and explore how FAN plays out among all Latina/o/x youth and young adults in distinct spaces and the resources available within these spaces, despite the growing institutional roadblocks. There is also a need to include the experiences of students in diverse contexts, which includes not only Hispanic Serving Institutions but also Historically White Institutions and Historically Black Colleges and Universities. While *The Chicana/o/x Dream* was centered in California, this anthology centers the experiences of Latina/o/x students in states with diverse ties with coloniality and immigration generations, such as Nebraska, Florida, Georgia, and/or Puerto Rico.

The edited book skillfully builds upon the parent book in three fundamental ways: (1) examines the experiences of Latina/o/x youth and young adults (instead of just Chicana/o/x students), including mix-race Latina/o/x populations (Afro-Latina/o/x, Asian-Latina/o/x, and *Indigenous* American ancestry) and students who navigate different areas of intersectionality; (2) examines the resources within school spaces from Pre-K-12, community college, four-year colleges, and graduate school; (3) and examines resources within familial spaces and other out-of-school spaces. In so doing, *We are Children of the Corn/Somos Hija/o/xs del Maíz: Husks of Hope, Resistance, and Latina/o/x Educational Success* emphasizes specific case study efforts that foster college access, readiness, and completion for Latina/o/x students with the aim of also addressing the PreK-12 and higher education divide.

*We are Children of the Corn/Somos Hija/o/xs del Maíz: Husks of Hope, Resistance, and Latina/o/x Educational Success* contributes to existing scholarship and serves as a unique resource that can help educators, educational leaders, community-based advocates, and researchers recognize the role of resources and assets within school spaces, familial spaces, and institutional spaces that are often overlooked or underexplored. In addition, *We are Children of the Corn/Somos Hija/o/xs del Maíz: Husks of Hope, Resistance, and Latina/o/x Educational Success* examines how FAN is activated in higher education settings as well as out-of-school contexts. Considering that Latina/o/x students experience the feeling of being labeled as *atravesada/os* from the very start of their educational journeys, there is a need to expand into settings outside of higher education and to locate the specific resources that enable the activation of FAN to foster college access, readiness, and completion for Latina/o/x students.

*We are Children of the Corn/Somos Hija/o/xs del Maíz: Husks of Hope, Resistance, and Latina/o/x Educational Success* is a powerful collection of research-based case studies examining the pillars and resources of support—the "husks"—that nurture Latina/o/x students. These resources provide the students with the necessary "nutrients" for navigating their educational journey through the barriers and challenges of the education borderlands. The edited book aims to provide practitioners and researchers with research-based case studies of the role of schools, families, and communities in assisting Latina/o/x students to pursue and succeed in higher education institutions. The book passionately highlights the lived experiences of Latina/o/x across PreK-16 and out-of-school spaces and identifies the pillars that enable their hope, resistance, and educational success in the borderlands. This hopeful book is in line with the major tenets of the **Ethnic Studies Revival Series.**

The mission of the **Ethnic Studies Revival Series** is to present volumes of current research and work focused on praxis and the effective implementation of critical ethnic studies educational experiences in diasporic communities of color and Indigenous communities while making connections between the local, national, and transnational settings. The book series seeks to provide an interdisciplinary intellectual space that inspires educators in schools and outside-of-schools to transform inequities based on race, ethnicity, nationality, gender, sexuality, ability, class, and the intersections among them, while advancing visions of social, political, and economic justice, and decolonial understandings of the global world. In particular, the series amplifies transformative ethnic studies models that seek to affirm the intellectual, social, racial, ethnic, and cultural being of ALL diverse groups (such as, but not limited to Pan African Americans, Pan Asian Americans, Indigenous Americans, Latinas/os, Arab Americans, and Muslim Americans). The book series draws attention to these groups' intersectional identities, histories, plights, and contributions and educators' dynamic roles in advancing efforts to pluralize the curriculum and instruction reflective of the diverse educational and social expectations of all learners in democratic schools and societies.

The timeliness and underlying rationale for the **Ethnic Studies Revival Series** is based on the growing cycles of ignorance, intolerance, racism, nativism, xenophobia, sexism, islamophobia, and homophobia, and all forms of *phobiasims* in today's America that must be confronted through promoting inclusive and global perspectives to empower all students and their communities. The book series is rooted in the understanding that Ethnic Studies paradigms and epistemologies contribute to educators, students, and educational leaders' development of a critical consciousness and can also be utilized to contextualize and understand the experiences of students of color and other marginalized groups in the institutions of PreK-12 schooling and higher education. This series will provide a thoughtful and rigorous platform for social justice–oriented educators to acquire and grapple with the knowledge and skills, and empower themselves with the political will to cultivate the community cultural wealth of all participants in a global society—including, but not limited to, the diverse educational experiences of students of color, under-resourced students, language minority students, students with disabilities, immigrant students, and other minoritized populations, such as LGBTQ+ students.

Drawing from the rich legacies of scholars such as Noam Chomsky (2003), Paulo Freire (2000), and their "dangerous" epistemologies, this series endeavors to transcend the boundaries of traditional education by embracing a pedagogy of liberation—a praxis that intertwines critical reflection with transformative action. Chomsky's insights into linguistic and political analysis, Freire's pedagogy of the oppressed, and our approach on the ubiquity of wars and the importance of literacy intersect to underscore the urgency of multicultural education and cultural proficiency in confronting systemic injustices (Suleiman, 2024). We hope this series will serve as a poignant reminder of the interconnectedness of global phenomena and local realities. In a world marked by conflicts and violence, the pursuit of education becomes not only a means of personal empowerment but also a pathway to peace and understanding (Suleiman & Huber, 2022). By shedding light on the complex relationship between warfare, literacy, and cultural identity, we seek to recognize the profound impact of local and geopolitical forces on educational practices and to engage in critical, courageous, and, yes, dangerous dialogue aimed at fostering a culture of peace and cooperation.

At the heart of this endeavor lies the principle of praxis—an iterative process of emancipatory reflection and action that empowers individuals to become agents of change in their own lives and communities (Suleiman, 2024). This requires our serious engagement in courageous and dangerous discourse that is good and necessary. As we navigate the complexities of ethnic studies and multicultural education, we are called not only to interrogate existing systems of oppression but also to actively participate in the creation of more just and equitable alternatives (Conchas & Acevedo, 2020). Through the good danger of praxis, theory is not divorced from practice; rather, it serves as a catalyst for transformative action, informed by the lived experiences and aspirations of those most affected by injustice.

We recognize that landmark research in the field of multicultural education has provided compelling evidence of its efficacy in fostering academic achievement, promoting positive intergroup relations, and nurturing the development of critical consciousness among students. For example, studies by researchers such as James A. Banks and Cherry M. Banks (2019), Sonia Nieto (2008), Gloria Ladson-Billings (2022), and Geneva Gay (2010) have underscored the importance of integrating diverse perspectives and experiences into the curriculum to enhance students' cultural competence and promote social justice (see also Muhammad, 2020; López & Sleeter, 2023; Sleeter & Grant, 1991). As such, we intend to establish continuity in transformative actions across the educational spectrums and provide new lenses that amplify the core elements of universal human needs and expectations educators are drafted to champion regardless of their diversity.

Thus, central to the principles of the **Ethnic Studies Revival Series** is the recognition of the interconnectedness of race, identity, ethnicity, culture, and power. As such, this series endeavors to explore the intersecting dimensions of identity and inequality, offering nuanced insights into the complex dynamics of privilege and oppression that shape our social realities. By centering the voices and experiences of historically marginalized communities, the volumes in the series will illuminate the often-overlooked contributions and struggles that have shaped our collective history.

The inaugural volume, *Repertoires of Racial Resistance* (Abad & Conchas, 2024), explores the integral role of dreaming and imagination in pursuing educational justice in distinct transborder educational spaces. The illuminating case studies in this book highlight how youth and adults utilize Transformative Methodologies not only to generate knowledge, but also to empower communities, combat all forms of inequality, and promote social change. The timely volume specifically highlights how BIPOC young people leverage their imaginations as part of their efforts to advocate for justice in their communities, families, and schools. Repertoires demonstrates the importance for researchers and practitioners to leverage youth imagination and freedom dreams in creating culturally sustaining educational settings and promoting transformative youth leadership.

As you embark on this journey through the myriad cultures, histories, and struggles presented in the series volumes, we hope to inspire readers and expand their intellectual horizons to engage actively in the pursuit of social change and empowerment. Each insight gained, each perspective embraced, brings us closer to a world where diversity is celebrated, and all individuals are valued for their inherent worth. In the spirit of inclusivity and solidarity, we delve into this series with open minds and compassionate hearts, knowing that through our collective efforts, we can build a more equitable and harmonious society for generations to come.

The volumes in the series fundamentally demonstrate that the field of Ethnic Studies is not just an academic discipline but a clarion call to action—albeit dangerous but necessary. It challenges us to confront uncomfortable truths, to interrogate systems of power and privilege, and to amplify voices that have been marginalized for far too long. It is through this critical examination that we can begin to dismantle the structures of oppression and forge a path toward genuine equity and justice.

Gilberto Q. Conchas, State College, PA
& Mahmoud Suleiman, Bakersfield, CA

## References

Abad, M. N., & Conchas, G.Q. (2024). *Repertoires of racial resistance: Pedagogical dreaming in transborder educational spaces.* Myers Education Press.

Banks, J. A., & Banks, C. M. (2019). *Multicultural education: Issues and perspectives.* Wiley.

Chomsky, N. (2003). *Chomsky on democracy and education.* Routledge.

Conchas, G. Q. (2024). *The color of success 2.0: Race and transformative pathways for high-achieving urban youth.* Teachers College Press of Columbia University.

Conchas, G. Q., & Acevedo, N. (2020). *The Chicana/o/x dream: Hope, resistance, and educational success.* Harvard Education Press.

Freire, P. (2000). *Pedagogy of the oppressed.* Bloomsbury Academic.

Gay, G. (2010). *Culturally responsive teaching: Theory, research, and practice.* Teachers College Press.

Ladson-Bilings, G. (2022). *The Dreamkeepers: Successful teachers of African American children* (3rd ed.). Jossey-Bass.

López, F., & Sleeter, C. E. (2023). *Critical race theory and its critics: Implications for research and teaching.* Teachers College Press.

Muhammad, G. (2020). *Cultivating genius: An equity framework for culturally and historically responsive literacy.* Scholastic Incorporated.

Nieto, S. (2008). *Affirming diversity: The sociopolitical context of multicultural education.* Pearson.

Sleeter, C. E., & Grant, C. A. (1991). Race, class, gender, and disability in current textbooks. *Theory Into Practice*, *30*(1), 42–49.

Suleiman, M. (2024). The ubiquity of wars and the "good danger" of praxis. *Journal of Leadership, Equity and Research*, *10*(1), 1–3.

Suleiman, M., & Huber, T. (Eds.). (2022). *Beyond provincialism: Promoting global competencies in teacher and educator preparation.* Information Age Publishing.

## FOREWORD

As I write this foreword to *We are Children of the Corn/Somos Hija/o/xs del Maíz: Husks of Hope, Resistance, and Latina/o/x Educational Success,* I am reflecting on a recent visit I made to a large school district in Texas that had invited me to share research and strategies focused on student belonging with school leaders. Prior to my segment of the day, I heard the superintendent welcome the leaders back from winter break, referring to them as *familia*. He provided highlights of the wonderful visits he had experienced in some of the schools and classrooms earlier in the week before turning to a series of important updates he had to share.

The first was to remind leaders that they were nearing the anniversary of a storm that resulted in HVAC system failures that forced the closure of 30 schools—and they were presently bracing for another storm on the anniversary. Last year's closures resulted in frustration among families and an onslaught of negative media attention. The superintendent elaborated that many of the district systems are over 100 years old and rely on boilers that take a very long time to heat up buildings. He reminded school leaders that despite their preparation for inclement weather, there were far too many buildings to attend to with far too few technicians who could work on the systems. Just this week, two of their technicians had resigned. The district salaries simply cannot compete with the private sector. They had, however, hired eight new technicians, but they had experience in residential, not commercial, HVAC systems. This will be a huge learning curve for them, as they are bracing for another round of storms that could potentially shut down schools again. The superintendent then reminded the leaders that addressing the issues of all the systems in their schools will cost $353 million, but they are dealing with a deficit of $51 million. He elaborated that even though Texas has a $32 billion surplus, the governor had withheld additional funds to schools as a political tactic to force school vouchers. "We will have to raise funds through bonds," the superintendent expressed.

The tone of the welcome became even more stark with the superintendent sharing with the group that they would hear from a deputy superintendent about a new system they have implemented to keep all their students safe regarding soon-to-be implemented U.S. Immigration and Customs Enforcement (ICE) policies. Citing a headline in the *Washington Post,* "Deportation at Light Speed," the superintendent shared that if ICE shows up to any school demanding that the school provide students, the protocol was to immediately call the deputy superintendent and the Chief of Police, as well as the district attorney. The information that was shared included the role of Child Protective Services (CPS), the protocol for students who are unaccompanied minors, and other scenarios the district was familiar with.

I decided to begin this forward with the information I am still processing from my visit to the district because I experienced firsthand the information shared with those charged with caring for K-12 students—90% of whom are Latina/o/x. I had been a teacher and school counselor in the state of Texas nearly three decades ago and was struck by the horrors educators are facing today, largely due to political ideologies rooted in racism, xenophobia, and white supremacy. It was exceedingly clear to me that politicians aiming to starve public schools of funds are succeeding in making the spaces uninhabitable so that their goals of privatizing education can be met. This is against the backdrop of Governor Abbott's buoys lined with razor wire to harm those attempting to cross the Rio Grande. The cruelty is unfathomable. Against this backdrop, the chapters in *We are Children of the Corn/Somos Hija/o/xs del Maíz: Husks of Hope, Resistance, and Latina/o/x Educational Success* could not be more urgent.

The empirically-supported evidence highlighted in each of the chapters in *We are Children of the Corn/Somos Hija/o/xs del Maíz: Husks of Hope, Resistance, and Latina/o/x Educational Success* provides the very resource needed that can help leaders and educators, as well as researchers and others who aim to reduce the disparities in college access and success of marginalized youth. The "husks" that provide the protection and nourishment of Latina/o/x youth will be ever more important given the context we are facing, which by all accounts may become acutely more hostile. However, this timely anthology aims to provide readers with the needed evidence for praxis that protects and nurtures youth as they navigate often-hostile contexts. More importantly, the chapters all align with the call to promote Latina/o/x K-12 and higher education students to resist inequality and arm themselves with the critical consciousness necessary to foster college access, readiness, and completion.

In their award-winning book, *The Chicana/o/x Dream,* Conchas and Acevedo (2020) initially coined the hopeful and insightful critical consciousness process among students as the Framework of *Atravesada/o/s Nepantleando* (FAN). As the illuminating chapters in this book demonstrate, FAN is essential across the educational trajectory to ensure that Latina/o/x youth are keenly aware of the systems that operate to both support and disrupt opportunities and develop the needed knowledge and skills to transform the opportunities that exist. The development of critical consciousness has historically been a target of those who seek to sustain systems of oppression, with schools being the primary contexts where what can be taught is met with disinformation and polarization. The ability of Latina/o/x students to contest marginalization serves as evidence of the power of educators who aim to develop critical consciousness and why *We are Children of the Corn/Somos Hija/o/xs del Maíz: Husks of Hope, Resistance, and Latina/o/x Educational Success* is such an invaluable contribution to educators, school leaders, and community stakeholders—especially in our current moment.

Francesca A. López,
Jim and Georgia Thompson Distinguished Professor of Education, at the University of Wisconsin, Madison, in the Department of Educational Leadership and Policy Analysis

INTRODUCTION

# Husks of Hope, Resistance, and Latina/o/x Educational Success

*Gilberto Q. Conchas, Victor DeAlba, and Nancy Acevedo*

> *Maíz (corn) is like a human being; it cannot grow without human care and human beings cannot grow without maíz ... the corn is rich and beautiful because it is sweet and tender, akin to a child. It later converts into a cob; it is when the kernels become hard and are ready to separate from the trunk. It is the representation of a mature human being, ready to become independent and to understand his/her role on earth. Finally, when the kernels are removed from the cob, they are ready to eat or to once again be planted and thus continue the species. It is similar to the human being becoming independent, who can provide for him- or herself, ready to procreate, to continue the human race. That is the life of the maíz and the life of a human being.*
>
> —Roberto Cintli Rodríguez, 2014

## Introduction

WE CHOSE THE title *We are Children of the Corn/Somos Hija/o/xs del Maíz: Husks of Hope, Resistance, and Latina/o/x Educational Success* because *maíz* connects with various aspects of Latina/o/x identity and culture. While Latina/o/x culture is not homogenous, we consider that domesticated *maíz* began in Mexico and became a key ingredient for communities in Mexico, Central America,

South America, and the Caribbean (Edwards, 2019). *Maíz* can be representative of the connection that Latina/o/xs have with their Indigenous ancestors as well as Mother Earth herself. The quote above by Roberto Cintli Rodríguez (2014) helps us better understand the symbolism between *maíz* and human beings. One must visualize society as the earth or soil where the crop initially sprouts. The roots of the crop are representative of Indigenous ancestors and cultural traditions that have been passed on from generation to generation. The cornstalk represents the opportunity structures that allow for the corn husks to grow and thrive. School, familial, and community-based support systems represent the corn husks that protect and nurture the *maíz*. The *maíz* itself is representative of Latina/o/x students who are cultivated through this process that will then continue the cycle by supporting the next generation of students.

On each stalk of *maíz*, the husks encapsulate the *maíz* to protect it. These husks not only protect the *maíz* from varying environmental conditions, but they also help it obtain necessary nutrients—or resources—as it grows. Once the *maíz* can withstand its environmental conditions, the husks open up, thus allowing the *maíz* to flourish, mostly on its own. That *maíz* then feeds people and animals across the world. Additionally, using a process known as nixtamalization, which was created by Mesoamericans thousands of years ago, *maíz* is transformed into a source of nourishment that creates many traditional Latina/o/x dishes (Goodman & Galinat, 1988). Even the husks, once removed from the *maíz*, are often repurposed as fertilizer to provide support to other plants or used in various types of cuisine. Latina/o/x students are the *maíz* that are being nurtured by resources from school, familial, and community-based support systems (the husks) within opportunity structures (the stalks) as they transform into nepantlera/o/x by building bridges for subsequent generations to access educational opportuniites.

*Somos Las Hija/o/xs del Maíz/We Are Children of the Corn* is a collection of research-based studies that examine the pillars and resources of support—the "husks"—that nurture Latina/o/x students. These resources provide the students with the necessary "nutrients" to navigate their educational journey through the barriers and challenges of the education borderlands. The edited book provides practitioners and researchers with research-based case studies of the role of schools, families, and communities in assisting Latina/o/xs to pursue and succeed in higher education institutions. The book highlights the lived experiences of Latina/o/xs across PreK-16 and out-of-school spaces, while identifying the "husks" as the pillars and resources of support that enable their hope, resistance, and educational success in the borderlands.

## *Maíz*-Based Philosophy and Scholarship

Since its creation and because of its versatility, *maíz* has been at the center of many Indigenous teachings and culture. Much of the existing research in mainstream academia has focused on the biology of the plant and its role as one of the world's most impactful economic staples (Staller, 2010). Ethnographic research conducted over the last century has only recently started to acknowledge the role of *maíz* as a critical component of Indigenous culture. Garcia-Weyandt (2023) shared that, according to oral tradition, the first farmer received *maíz* from Mother Earth, but it came with a set of "instructions, protocols, and principles to follow Traditional Ecological Knowledge (TEK) or local understanding of the environment and the applicability of this knowledge in daily life" (p. 1–2). Since then, Indigenous families have embodied these practices to maintain and sustain a reciprocal relationship with *maíz*. Thus, Indigenous cultural knowledge and traditions relating to *maíz* have been passed down from generation to generation to balance the interaction between people and the environment (Garcia-Weyandt, 2023). Rodríguez (2019) referred to this as a *maíz*-based philosophy that has existed for centuries. Due to active efforts made by European colonizers to undermine and erase Indigenous knowledge and teachings, this philosophy has only recently begun to get the recognition it deserves in academia.

This philosophy became a central tenant in Mexican American Studies (MAS) that sought to reconnect students to Indigenous teachings. Using Tucson's MAS program as an example, Rodríguez (2017) shared:

> At the heart of Tucson's highly successful Mexican American Studies (MAS) department were several Indigenous philosophical concepts, including two Maya or maiz-based ones: In Lak' Ech—Tu eres mi otro yo—you are my other me; and Panche Be—Buscar la raiz de la verdad—To seek the root of the truth. (p. 126)

The MAS program in Tucson encountered contentious legal battles due to efforts by conservative lawmakers to ban it from being taught. Similar Ethnic Studies and Indigenous teachings across U.S. schools face significant pushback, which reflects the colonial mechanisms that continue to operate within the country's public education system. These Indigenous philosophical concepts and the remnants of colonization that they seek to counter are at the core of our anthology. The authors in this book continue to build on *maíz*-based philosophy and scholarship by honoring the traditions of our Indigenous ancestors and the work of the scholars that have amplified them.

## Building on *The Chicana/o/x Dream*

Chicana/o/x communities in the United States have faced significant barriers when attempting to reach the "American Dream." Education has been a means for Chicana/o/x students to access power and pathways for social mobility. Despite this, Chicana/o/x students have had to navigate challenging educational borderlands, which are filled with racism and deficit-based stereotypes that are the residue of colonialism. In the book *The Chicana/o/x Dream,* Conchas and Acevedo (2020) emphasized that colonialism functions to label Chicana/o/x students as *atravesada/o/xs,* as transgressors, who are made feel that they do not belong within these educational spaces.

*The Chicana/o/x Dream* pulls from the individual perspectives and identities of first-generation Chicana/o/x college students, *atravesada/o/xs,* who are impacted by racism, racist nativism, capitalism, and inequities in educational opportunities. Their *testimonios* show that these students enact *la facultad,* a critical consciousness, which helps them to see and understand the marginalization that they face regularly. Through the development and enactment of *la facultad,* they become *nepantlera/o/xs* who actively tap into limited institutional resources, navigate the inequities that they confront, and build bridges for subsequent generations.

In the book, Conchas and Acevedo (2020) coined this process as the Framework of *Atravesada/o/xs Nepantleando* (FAN), which acknowledges the resistance of Chicana/o/x students within the education borderlands to pave pathways for educational success for themselves and others. This groundbreaking and award-winning book has helped to highlight hope and resistance while reframing success for Chicana/o/x students in a rapidly changing U.S. society. A foundational element in the book is critical race theory in education (Solorzano, 1998), which includes Derrick Bell's (1991) notion of racial realism to account for the persistent racism present in U.S. society. As evidenced by recent U.S. Supreme Court decisions and the presidential executive orders, the pendulum continues to swing away from justice toward racism. *The Chicana/o/x Dream* has served as a tool for educators, educational leaders, and education researchers to operationalize their work in a way that actively intervenes in the systems that have contributed to the marginalization and oppression of all Chicana/o/x students.

*We are Children of the Corn/Somos Hija/o/xs del Maíz: Husks of Hope, Resistance, and Latina/o/x Educational Success*, builds on and is guided by *The Chicana/o/x Dream* within an era when affirmative action in higher education is outlawed, anti-immigrant state legislations persist, legislators ban critical race theory, and both the U.S. President and state leaders enact dehumanizing laws against LGBTQIA+ populations. In *The Chicana/o/x Dream*, FAN was used to examine how first-generation Chicana/o/x college students understand the inequalities they experience and the steps they take to counter that marginalization in community college and other higher education spaces. While FAN continues to guide *We are Children of the Corn/Somos Hija/o/xs del Maíz: Husks of Hope, Resistance, and Latina/o/x Educational Success*, there is a need to expand the framework beyond Chicana/o/x college student identities and perspectives; there is a need to explore how FAN plays out among all Latina/o/x youth and young adults in distinct spaces and the resources available within these spaces, despite the growing institutional roadblocks. There is also a need to include the experiences of students in diverse contexts, which includes not only Hispanic-Serving Institutions but also Historically White Institutions and Historically Black Colleges and Universities. While *The Chicana/o/x Dream* focused on California, we center the experiences of Latina/o/x, Afro-Latina/o/x, and Indigenous students with diverse ties to coloniality and immigration generations.

The edited book builds upon the parent book in three fundamental ways: (1) examines the experiences of Chicana/o/x and Latina/o/x youth and young adults who navigate different contexts of intersectionality; (2) examines the resources within school spaces from Pre-K-12, community college, 4-year colleges, and graduate school; and (3) examines resources within familial spaces and other out-of-school spaces. In so doing, the edited book highlights specific examples of efforts that foster college access, readiness, and completion for Chicana/o/x and Latina/o/x students with the aim of also addressing the PreK-12 and higher education divide.

Thus the anthology places FAN as the theoretical framework and speaks to how FAN is activated through resources in distinct spaces within schools, familial contexts, and community-based institutions. *We are Children of the Corn/Somos Hija/o/xs del Maíz: Husks of Hope, Resistance, and Latina/o/x Educational Success* contributes to existing scholarship, but it will also serve as a unique resource that can help educators, educational leaders, community-based educators, and researchers recognize the role of resources and assets within school spaces, familial spaces, and institutional spaces that are often overlooked or underexplored. In addition, *We are Children of the Corn/Somos Hija/o/xs del Maíz: Husks of Hope, Resistance, and Latina/o/x Educational Success* examines how FAN is activated in higher education settings as well as out-of-school contexts. Considering that Latina/o/x students experience the feeling of being labeled as *atravesada/o/xs* from the very start of their educational journeys, there is a need to expand into settings outside of higher education and to locate the specific resources that enable the activation of FAN to foster college access, readiness, and completion for Latina/o/x students.

## Framework of *Atravesada/o/xs Nepantleando*

FAN was built on an interdisciplinary foundation using Anzaldúan concepts (Anzaldúa, 1987) and Chicana feminist theories that sought to examine the experiences of Latina/o/x students (Conchas & Acevedo, 2020). Since the 1980s, the theories developed by Gloria E. Anzaldúa have had an impact on education research, especially as it relates to the experiences of historically marginalized students. Chicana feminist perspectives have also provided valuable insight to researchers as they develop and build on existing scholarship seeking to center the voices of communities of color.

*Nepantla* is a Nahuatl word representing the in-between space of multiple and overlapping worlds, which resembles the space of borderlands. Thus, when in *nepantla*, a *nepantlera/o/x* has the ability to see multiple cultures in their overlapping, complementing, or conflicting relationships. *Nepantlera/o/xs* are susceptible to wounds, including isolation and rejection from their conflicting worlds. Nevertheless, a *nepantlera*/o/x aims to transform perspectives and possibilities. In being able to see multiple perspectives and identify with multiple cultures, *nepantlera/o/xs* also aim to build bridges between these worlds.

FAN provides a lens for examining the intersecting identities that allow students to see the colonial mechanisms and intersecting systems of power that reproduce marginalization. The framework accounts for students critiquing such institutional processes as they navigate their educational journeys. By recognizing these inequities and actively working to intervene on these systems, Latina/o/x students enact *la facultad*. In other words, *la facultad* informs the development of a student's critical consciousness. Once students enact *la facultad*, they go from the label of *atravesada/o/xs* to navigating the education system as *nepantlera/o/xs*. This does not occur in an isolated vacuum; students in these structures have access to at least one individual who brokers institutional resources and power. In this process, *la facultad* facilitates the transformation of the hope maintained as *atravesada/o/xs* to resist as *nepantlera/o/xs* and successfully navigate systems of higher education by accessing institutional resources. Nevertheless, the transition is not permanent and individuals can continue to navigate both as *atravesada/o/xs* and *nepantlera/o/xs*.

With the development of FAN, Conchas and Acevedo (2020) aimed to counter traditional education theories and frameworks that contributed to the academic apartheid of knowledge. The apartheid of knowledge includes academic research that centers Eurocentric methodologies and pedagogies while contributing to inequity by excluding those of Black, Indigenous, People of Color (Delgado Bernal & Villalpando, 2002; Pérez Huber, 2009, as cited in DeAlba, 2023). Additionally, due to the intersectional nature of Latina/o/x students navigating systems of intersectionality (Crenshaw, 1989), critical race theory provides an epistemological lens through which FAN operates to acknowledge the racialized inequalities in the schooling system that are colonial, racist, intentional, and ever-present.

With FAN, Conchas and Acevedo (2020) applied coloniality, deservingness, and borderlands to contextualize the schooling experiences of Latina/o/x students and to account for the colonial mechanisms that persist within the

U.S. schooling system. The mechanisms rooted in San Miguel's (1999) conceptualization of coloniality include the majority white teacher workforce in U.S. public schools, the absence of bilingual or dual-language education, a Eurocentric curriculum, and the continual *de facto* racial segregation of schools. Existing textbooks and school curricula in U.S. schools fail to acknowledge these mechanisms and often exclude the true and documented history of Latina/o/xs and the root of their current schooling conditions. Conchas and Acevedo (2020) developed FAN in a manner that asks scholars and practitioners to reflect on their approaches and self-assess what necessary changes are needed to avoid engaging in the marginalization of Latina/o/x students.

As such, this anthology is guided by the Framework of *Atravesados Nepantleando* to highlight the continued resistance efforts of Latina/o/xs as they access limited institutional opportunities and build bridges for themselves, their communities, and others within higher education. The authors in this book build on those theories, concepts, and frameworks to shine a light on the experiences and amplify the voices of Latina/o/x students across the United States.

## The Husks that Nurture Access, Readiness, and Completion Around Three Themes

This book is organized around three questions related to three themes that underscore the importance of planting, cultivating, and harvesting the seeds for Chicana/o/x and Latina/o/x students to succeed throughout their entire educational journeys. The questions we seek to engage within each theme are:

1. How and why do college access efforts plant the seeds to overcome educational inequality and foster college access?
2. How and why do college readiness policies, practices, and initiatives cultivate and support the academic and metacognitive development of Latina/o/x students?
3. How can schools, families, and communities be leveraged to Latina/o/x students in achieving college completion and preparing for postgraduation success?

From college *access* to *readiness* to *completion* the aforementioned questions guide these themes to capture the impact of community, mentorship, and targeted support programs. Through these three themes, we illuminate college access, readiness, and completion present along the educational journeys of Latina/o/x students.

### Theme 1: *Planting the Seeds to Foster College Access: Pillars and Resources of Support that Nurture College Preparation*

The first theme focuses on the importance of fostering college *access* efforts that both prepare students academically for higher education and to make informed postsecondary decisions. Within this theme, authors use qualitative research methods to uncover the challenges faced by Latina/o/x students as they navigated their educational journeys. The examples in this section include the utilization of reflections from undocumented students to shine light on their experiences in public high schools as they prepare for higher education, the impact of a Grow-Your-Own (GYO) teacher pipeline program on students' ability to recognize inequities and become active agents of change, and the approaches used to amplify students' pedagogies of the home by bridging the classroom space to its surrounding community wealth. Within this section, we're able to capture the experiences and perspectives of Latina/o/x students as they access and seek opportunities in college preparation programs.

### Theme 2: *Cultivating to Foster College Readiness: Pillars and Resources of Support that Nurture Student Development and College Navigation*

The second theme encompasses the critical nature of fostering college *readiness* programs, which emphasize the academic and metacognitive skills that prepare students to navigate postsecondary education. The examples within this include the use of *testimonios* to highlight the way students describe both their positive and negative experiences in Science, Technology, Engineering, and Mathematics (STEM). Additionally, within this section, there are insights derived from a pedagogical *testimonio* that recount the experiences of students participating in a summer bridge program. Lastly, this theme includes an examination of the implementation of California Assembly Bill 705 as it relates to equitable outcomes for Latina/o/x students in community college. In this section, we get a glimpse of the programs, initiatives, and legislation that cultivate, support, and nurture college readiness for Latina/o/x students across the United States.

**Theme 3: *Harvesting for College Completion: Nurturing Students for Post-Graduation to Plant Future Seeds***

In the third theme, the focus is on the resources that foster college *completion* in college and outside of college that prepare students for postgraduation decisions. The examples within this theme include the use of an asset-based lens to emphasize the importance of schools, families, and communities in assisting Chicana/o/xs to pursue the Chicana/o/x Dream. In addition, this section showcases the utilization of *platicas* methodology to highlight the experiences and challenges faced by Chicana/Latina graduate students as they navigate through McNair undergraduate research programs (URPs). Lastly, within this theme are the examples of Chicana/o/xs and Latina/o/xs who are thriving and the institutional practices, processes, and commitments that facilitate their success through Academic *Familias*. This section emphasizes the need for institutional resources to build on the strengths of Latina/o/x students and contribute to building the next generation of scholars and leaders.

## Organization of the Anthology

The book includes an Introduction, three sections with three chapters in each section, and a Conclusion. This edited anthology builds on the parent book, *The Chicana/o/x Dream*, but also emphasizes specific case study efforts around three main areas that foster college access, readiness, and completion for Latina/o/x students inside of school and outside of school settings. The cutting-edge examples in this book showcase the learning spaces (formal or informal) that support Latina/o/x young peoples' college access, readiness, and completion. Thus, the volume is divided into the following three sections.

Section 1, *Planting the Seeds to Foster College Access: Pillars and Resources of Support that Nurture College Preparation*, includes chapters that focus on the experiences of Latina/o/x students prior to arriving in higher education and the opportunities created that allowed them to gain greater access. In Chapter 1, Eduardo Mosqueda and Raul Meneses Samperio draw from a larger qualitative research project to examine the persistent challenges faced by undocumented Chicana/o/x and Latina/o/x students while they were in high school. Using a narrative inquiry approach, the authors conducted semi-structured interviews with four participants to capture the reflections of these students as they navigated varying geographical spaces. Mosqueda and Samperio highlight how participants described instances of marginalization that directly hindered their sense of belonging, as well as how they straddled liminal spaces to carve out spaces to belong. This chapter brings to light the myriad of challenges that undocumented students face while enrolled in public high schools before they matriculate in college.

In Chapter 2, Omar Davila Jr., Thalia Rodriguez, Mikaela Dacanay, Brianna Roberto, Donna Garcia, and Aaron Rivas examine the experiences of four Latina/o/x youth—three primarily of Mexican descent and one of Mexican and Salvadoran descent—taking part in a GYO teacher pipeline program for high school students. The qualitative study highlighted in this chapter was a collaborative effort among current and future educators at multiple levels—professorial, undergraduate, and high school. The focus of the study had a threefold purpose: (1) examine how Latina/o/x youth might become active agents, as opposed to passive recipients, in the production of knowledge; (2) examine how Latina/o/x youth make sense of and present solutions to educational inequality; and (3) examine how teacher pipeline programs might better prepare Latina/o/x youth to become transformative educators. This chapter aims to provide insight to a broad readership, including scholars in the fields of teacher preparation, urban education, ethnic studies, and sociology of education.

In Chapter 3, Jacey de la Torre offers insights from an investigation of students' pedagogies of the home during their teacher education program at UC Berkeley. de la Torre contends that students' plural affinities and identities must be honored by similarly plural modes of classroom teaching. Their stance ushers in a pedagogy that is "porous," or that affirms the role of the relationship between the classroom and the geopolitical context of the local community. de la Torre emphasizes that students' senses of self are in an ongoing state of becoming and that classrooms provide a generative space to impart tools for navigating students' many transformational processes of identity-and world-making. In this chapter, de la Torre details the methods used to amplify students' home pedagogies by bridging the classroom space to its surrounding community wealth (Yosso, 2005) of knowledge and cultural production. These methods attempt to honor the students' unique positions within the Framework of *Atravesada/o/xs Nepantleando*, as primarily Latina/o/x, Afro-Latina/o/x, and Indigenous Mayan children in K-12 American education. Such consideration may be a conduit for students' articulation of their freedom dreams (Kelley, 2002) for themselves and their communities.

Section 2, *Cultivating to Foster College Readiness: Pillars and Resources of Support that Nurture Student Development and College Navigation*, includes chapters that examine the role of college *readiness* programs that prepare students to navigate postsecondary education. In Chapter 4, Brianna R. Ramirez shares data from a qualitative study conducted with 24 Chicana/o/x and Latina/o/x students who participated in a summer bridge program. Braiding together the student interview data and insight from a pedagogical *testimonio*, the author makes visible curricular strands that activated student *facultad*. Additionally, this chapter highlights how the curriculum in the summer bridge program served to support student preparation for navigating institutionalized racism and the marginalities they experienced as *atravesada/o/xs* in higher education. The author also underscores the importance of the summer bridge curriculum centering on racial and intersectional justice to strengthen Latina/o/x student *facultad* as students begin their journey of *nepantleando*.

In Chapter 5, Luis Andrade draws from *testimonios* of 14 undocumented Chicana/o/x, Salvadoran, Guatemalan, and Zapotec students majoring in distinct STEM fields at a community college to understand their experiences during the COVID-19 pandemic. In this chapter, the author describes the students' ambivalent experiences as they inhabited states as *atravesada/o/s nepantleando* in STEM. These student's *testimonios* highlight both the positive and negative descriptions of their experiences in STEM. The chapter ends with practical recommendations for higher education leadership to cultivate college readiness and better address their needs during the pandemic and beyond.

In Chapter 6, Audrey Baca Lopez and Victor DeAlba examine the implications of implementing California Assembly Bill 705 as it relates to equitable outcomes for Chicana/o/x and Latina/o/x students. With the research site being a Hispanic-Serving Community College with a majority Latina/o/x student population, the study sought to understand the process of implementing A.B. 705 from the perspectives of those who were tasked with making changes. The data from this chapter were derived from semi-structured interviews with 11 participants and document collection and analysis. The findings elucidate three primary themes: institutional commitment to equity and access, removing institutional barriers as a form of student empowerment, and enacting *la facultad* to navigate threats to equitable outcomes. The themes highlight the transformative changes made to improve college readiness, equity, and access in response to the A.B. 705 legislation. The findings in this chapter also expose underlying problems of practice that persist in higher education, such as implicit biases and race-neutral and color-evasive approaches to understanding equity.

Section 3, *Harvesting for College Completion: Nurturing Students for Postgraduation to Plant Future Seeds,* includes chapters that focus on resources in college and outside of college that prepare students for college *completion.* In Chapter 7, Gilberto Q. Conchas and Victor DeAlba use an asset-based lens to emphasize the importance of schools, families, and communities in assisting Chicana/o/xs to pursue the Chicana/o/x Dream and to counter longstanding deficit-based perspectives and systems of oppression within the education borderlands. The authors introduce the chapter with an overview of the historical experiences faced by Chicana/o/x students who have been repeatedly banned and often excluded from mainstream curriculum in U.S. schools. Conchas and DeAlba use interview data and *testimonios* from Chicana/o/x students to center their voices and amplify the unique perspective they have for helping educational researchers, policymakers, and practitioners to transform the U.S. schooling system.

In Chapter 8, Arlene Cano-Matute, Alexis Meza, Elizabeth Claassen Thrush, and Louie F. Rodriguez share a story of Chicana/o/xs and Latina/o/xs who are thriving and the institutional practices, processes, and commitments that facilitate their success. The authors argue that the success of Chicana/o/xs and Latina/o/xs in higher education is a harvest realized with a collection of institutional agents, culturally-validating practices and structures, and intentionally to created university pathways that foster Academic *Familias*. Cano-Matute and colleagues explain that this harvest is based on a history of nurturing Academic *Familias* at that particular institution and community over the last few decades. Drawing on this history, the authors focus on the voices and experiences of recent academically successful Chicana/o/x and Latina/o/x students. The chapter emphasizes that Hispanic Serving Institutions have the potential to harvest college completion through Academic *Familias*.

In Chapter 9, Samantha Prado Robledo uses a *platicas* methodology to highlight the experiences and challenges faced by Chicana and Latina graduate students as they navigate through McNair URPs. The author shares that because Chicana/Latina students are made to feel that they do not belong in educational spaces, this chapter examines how two graduate students overcame limited institutional resources and built bridges for subsequent generations navigating as *nepantleras* in URPs to nurture postgraduate decisions. The authors underscore listening to student voices on each campus as a way to illuminate the people, practices, and structures that exist or may exist in the future. Prado Robledo also emphasizes the importance of utilizing multiple tools, such as qualitative data collection, mapping, and art to help campuses envision the next steps for nurturing *nepantleando en la universidad*.

In Chapter 10, Nancy Acevedo, Gilberto Q. Conchas, and Victor DeAlba reiterate the important and symbolic nature of *maíz* as a central tenant of Latina/o/x culture and identity. This chapter emphasizes the impact of fostering college pathways for Latina/o/x students by providing examples from the anthology. The authors provide recommendations for scholars, educators, and educational leaders to consider when creating opportunities for Latina/o/x students. Lastly, Acevedo, Conchas, and DeAlba conclude with critical reflections to build on this scholarship.

## Hope, Resistance, and Educational Success

The research-based studies in this book explore the transformative systems of support that seek to nurture college aspirations and promote college completion for Latina/o/x students. Grounded in critical race theory and guided by the Framework of *Atravesada/o/xs Nepantleando*, these examples highlight the impact of transformative approaches for understanding and intervening on the underlying causes of inequitable and oppressive schooling systems. The students, community members, and educators highlighted within this book demonstrate the importance of the in-school and out-of-school resources necessary to break down existing barriers and support the ongoing struggle for equity. Throughout the chapters, we emphasize our commitment to promote social justice within the U.S schooling system and equip Latina/o/x students with the necessary tools for navigating their experiences.

This timely anthology provides a close look at the transformative and Indigenous-centered approaches utilized by scholars who are working to amplify existing research in a way that centers the experiences of Latina/o/x students at all levels of the U.S. educational system. Student voice and experience are a core part of this book as their perspectives provide valuable insights to scholars and practitioners. Each chapter emphasizes the critical nature of fostering college access, readiness, and completion.

As explained by Roberto Cintli Rodríguez (2014) in the introductory quote, the symbolism of *maíz* has a fundamental link to the human experience. The book, therefore, utilizes Indigenous knowledge and teachings to understand the experiences of Latina/o/x students throughout their educational journeys. The symbolic nature of *maíz* and their husks allows us to examine hope, resistance, and success in a way that honors and amplifies the epistemologies passed down by our ancestors, families, and communities. The authors within this volume provide insights and tools that will provide students and their adult allies with growth opportunities in their personal and professional endeavors.

## References

Anzaldúa, G., E. (1987). *Borderlands/La frontera: The new mestiza* (2nd ed). Aunt Lute Books.

Bell, D. (1991). Racial realism. *Connecticut Law Review, 24*, 363.

Bernal, D. D., & Villalpando, O. (2002). An apartheid of knowledge in academia: The struggle over the "legitimate" knowledge of faculty of color. *Equity & Excellence in Education, 35*(2), 169-180.

Conchas, G. Q., & Acevedo, N. (2020). *The Chicana/o/x dream: Hope, resistance, and educational success.* Harvard Education Press.

Crenshaw, K., (1989). Demarginalizing the intersection of race and sex: A Black feminist critique of antidiscrimination doctrine. *University of Chicago Legal Forum, 1989*, 139–168.

DeAlba, V. (2023). *Amplifying Latina/o/x student voice through critical pedagogy.* [Unpublished doctoral dissertation proposal]. Pennsylvania State University.

Delgado Bernal, D., & Villalpando, O. (2002). An apartheid of knowledge in academia: The struggle over the "legitimate" knowledge of faculty of color. *Equity & Excellence in Education, 35*(2), 169-180.

Edwards, D. (2019). The surprising history of maize. *Bright Maize. https://www.brightmaize.com/surprsing-history-maize/#:~:text=Domesticated%20maize%20initially%20spread%20south,South%20America%20and%20the%20Caribbean*

Garcia-Weyandt, C. (2023). Teachings of Tatéi Niwetsika: Native Maize from Northern Mexico. In P. Kaushik (Ed.), *New prospects of Maize.* IntechOpen.

Goodman, M. M., & Galinat, W. C. (1988). The history and evolution of maize. *Critical Reviews in Plant Sciences, 7*(3), 197–220.

Kelley, R. D. (2002). Beyond the "real" world, or why Black radicals need to wake up and start dreaming. *Souls, 4*(2), 51-64.

Rodríguez, R. (2017). Ixiim: A Maiz-based philosophy. *Journal of Latinos and Education.* DOI: 10.1080/15348431.2017.1373649.

Rodríguez, R. (2019). Ixiim: A Maiz-based philosophy. *Journal of Latinos and Education.*

Rodríguez, R. C. (2014). *Our sacred maíz is our mother: Indigeneity and belonging in the Americas.* University of Arizona Press.

San Miguel, G. (1999). The Schooling of Mexicanos in the Southwest, 1848–1891. In J.F. Moreno (Ed.), *The elusive quest for equality: 150 years of Chicano/Chicana Education* (pp. 31–51). Harvard Education Press.

Solórzano, D. G. (1998). Critical race theory, race and gender microaggressions, and the experience of Chicana and Chicano scholars. *International Journal of Qualitative Studies in Education, 11*(1), 121-136.

Staller, J. E. (2010). *Maize cobs and cultures: History of Zea mays L.* Springer.

Yosso, T. J. (2005). Whose culture has capital? A critical race theory discussion of community cultural wealth. *Race ethnicity and education, 8*(1), 69-91.

CHAPTER 1

# Undocumented Latina/o/x Students Straddling High School Borderlands:

## Nepantleando, A Sense of Belonging

*Eduardo Mosqueda and Raul Meneses Samperio*

> When Trump was president, I was kind of like, what if I don't even stay here and I gotta go to Mexico? I felt like everything that I'm doing here was for nothing, right? Because I have to start over with everything, like building relationships [and] classes. Yeah, that was a big possibility for me. I genuinely thought, that's probably gonna happen one day. ICE is probably gonna bust through the door, and we're gonna have to leave.
>
> —Isabel, Narrative Interview

## Introduction

THE QUOTE ABOVE was from an interview with Isabel, an undocumented college student, whose family migrated to the United States from Mexico when she was only 2 years old. For Isabel, and other students in similar situations, the election of former president Donald Trump in 2016 intensified what has become known as the *Trump Effect,* or a heightened sense of fear and uncertainty brought forth by an increase in anti-immigrant sentiment and consequences that have harmed and criminalized undocumented migrants (Southern Poverty Law Center, 2017). The *Trump Effect* has been linked to increased deportations for undocumented people, a push to expand the development of a wall on the border with Mexico, a reversal of the policy of Advanced Parole for Deferred Action for Childhood Arrivals (DACA) recipients, as well as numerous attempts to repeal the DACA program altogether. Trump's amplification of nativist ideology and policies that were also promoted by the rest of the administration have served to deeply marginalize undocumented students. As students attempt to make sense of the reemergence of racist discourses and ideologies that are alienating them, their perspectives reflect feeling unprotected by the schools they attend.

Although the landmark U.S. Supreme Court decision, *Plyler v. Doe, 457 U.S. 202 (1982)*, secures the educational rights for undocumented children to access a free public education, the safety and protections offered by this mandate have been elusive. For instance, a survey of teachers found that undocumented students suffered an increase in anxiety related to the negative school climate that the *Trump Effect* has intensified (Southern Poverty Law Center, 2017). These anxieties are clearly emphasized in the epigraph above. In fact, Isabel's narrative clearly points to Donald Trump's anti-immigrant discourse and policies as the source of her fear and anxiety about the possibility of being deported by Immigration and Customs Enforcement (ICE), even though she has grown up most of her life in the United States. The sociopolitical messaging during the Trump administration seems to be a stark reminder for undocumented students of the looming specter of undocumented Latina/o/x students' deportability, which is a source of fear and worry for students with this status (De Genova, 2013; Ee & Gándara, 2020; Jefferies, 2014; Negrón-Gonzales, 2014).

Even prior to the reelection of Trump, the immigration political climate had not changed significantly. Presently, there continues to be a crisis at the U.S.-Mexico border owing to the inhumane treatment of migrant youth and the continued practice of family separation (Rodriguez, 2020). Additionally, the COVID-19 pandemic which deepened preexisting educational inequities (Gee et al., 2023), coupled with heightened racial unrest across the United States, have further exacerbated challenges faced by marginalized communities in general, and undocumented youth in particular. This multifaceted context underscores the urgency of understanding how undocumented Latina/o/x students navigate and seek out a sense of belonging within the educational borderlands, which are defined as "the nexus of deficit and marginalizing practices, policies, and ideologies present in the education system" (Conchas & Acevedo, 2020, p. 23). Understanding how undocumented immigrants, as *hija/o/xs del maiz* (children of the corn), navigate and seek out a sense of belonging in schools can help illuminate the pillars and resources of support that can help improve their chances of successfully navigating and completing secondary education, ultimately placing them on a pathway toward higher education. This study is guided by the following three research questions:

1. How do undocumented Latina/o/x students navigate educational borderlands?
2. How do undocumented Latina/o/x students talk about the challenges and opportunities they encounter in the educational borderlands?
3. What do undocumented Latina/o/x student experiences teach us about seeking a sense of alienation and belonging?

To answer these research questions, this chapter closely examines how Latina/o/x high school immigrant youth straddling educational borderlands navigate liminal spaces to carve out places to belong. The narratives shared by participants center on feelings of marginalization in school related to their undocumented status, their placement in English Language Development (ELD) courses, and being singled out because of their emergent levels of English proficiency. We examine the possibilities of finding ways to improve relationships between school personnel and undocumented youth to foster a sense of belonging. In addition, we consider the role of multilingualism and discuss the possibility of establishing translanguaging practices within the school that respect and value the full repertoire of linguistic skills, knowledge, and practices that students bring (García & Wei, 2014), in order to avoid the marginalization of immigrant students that often arises as a result of the stigma related to emergent English-speaking skills.

## Conceptual Framework

This chapter adapts the Framework of *Atravesada/o/x Nepantleando* (FAN), which acknowledges the structural challenges (racism, racist nativism, discrimination, and inequities in educational opportunities) and allows students to critique educational processes that reproduce marginalization (Conchas & Acevedo, 2020). As a borderlands framework, FAN provides a lens for understanding how both physical and symbolic boundaries between groups that are hierarchically organized can "affect the material conditions, sociopolitical realities, and hybrid identities of those at the bottom of the hierarchies" (Delgado Bernal et al., 2009, p. 565). Thus, FAN allows us to examine the positioning of undocumented Latina/o/x students as *atravesada/o/x* or transgressors, who are often relegated to low social status positions and consistently reminded that they do not belong within the United States as noncitizens nor within educational spaces that are supposed to educate and protect them.

We use FAN to illuminate how undocumented Latina/o/x students use *la facultad* (a sixth sense of awareness that allows individuals to recognize structures below surfaces) to navigate the educational system as *nepantlera/o/xs. Nepantlera/o/xs* are able to navigate conflicting worlds in order to transform perspectives and possibilities and successfully straddle the multiple and colliding cultures and liminal spaces in educational institutions (Conchas & Acevedo, 2020). In so doing, we examine how undocumented youth successfully navigate spaces of exclusion and inclusion by using the cultural resources at their disposal to rewrite the rules that attempt to deny their experiences and marginalize them. FAN provides a window into the school spaces that often exclude rather than embrace undocumented Latina/o/x students and therefore compels us to reexamine the role of school personnel, such as school administrators, teachers, and counselors, in affording students' spaces and opportunities that include undocumented Latina/o/x youth. Having access to such spaces and opportunities can provide undocumented students with pillars and resources of support, which include the necessary "nutrients" for successfully navigating educational spaces to achieve school success in high school as well as prepare them for a productive college experience.

## Literature Review

### *Undocumented Latina/o/x Students in Secondary Schools*

This chapter focuses on critical themes that contribute to our understanding of the experiences of undocumented Latina/o/x secondary school students. First, we highlight prevailing challenges in the literature: academic, emotional, social, and political. Next, we review the literature on undocumented students' agency and resistance. Lastly, we examine the literature on belonging for undocumented Latina/o/x immigrant students.

### *Challenges: Academic, Emotional, and SocioPolitical*

Researchers have examined the ways that undocumented status impacts students' academic experiences. For instance, in a study of educator responses on a survey of more than 3600 participants, Ee and Gándara (2020) found that educators reported declining academic performance from undocumented students amidst contentious anti-immigrant contexts. Norrid-Lacey and Spencer (2000) reported that the graduation rate for Latina/o/x immigrants was low compared to other groups. These academic challenges are just some of the many academic obstacles that undocumented students face in schools.

Scholars have also pointed out the ways undocumented status impacts students' emotional and psychological well-being. Torres and Wicks-Asbun (2014) found that undocumented students experienced "great anxiety, frustration, sadness, and fear regarding their higher education prospects" (p. 200). Similarly, Castro-Salazar and Bagley (2010) found that undocumented students from Mexico experienced feelings of anxiety and depression due to their undocumented status. Other research has reported that undocumented students are in constant fear of deportation (Jefferies, 2014; Negrón-Gonzales, 2014). Similarly, Ee and Gándara (2020) reported that 85% of their respondents expressed fear due to harsh immigration policy context.

The literature on undocumented Latina/o/x youth has also examined their sociopolitical challenges. First, undocumented Latina/o/x students felt stymied by the reality of their limited social mobility prospects (Abrego 2006; Gonzales et al., 2015). Despite legislation that protects undocumented students' access to K-12 schools, such students felt blocked as they started thinking about their post-high school future (Gonzales, 2011; Lara & Nava, 2018). Additionally, Torres and Wicks-Asbun (2014) found that once undocumented students realized that a high school diploma did not guarantee upward mobility, they felt the need to drop out. Moreover, Gleeson and Gonzales (2012) found that young undocumented students are socialized into an ideology of meritocracy that can lead to a very complex relationship with their undocumented status. When undocumented youth arrive in the United States at an early age and attend school, they share similar experiences with their U.S.-born peers. However, once they graduate from high school, their status becomes a barrier to paying for college (undocumented students do not qualify for financial aid) or they are not able to secure high-paying jobs that require a social security number (Gonzales, 2011; Súarez-Orozco et al., 2015).

Racist/nativist experiences are another sociopolitical challenge that is present in the literature. Rodriguez (2020) described how undocumented youth are racialized and targeted in schools. Similarly, Szlyk et al. (2020) found that non-English speakers were targets of bullying, and Ee and Gándara (2020) found that the bullying of immigrant youth was more common in schools with higher percentages of white students. Furthermore, Michaels (2020) found that school officials employed anti-immigrant messages to exclude students from enrollment or to push them out. Thus, when it comes to racist/nativist experiences in schools, undocumented Latina/o/x youth confront such challenges from multiple actors in school settings.

This review acknowledges multiple challenges that undocumented Latina/o/x students experience in secondary schools. Next, we review research that highlights the agency and resistance practices undocumented students engage with in schools.

### *Agency and Resistance*

Beyond the challenges that undocumented immigrant youth face in schools, other studies have emphasized how these students exercise agency and resistance, but this area of focus is highlighted less frequently in the literature. Agency and resistance studies argue that undocumented Latina/o/x students are not passive subjects in their schools, but instead are actively engaging in behaviors that challenge inequitable structures. For example, Gonzales et al. (2015) found that most undocumented students in K-12 schools hide their status as a way of avoiding negative reactions from school personnel and their peers. In contrast, Allard (2015) showed that the 1.25 generation (young people who migrated to the United States during their teenage years) engaged in agentic and resisting behaviors by "surprisingly being vocal about the fact they were in the US without authorization" (p. 491). These examples challenge the deficit narrative, which blames immigrant parents and portrays immigrant youth as passive victims of their parent's immigration decisions. Furthermore, Negrón-Gonzales (2013) demonstrated how youth engaged in oppositional consciousness, which is "an empowered mental state that prepares members of an oppressed group to act to undermine, reform, and overthrow a system of human domination" (as cited in Negrón-Gonzales, 2015, p. 1286). Moreover, Rodriguez (2020) described how undocumented immigrant youth engaged in telling their stories as a form of empowerment and resistance.

### *Sense of Belonging in Latina/o/x Immigrant Contexts*

This chapter expands on Hagerty et al.'s (1992) definition of belonging, which integrates psychological and sociological perspectives that emphasize the centrality of the "internal affective or evaluative feeling or perception" relative to other adults and peers in school (p. 174). We also build on a more generalized definition of belonging that emphasizes students' perceptions of being "accepted, valued, included and encouraged by others (teachers and peers) in the academic classroom setting and of feeling oneself to be an important part of the life and activity of the class" (Goodenow, 1993, p. 25). Multiple studies have demonstrated that positive perceptions of belonging in schools were associated with an improved sense of motivation and academic achievement (Goodenow, 1993; Goodenow & Grady, 1993), improved help-seeking behaviors, and higher participation in the social life of school (Gibson & Koyama, 2004). In an important study of belonging, Osterman (2000) found that students who experience inclusion and acceptance within schools are more engaged, motivated, and invested in their academic experiences. However, research on immigrant students' sense of belonging is limited, and until recently, has largely ignored the experiences of undocumented students.

The sense of school belonging for undocumented Latina/o/x youth has been studied and conceptualized in different ways. For instance, several studies have examined the link between undocumented immigrants' sense of belonging and their psychological well-being (Bazo Vienrich & Torres Stone, 2022; Kia-Keating & Ellis, 2007). Gonzales et al. (2013) found that undocumented status was associated with higher-than-normal elevated levels of anxiety, but helping youth to identify options for education, community participation, civic engagement, and continued belonging can reduce their mental distress. Other research has examined how perceptions of safety relate to belonging and calls for establishing school cultures that can buffer immigrant students from threats outside of the school (Lowenhaupt et al., 2021). Souto-Manning et al. (2021) have admonished us to consider how the pseudo-neutrality of belonging can be harmful to students and lead to their marginalization. DeNicolo et al. (2017) have argued for rethinking sense of belonging beyond notions of involvement or inclusion, and to also consider providing support in ways that challenge and disrupt inequalities through *cariño conscientizado,* or critical and authentic care. They argue that belonging as *cariño conscientizado* provides guidelines for school staff for engaging structural racism through multifaceted approaches that facilitate practices to view, learn, collaborate, and incorporate "immigrant communities as democratic partners in supporting the education of all students" (DeNicolo et al., 2017). The research literature on undocumented Latina/o/x students' sense of belonging highlights unique features of their experience that call for a need to also address their fears, issues of safety related to undocumented status, incorporating immigrant communities, and attention to their mental well-being.

The literature reviewed here attempts to highlight critical themes that contribute to our understanding of the experiences of undocumented Latina/o/x secondary school students. The FAN framework guiding this chapter helps us make the argument that structural challenges position undocumented Latina/o/x students as *atravesada/o/x* or transgressors. The agency and resistance enacted by undocumented students illuminate how students as *nepantlera/o/xs* use *la facultad* to navigate these challenges. Lastly, the literature on belonging for undocumented Latina/o/xs helps us conceptualize spaces that can become pillars and resources of support for undocumented students as they complete secondary education and also prepare for higher education.

## Our Methods: Understanding Undocumented Student Experiences

This chapter examines the reflections of four undocumented college students who revisit their lived experiences during their high school years. The data for this chapter was drawn from a narrative inquiry qualitative research project that was conducted in 2021 by one of the authors. That project examined the reflections of undocumented Latina/o/x college-going students and how they navigated different geographical spaces when they were enrolled in high school. In this chapter, we reanalyzed the data to focus on participants' experiences where they either felt excluded or experienced a sense of belonging in their secondary school spaces (Bazo Vienrich & Torres Stone, 2022; DeNicolo et al., 2017; Kia-Keating & Ellis, 2007).

### *Study Design*

The original project employed a qualitative research approach because the author was interested in understanding how Latina/o/x undocumented students made sense of, described, and reflected on their experiences when they were enrolled in their respective high schools (Merriam & Tisdell, 2016). Additionally, the project used a narrative inquiry approach that elicited and analyzed participants' first-person stories. Narrative inquiry as a qualitative research approach allows for the use of first-person accounts of stories as data (Merriam & Tisdell, 2016). For this chapter, a qualitative narrative inquiry approach is especially appropriate given undocumented students' experiences navigating academic borderlands as *atravesada/o/x* or transgressors, as described by FAN.

### *Data Collection*

The data for the original project were collected through narrative inquiry, semi-structured interviews with four participants (Brenner, 2006). The author used convenience sampling to intentionally select respondents with the life experiences and characteristics most relevant to the research project. A snowball sampling technique was used to recruit all of the participants. The selection criteria for participants included: identifying as an undocumented Latina/o/x student, age of 18 years or older, and having been enrolled in a high school within the last 2 years from the time of the interview. All of the respondents lived in the western part of the United States, attended public high schools, and were enrolled in higher education institutions in that same region (see Table 1.1).

**Table 1.1** *Study Participants Details*

| Pseudonym | Age of Arrival | Educational Level | Institution Type |
|---|---|---|---|
| Isabel | 2 | Undergraduate | 4-Year University |
| Bianca | 4 | Undergraduate | 4-Year University |
| Sam | 14 | Undergraduate | Community Coll. |
| Rodrigo | 15 | Undergraduate | 4-Year University |

### *Data Analysis Procedures*

For this study, we reanalyzed the existing data from the earlier project using a different analytical approach to focus on participants' experiences navigating secondary school spaces and specifically highlighting moments when participants described instances where they either felt excluded or perceived a sense of belonging. Thus, we employed a grounded theory approach to identify key patterns, themes, and significant processes that we interpreted in the data (Charmaz, 2006). This grounded theory approach involved two phases of analysis: (1) during the initial coding phase, each author closely analyzed lines or segments of data to identify initial codes, themes, and areas for further exploration (each author conducted this analysis separately); and (2) during the focused coding phase, the authors jointly identified the most salient codes and/or themes from the initial coding phase to organize and synthesize the data (Charmaz, 2006). Following this grounded theory approach to data analysis, the theme of (un)belonging was particularly prevalent in the narratives, and this particular theme helped us highlight how participants' narratives described instances of marginalization ((un)belonging), as well as how they carved out spaces to belong.

## Our Study: Latina/o/x Undocumented Youths' High School Experiences

The results of this study highlight how participants described instances of marginalization that directly hindered their sense of belonging, as well as how they straddled liminal spaces to carve out spaces to belong. The results suggest that participants in this research study experienced a myriad of challenges while enrolled in public high schools before they matriculated into college. We specifically present students' narratives detailing how they navigated places of inclusion and exclusion as they straddled spaces to belong and located pillars that nurtured their college preparedness in high school. Our findings are divided into two parts. The first part of our analysis focuses on students' perceptions of marginalization and (un)belonging, and the second part focuses on how students created spaces of belonging with their peers.

### *(Un)Belonging in School: Undocumented Students' Perceptions of Marginalization*

Latina/o/x undocumented youth faced a set of unique challenges as they navigated high school and attempted to "fit in" and experience a sense of belonging. School belonging has important implications for immigrant students' school engagement (Osterman, 2000), feeling safe at school (Lowenhaupt et al., 2021), and a particular focus on undocumented Latina/o/x youth (Gonzales et al., 2013; DeNicolo et al., 2017). For the undocumented Latina/o/x youth in this study, their perceptions of (un)belonging were shaped by negative interactions with school personnel that left them feeling alienated because they were ignored, demeaned, or relegated to a marginalized position. As a result of negative interactions with school personnel, students experienced marginalization and expressed feeling like "outsiders" in school. In addition, students also described experiencing marginalization resulting from the stereotypes and stigma related to being placed in an ELD program. On the one hand, students felt that the stigma related to being assigned to the ELD program and being called an "ELD" student was an identity label that separated and distinguished Latina/o/x immigrant students from English-speaking mainstream students in ways that reified their marginalized status by positioning them to the lower echelons of the student social hierarchy. On the other hand, the stigma related to the ELD label also marked students as not proficient in English, which also resulted in feelings of linguistic marginalization that resulted from their perceptions of being viewed as having lower learning ability, being poorly behaved, and undesirable, in relation to privileged views toward their mainstream peers within their schools.

We present our analysis of students' perceptions of marginalization and (un)belonging in two sections. In the first section, we discuss the challenges such as the lack of support and mistrust of both teachers and administrators resulting from negative and demeaning interactions, which resulted in undocumented students experiencing mistrust and alienation. In the second section, we focus on students' perceptions of linguistic marginalization. We highlight participants' experiences of linguistic marginalization related to ELD being used to draw distinctions between them and English-speaking students in mainstream courses, and we also discuss how "ELD" students were positioned in the lower rungs of the school's social ladder owing to their emergent levels of English proficiency.

### *Perceptions of (Not) Belonging: Experiences of (Mis)Trust and Alienation in School*

The data suggest that the experiences of Latina/o/x undocumented youth in high school were shaped by an anti-immigrant sociopolitical context, but also by experiences of feeling degraded, devalued, and not prioritized by school administrators, teachers, and counselors. For example, when asked about her relationship with her school's administration, Isabel responded, "They definitely weren't a resource for me, or a place to like, talk about things," and when asked if she could elaborate, she replied with the following:

> there was this ... vice principal that I was not ... I didn't have good vibes from her. I felt like she, I mean, in general, the administrative staff wasn't

> very ... they were very much about hierarchy ... I feel like there was this one vice principal that ... would kind of look at students in a childish way ... like those moms that always look at you like small, if that makes sense. Like, they think you're not developed or like you're not capable of making mature decisions.

In this excerpt, Isabel describes how school administration was not a supportive resource for her, and that she felt disparaged by administrators, particularly the vice principal. She also describes how administrators seemed to value a type of social hierarchy, and she felt that she was positioned at the bottom because she felt looked down upon. As a result of these negative experiences, Isabel did not feel "good vibes" from this and other administrators, which appears to have resulted in distrust of the vice principal and other school personnel.

Further, this type of mistrust of administrators is also clearly articulated by Bianca when she reached out to them for support for a Chicana/o/x Studies class event. She felt that they were not helpful and continually rejected her paperwork or proceeded to tell her that she needed other forms, without providing clear direction. In explaining why she thought they made it difficult to get her class activity approved, she stated:

> They were not really pleasant I guess, ... they would always make it difficult, which I thought was really unfair. Because whenever ASB (Associated Student Body) had to get something approved, they would get it approved really easily. So, I didn't really enjoy talking to them. I feel like they had favorite students.

Bianca explained her frustration with administrators when she needed their support to approve an activity for the *Dia de Los Muertos* event that involved students and parents through her Chicana/o/x Studies class. She described that she felt unsupported, overlooked, and disparaged because of the difficulties with filing paperwork throughout the approval process. Bianca also noted that, in contrast, ASB students were treated favorably and had their activities approved with much more ease; this contrast also reflected the student hierarchy described by Isabel previously.

Another student, Sam, shared feeling unsupported and disparaged by a school counselor when he was asking for help with financial aid for college. Sam recalled:

> I really wanted to go to college and I got very little help. And I remember we were filling out the financial aid papers and the [counselor] was making fun about how much money my mother makes. And yeah. I felt like, "Okay, don't help me anymore, I will do it myself." Yeah, I did feel bad, especially for my mother.

This excerpt highlights the blatant disrespect and denigration a counselor showed towards both Sam and his mother. Through this excerpt, Sam helps us understand that the counselor valued a social hierarchy rooted in social class status because they laughed at his mother's low-income level. This, in turn, resulted in Sam developing a mistrust of a school adult. Without trust, Sam would need to figure out the financial aid process on his own. Three students, Sam, Isabel, and Bianca, expressed feeling overlooked and put down, which led them to be wary of school personnel.

### *Linguistic Marginalization: ELD Placement as an Identity Label and Status Marker*

Two of the four participants arrived in the United States after the age of 14, so when they enrolled in secondary school, they were considered emergent bilingual learners and placed in "ELD" courses. Thus Sam and Rodrigo's challenges navigating high school were predominantly tied to their recent arrival status and their English language and academic proficiency. When asked about some of the challenges he experienced in school, Rodrigo replied:

> I think it was all about language. And like, I didn't encounter other problems than that. Maybe like the regular classes ... there were some problems, like in the beginning, because I had to get used to them, I had to get used to, like, the way they used to teach because they were different from my ELD classes, you know, they wouldn't describe like

> everything with details for me to understand because they will like … think that I [already] knew the language.

In this excerpt, Rodrigo expressed his difficulty with the academic language when his English proficiency was at an emergent level and when he specifically stated that it was "all about language." The linguistic challenge Rodrigo described was particularly salient for students who enrolled in school at a secondary school age level. Rodrigo recalls that once he was reclassified from the ELD program and placed in mainstream courses, he struggled to understand the academic language because he did not receive language support similar to what he received when he was in the ELD program. The English proficiency of emergent speakers like Rodrigo limit access to academic content after placement in mainstream classes. He also felt ignored because teachers assumed that he understood English fully.

Moreover, Sam experienced a negative teacher interaction related to ELD status that he described after he was asked to recall an incident that made him sad when he was in high school.

> "During my first year, when I had algebra 1, and my teacher, I don't know, she wasn't really racist, but I will say she kinda treated us differently. Because the ELD students, we will all go together into like the different math or science classes. And she would always say things like, 'You guys are so' … I really don't remember the word, but 'Compared to my sixth period, they're so sweet, they're so quiet,' things like that."

Though Sam was careful to describe the teacher in this incident as not "racist," it can be argued that the teacher engages in a racial microaggression when she compares her ELD students presumably to students in mainstream classes who the teacher implied were "sweet" and "quiet." This excerpt also describes that ELD students were often segregated and treated differently by teachers. Additionally, when Sam was asked about the places in school that made him feel uncomfortable, he replied:

> I would say transferring from … the ELD department into standard classes, where you wouldn't have the immigrant type of people in your

> classroom, and you would feel like a completely different person. Like in those standard classrooms with people that were born here.

When asked to elaborate on what he meant by "feeling like a completely different person," Sam responded, "Umm, like an outsider, maybe." Sam stated openly that he felt like an outsider in "standard" classrooms compared to his former ELD department, where he was in class with other immigrant students whom he was more familiar with. Additionally, Sam's description of being transferred from ELD to the mainstream "standard classes" highlights his understanding of the hierarchical positioning of ELD versus mainstream courses, which reinforces the linguistic marginalization of immigrant students who were marked with the ELD label, and the stereotypes and stigma it carried.

### *Carving Out Spaces of Belonging*

The analysis of the narrative data also revealed that undocumented Latina/o/x students sought out opportunities to experience belonging. To find spaces to belong, students exercised agency with peers to carve out liminal spaces because of their negative interactions with school personnel and to avert the stigma of being labeled as "ELD" students, because this stigma gave rise to treatment and experiences where they instead felt marginalized and a sense of not belonging. Thus it was through their interactions with peers that participants carved out spaces for belonging. For example, when Rodrigo was asked what it was about hanging out with friends that he liked the most, he responded:

> I think it was just because I was with my friends, like eating lunch and then talking about our experiences, like "How was your class?" "How was your ELD class?" "How was your teacher?" "What did they teach you?" And I remember that we used to laugh when someone, like, try [sic] to speak English because they didn't know how to pronounce, like the correct way. Yeah, so even though we were making fun of everyone, we were learning at the same time.

Rodrigo describes how he and his friends developed an empathizing, supportive, and trusting peer community. The trusting relationships ELD students developed brought them together as friends who support one another in learning the English language. Outside of the classroom and among friends, immigrant students translanguaged and drew from each other's linguistic repertoires to refine their own English skills. These instances of translanguaging practices appear to help expand each other's linguistic repertoire and also reflect mutual trust among peers, given how some students supported and sometimes "made fun" of each other when they (mis)pronounced and corrected the pronunciation of certain words. Together, they created a space where they became *nepantlera/o/xs*, by being able to be themselves authentically and moving away from the feelings of not belonging.

A feature of the relationships with peers was not just limited to trust, but how trust created a different sense of self that fostered a sense of belonging. For example, when asked about feeling different in distinct school areas, Rodrigo replied:

> During class, I was usually quiet. I will [sic] always be listening. I didn't like to participate at all. And then when I was on my break time, I was picking up my friends. So I felt like I had two different lives. One where I'm quiet and the other where I am very open.

Rodrigo's response reflects how he was an *atravesado nepantleando* as he describes how he deliberately straddled two "lives" within his high school. Rodrigo discusses how he was intentional about being "silent" yet "always listening" in class, but outside of class among his trusted friends, where he presumably felt a higher sense of belonging, he was his authentic self and "very open."

Similarly, when elaborating on a comment where he stated he felt like a different person in different school spaces, Sam said:

> There was a time where I was moving forward very fast. And, they wouldn't really recognize at one point that I was an immigrant. And I felt like then I shouldn't tell anybody. It's not that I don't look, but I didn't ... It wasn't that I didn't feel like that ELD "1" student anymore ... I even remember, the person I used to physically look like, in my freshman year,

> was completely different than what I could look like now. So, I started to dress differently, more like the people that are from here.

In this narrative, Sam describes how he felt the need to distance himself from the stigma of the ELD label by changing his physical appearance to fit in with the mainstream students. At a later point in the interview, Sam describes how he tried to fit in linguistically:

> I didn't try to complicate my English as much, like I kept it very simple ... And I felt like I started to lose that Spanish accent more, while practicing a lot more. And yeah, at one point, nobody would have ever expected that I was an immigrant ... it's not that I left the ELD community behind. But I felt like I was a completely different person from one year to another. And I did like it because all the high school experience changed for me ... I even remember practicing with my cousins because I didn't want to have the accent as much. Like, it's not that I hated it, but you could easily get pointed out immediately, if you have that.

This excerpt describes Sam's agentic decisions of dressing and speaking differently to avoid the marginalizing labels and stigma typically aimed at immigrant "ELD" students. In the end, Sam states that the process of transforming his physical appearance and his accent had the effect of changing his whole high school experience as he was able to straddle mainstream spaces and find a sense of belonging. Since translanguaging was not a feature of the classroom nor the school culture, students had to instead engage in agentic actions and straddle liminal spaces of *nepantla* to avoid linguistic marginalization. It seems clear that both a sense of trust and distancing themselves from being labeled as ELD were critical for undocumented Latina/o/x students to avoid marginalization and foster a sense of belonging.

## Discussion

There is a great need to understand how undocumented Latina/o/x students navigate and seek a sense of belonging within the educational borderlands. The results of this study highlight how participants described instances of marginalization that directly hindered their sense of belonging, as well as how they carved out spaces to belong by straddling liminal areas within school. The framework of FAN (Conchas & Acevedo, 2020) provides a critical lens to analyze this study's results. First, we employ FAN to point out how our participants are positioned as *atravesada/o/xs* in the academic borderlands. Secondly, FAN offers us a unique lens that allows us to better understand how these students as *atravesada/o/xs,* carved out spaces to belong by straddling liminal spaces. Lastly, applying a FAN framework allows us to identify and offer a reconceptualization of belonging for *atravesada/o/x* undocumented Latina/o/x students.

The students' narratives describe their perceptions of feeling marginalized by school personnel who failed to provide support and instead disparaged, belittled, and demeaned them. Conchas and Acevedo (2020) argued that Latina/o/x students represent *atravesada/o/xs* because they navigate subjugating experiences within the education borderlands. Our study's results highlight how undocumented Latina/o/x students experience instances of alienation and mistrust predominantly through interactions with school leaders, as well as how the stigma of an ELD assignation created an identity label and status-marker generated and reinforced linguistic marginalization. Unsurprisingly, instances of marginalization are a dominant theme in the literature on undocumented students in secondary schools (Castro-Salazar and Bagley, 2010; Ee & Gándara, 2020; Norrid-Lacey & Spencer, 2000; Torres & Wicks-Asbun, 2014), and there is also some attention to the ways that such challenges impact their sense of belonging (DeNicolo et al., 2017; Gonzales et al., 2015; Lowenhaupt et al., 2021). Thus, following FAN, we contend that undocumented students as *atravesada/o/xs* activate *la facultad* to straddle or *nepantlear* the educational borderlands and carve out spaces for belonging, particularly through trusting relationships with peers.

Our study of how undocumented Latina/o/x youth as *atravesada/o/xs nepantleando* illuminates the absence of critical elements of belonging that, if made transparent, could offer a way to rethink and expand on how we define this belonging in school contexts that serve such populations of students. Traditional notions of belonging emphasize students' perceptions of feeling accepted and included by adults and peers in schools. However, for undocumented youth straddling educational borderlands, where the uncertainty of being undocumented can thwart students' academic achievement hopes (Garcia, 2011) and aspirations for higher education (Lara & Nava, 2018), the need for trust appears to be a significant element that was not available to them. Thus, trust in belonging becomes a pillar of support for undocumented Latina/o/x students who are *nepantleando* the academic borderlands.

Given our findings, the narrative analysis suggests that we conceptualize belonging as trust in addition to acceptance. Thinking about belonging as trust can help make the culture of schools more receptive, safe, and integrative. Undocumented Latina/o/x youth receive plenty of messages from socio-political spaces that are a source of alienation and communicate to them that they do not belong. Schools need to provide integrative social and learning environments where students feel protected and incorporated into the fabric of the community. Fostering these social and learning environments with trust can support students in successfully completing their secondary education, but they also become pillars or "husks" that nurture Latina/o/x students to foster college access and prepare them for higher education. However, undocumented Latina/o/x youth are experiencing marginalization through interactions with adults and through the stigma the ELD assignation carries. In our study, a great deal of energy was expended by Latina/o/x undocumented youth in transforming their identities away from the ELD label because they perceived the stigma related to this label to be a source of marginalization, given they were singled out as "deficient" in English as well and other connotations such as not smart, uncommitted to schools, low income, and also were marked as low status.

Reconceptualizing belonging to include trust as a central feature of belonging leads us to believe that school personnel play a critical role in establishing a school culture that incorporates undocumented Latina/o/x youth equitably (Lowenhaupt et al., 2021). School personnel can become the key actors in planting the seeds and fostering college access for undocumented youth. We also believe that to eliminate the borders and borderlands erected by the stigma and stereotypes related to the ELD label, the school culture needs to eliminate factors that contribute to the linguistic marginalization of students. To remove such linguistic barriers and divisions, one approach is to establish an equitable linguistic environment by remaking the culture of schools as translanguaging learning spaces. Translanguaging is how bilingual or multilingual students combine and innovate within and across languages and discourses and pull from their available language resources to comprehend and produce language (García & Wei, 2014). Translanguaging is also embedded in a historical struggle of separating languages in society, communities, and institutions based on social status and historical suppression of certain forms of bilingual or multilingualism (García & Wei, 2014). Therefore, establishing translanguaging practices as a cornerstone of the school culture, in ways that leverage and validate all students' cultural and linguistic knowledge, as a central feature of the learning environment within the school, to effectively eliminate the linguistic borderlands that, if left in place, will continue to further marginalize undocumented immigrant youth. Thus, having access to school personnel that undocumented youth can trust and those that can help them feel welcomed and secure, coupled with practices that eliminate linguistic borderlands, can foster the pillars and recourses that nurture successful secondary school completion, as well as their preparation for higher education.

## Conclusion

This study illuminates how undocumented Latina/o/x youth's perceptions of both not belonging and linguistic marginalization can stymie opportunities to feel included in the school culture and community. Participants' experiences with school adults contributed to distrust, and as a result, students effectively gave up on school personnel. Additionally, the placement of emergent bilingual immigrant students in ELD and the stigma it carries added another layer of marginalization as students felt singled out by this label as well as their experiences being demeaned, positioned as lower status, and viewed as undesirable relative to mainstream students. Experiencing exclusion and marginalization rather than belonging can affect school engagement and academic performance, for undocumented Latina/o/x students already vulnerable to dropping out of school (Gonzales, 2011; Mosqueda & Tellez, 2016). Creating school spaces where immigrant students feel a sense of belonging should help reinforce their aspirations and hopes for pursuing higher education (Abrego, 2006) and cultivate their motivation to pursue college and a career that may provide them with social mobility (Torres & Wicks-Asbun, 2014).

In schools that serve undocumented Latina/o/x students, it is imperative that adults receive training and commit to fostering a sense of belonging that is based on trust and helps make students feel accepted, included, and valued. In addition, school personnel must work to eliminate the marginalization that can result from the stigma and stereotypes created by the ELD assignation, by establishing translanguaging learning environments where students' native language is a valuable skill for learning and teaching. In establishing translanguaging practices as central features of the classroom and the school culture, such a shift can help eliminate the linguistic marginalization experienced by "ELD" students, and perhaps the status hierarchies attributed to language (English proficiency) can be diminished or even erased.

The sociopolitical messaging that excludes and marginalizes undocumented Latina/o/x students is in itself a huge weight for students to bear. By establishing belonging as trust, school personnel can build positive relationships and work to create a translanguaging school environment and culture where learning is viewed as a bilingual or multilingual endeavor. An approach that validates bilingualism and at the same time helps schools and school personnel foster a sense of belonging with trust can be seen as the conduit that plants the seed for college access and nurtures college preparation. Latina/o/x undocumented students as *Hija/o/xs del Maiz* need to feel a sense of school belonging with trust, which can serve as a "husk" to protect and nurture their academic growth. It is critical for educators to offer classroom and school cultures that promote the safety and equitable treatment to support Latina/o/x immigrant success in ways that make up for the broken promise of the protections for undocumented students purported by the 1982 *Plyler v. Doe* Supreme Court decision (Gonzales et al., 2015).

## References

Abrego L. J. (2006). "I can't go to college because I don't have papers": Incorporation patterns of Latino undocumented youth. *Latino Studies, 4*, 212–231.

Allard, E. (2015). Undocumented status and schooling for newcomer teens. *Harvard Educational Review, 85*(3), 478–501. https://doi.org/10.17763/0017-8055.85.3.478

Bazo Vienrich, A., & Torres Stone, R. A. (2022). The educational trajectories of Latinx undocumented students: Illegality and threats to emotional well-being. *Socius, 8*. https://doi.org/10.1177/23780231221135966

Brenner, M. E. (2006). Interviewing in educational research. In J. Green, G. Camilli, & P. Elmore (Eds.), *Complementary methods for research in education* (pp. 357–370). American Educational Research Association.

Castro-Salazar, R., & Bagley, C. (2010). "Ni de aquí ni from there." Navigating between contexts: Counter-narratives of undocumented Mexican students in the United States. *Race, Ethnicity and Education, 13*(1), 23–40. https://doi.org/10.1080/13613320903549651

Charmaz, K. (2006). *Constructing grounded theory: A practical guide through qualitativeanalysis.* Sage Publications, Inc.

Conchas, G. Q., & Acevedo, N. (2020). *The Chicana/o/x dream: Hope, resistance, and educational success.* Harvard Education Press.

De Genova, N. (2013). Spectacles of migrant "illegality": The scene of exclusion, the obscene of inclusion. *Ethnic and Racial Studies, 36*(7), 1180–1198. https://doi.org/10.1080/01419870.2013.783710

Delgado Bernal, D., Alemán Jr, E., & Garavito, A. (2009). Latina/o undergraduate students mentoring Latina/o elementary students: A borderlands analysis of shifting identities and first-year experiences. *Harvard Educational Review, 79*(4), 560–586.

DeNicolo, C. P., Yu, M., Crowley, C. B., & Gabel, S. L. (2017). Reimagining critical care and problematizing sense of school belonging as a response to inequality for immigrants and children of immigrants. *Review of Research in Education, 41*(1), 500–530. https://doi.org/10.3102/0091732X17690498

Ee, J., & Gándara, P. (2020). The impact of immigration enforcement on the nation's schools. *American Educational Research Journal, 57*(2), 840–871. https://doi.org/10.3102/0002831219862998

García, O., & Wei, L. (2014). *Translanguaging: Language, bilingualism and education.* Palgrave Pivot.

Garcia, S. J. (2011). The social realities of undocumented Mexican immigrant women and the broader implications for adult educators [Conference paper]. Adult Education Research Conference, Toronto, ON, Canada.

Gee, K. A., Asmundson, V., & Vang, T. (2023). Educational impacts of the COVID-19 pandemic in the United States: Inequities by race, ethnicity, and socioeconomic status. *Current Opinion in Psychology, 52*, 101643.

Gibson, P. G., & Koyama, J. P. (2004). *School connections: U.S. Mexican youth, peers, and school achievement.* Teachers College Press.

Gleeson, S., & Gonzales, R. G. (2012). When do papers matter? An institutional analysis of undocumented life in the United States. *International Migration, 50*(4), 1–19. https://doi.org/10.1111/j.1468-2435.2011.00726.x

Gonzales, R. G. (2011). Learning to be illegal: Undocumented youth and shifting legal contexts in the transition to adulthood. *American Sociological Review, 76*(4), 602–619. https://doi.org/10.1177/0003122411411901

Gonzales, R. G., Heredia, L. L., & Negrón-Gonzales, G. (2015). Untangling Plyler's legacy: Undocumented students, schools, and citizenship. *Harvard Educational Review, 85*(3), 318–341. https://doi.org/10.17763/0017-8055.85.3.318

Gonzales, R. G., Suárez-Orozco, C., & Dedios-Sanguineti, M. C. (2013). No place to belong: contextualizing concepts of mental health among undocumented immigrant youth in the United States. *American Behavioral Scientist, 57*(8), 1174–1199. https://doi.org/10.1177/0002764213487349

Goodenow, C. (1993). Classroom belonging among early adolescent students: Relationships to motivation and achievement. *Journal of Early Adolescence, 13*(1), 21–43. https://doi.org/10.1177/0272431693013001002

Goodenow, C., & Grady, K. E. (1993). The relationship of school belonging and friends' values to academic motivation among urban adolescent students. *Journal of Experimental Education, 62*(1), 60–71. https://doi.org/10.1080/00220973.1993.9943831

Hagerty, B. M. K., Lynch-Sauer, J., Patusky, K. L., Bouwsema, M., & Collier, P. (1992). Sense of belonging: A vital mental health concept. *Archives of Psychiatric Nursing, 6*(3), 172–177. https://doi.org/10.1016/0883-9417(92)90028-h

Jefferies, J. (2014). Fear of deportation in high school: Implications for breaking the circle of silence surrounding migration status. *Journal of Latinos and Education, 13*(4), 278–295. https://doi.org/10.1080/15348431.2014.887469

Kia-Keating, M., & Ellis, B. H. (2007). Belonging and connection to school in resettlement: Young refugees, school belonging, and psychosocial adjustment. *Clinical Child Psychology and Psychiatry, 12*(1), 29–43. https://doi.org/10.1177/1359104507071052

Lara, A., & Nava, P. E. (2018). Achieving the dream, uncertain futures: The postbaccalaureate decision-making process of Latinx undocumented students. *Journal of Hispanic Higher Education, 17*(2), 112–131. https://doi.org/10.1177/1538192718758855

Lowenhaupt, R., Dabach, D. B., & Mangual Figueroa, A. (2021). Safety and belonging in immigrant-serving districts: Domains of educator practice in a charged political landscape. *AERA Open, 7*, 23328584211040084.

Merriam, S. B., & Tisdell, E. J. (2016). *Qualitative research: A guide to design and implementation*. John Wiley & Sons.

Michaels, E. (2020). Beyond academic achievement outcomes: The impact of school on the immigrant political incorporation of undocumented Latinx youth. *Youth & Society, 52*(7), 1285–1311. https://doi.org/10.1177/0044118X20913733

Mosqueda, E., & Tellez, K. (2016). Contesting racism, marginalization, and Mexican immigrant youth: Examining the elusive path toward earning a diploma from a nontraditional high school. In G. Q. Conchas (Ed.), *Critical case studies in Latino education: Narratives of inequality and school success* (pp. 96-111). Teachers College Press.

Negrón-Gonzales, G. (2013). Navigating "illegality": Undocumented youth & oppositional consciousness. *Children and Youth Services Review, 35*(8), 1284–1290. https://doi.org/10.1016/j.childyouth.2013.04.016

Negrón-Gonzales, G. (2014). Undocumented, unafraid and unapologetic: Re-articulatory practices and migrant youth "illegality." *Latino Studies,12*(2), 259–278.

Negrón-Gonzales, G. (2015). Undocumented youth activism as counter-spectacle: Civil disobedience and testimonio in the battle around immigration reform. *Aztlán: A Journal of Chicano Studies, 40*(1), 87-112.

Norrid-Lacey, B., & Spencer, D. A. (2000). Experiences of Latino immigrant students at an urban high school. *NASSP Bulletin, 84*(619), 43–54. https://doi.org/10.1177/019263650008461905

Osterman, K. F. (2000). Students' need for belonging in the school community. *Review of Educational Research, 70*(3), 323–367. https://doi.org/10.3102/00346543070003323

*Plyler v. Doe*, 457 U.S. 202. (1982). Justia Law. https://supreme.justia.com/cases/federal/us/457/202/

Rodriguez, S. (2020). "I was born at the border, like the 'Wrong' side of it": Undocumented Latinx youth experiences of racialization in the US South. *Anthropology & Education Quarterly, 51*(4), 496–526. https://doi.org/10.1111/aeq.12357

Southern Poverty Law Center. (2017). *The Trump effect*. https://www.splcenter.org/resources/reports/trump-effect/

Souto-Manning, M., Malik, K., Martell, J., & Pión, P. P. (2021). Troubling belonging: The racialized exclusion of young immigrants and migrants of color. *International Journal of Early Childhood, 53*(1), 101–118. https://doi.org/10.1007/s13158-021-00286-8

Suárez-Orozco, C., Katsiaficas, D., Birchall, O., Alcantar, C. M., Hernandez, E., Garcia, Y., Michikyan, M., Cerda, J., & Teranishi, R. T. (2015). Undocumented undergraduates on college campuses: Understanding their challenges and assets and what it takes to make an undocufriendly campus. *Harvard Educational Review, 85*(3), 427–463. https://doi.org/10.17763/0017-8055.85.3.427

Szlyk, H. S., Berger Cardoso, J., Barros Lane, L., & Evans, K. (2020). "Me perdía en la escuela": Latino newcomer youths in the US school system. *Social Work, 65*(2), 131–139. https://doi.org/10.1093/sw/swaa001

Torres, R. M., & Wicks-Asbun, M. (2014). Undocumented students' narratives of liminal citizenship: High aspirations, exclusion, and "in-between" identities. *The Professional Geographer, 66*(2), 195–204. https://doi.org/10.1080/00330124.2012.735936

CHAPTER 2

# Cultivating Nepantlera/o/x Teachers:

## Planting the Seed for Knowledge Production and College Preparation Among Latina/o/x Youth

*Omar Davila Jr., Thalia Rodriguez, Mikaela Dacanay, Brianna Roberto, Donna Garcia, and Aaron Rivas*

> Recently one of our district officials came and told us, 'Your school is the least funded of the district. Your school has the lowest percentage of graduation rates in our district on the east side.' They wanted to come in and identify the problems, but it's like, 'Every time we tell you guys what to do, you don't do it.' We tell them, 'Hey, our teachers don't really care. We want more tutoring opportunities. Much of the in-class curriculum, teachers have to make themselves.' How can you change an education system when there's no system?
>
> —Mario

### Introduction

ACROSS THE UNITED States, thousands of students, like Mario, are taking part in Grow-Your-Own (GYO) teacher programs, with the goal of increasing diversity and addressing the so-called "teacher shortage" (Gist et al., 2019). Mario was selected for the GYO program, *Academy for Future Educators* (a pseudonym), at a private university in the Bay Area of Northern California. Like Mario, many of these students are seeking to return to their communities as teachers. Furthermore, based on previous research, many students like Mario come from urban neighborhoods where they feel denigrated, unheard, and invisible (Conchas, 2012; Rios, 2017; Shedd, 2015). This Youth Participatory Action Research (YPAR) study highlights Latina/o/x youth voices and calls on them, as authors and participants, to construct knowledge in an effort to strengthen GYO programs and create transformative learning spaces that nurture college preparation.

This chapter focuses on the experiences of four Latina/o/x youth participating in a GYO summer program for high school students. Founded in 1995, the *Academy for Future Educators* provides academic, financial, and social support for students from the surrounding communities who wish to become teachers. Students are recruited for this program as early as senior year of high school and as late as junior year of college. They receive $8500 per year for tuition and full funding to pursue their master's degree and teaching credential. Students participate in a weekly seminar where they read, reflect, and discuss scholarship on educational inequality. In addition, students take part in research and leadership initiatives, such as organizing summer programs for high school youth and publishing peer-reviewed manuscripts. The central aim of this program is to prepare critically conscious educators and leaders who return to their communities and implement transformative teaching practices. Our research examines the following questions:

- How might Latina/o/x youth become active agents, as opposed to passive recipients, in the construction of knowledge?
- How are Latina/o/x youth making sense of educational inequality?
- How might teacher pipeline programs create transformative learning spaces that nurture college preparation?

This study explores the possibilities that arise when we center youth voices and, simultaneously, enable youth to become authors engaged in the knowledge creation process. The authors of this chapter are all affiliated with the *Academy of Future Educators* at multiple levels, including professorial, undergraduate, and high school. Our collaborative effort aims to critically examine teacher preparation and imagine new educational possibilities.

In the award-winning book, *The Chicana/o/x Dream: Hope, Resistance and Educational Success,* Conchas and Acevedo (2020) deploy critical scrutiny on traditional higher education scholarship, showing how it fails to account for systems of power and social context. Conchas and Acevedo (2020) put forth the Framework of *Atravesada/o/xs Nepantleando* to underscore the way Chicana/o/x students are (1) relegated to the status of *atravesada/o/xs* (i.e., transgressors) who do not belong in the education system, as evidenced by Mario's opening statement; (2) draw from their *facultad* (i.e., critical consciousness, strength, and resistance) to become *nepantlera/o/xs,* who tap into various institutional resources to navigate college; and (3) redefine success to ensure their communities have access to higher education. Our chapter embraces these insights to achieve greater analytical precision, as we learn from Latina/o/x youth, who wish to become future teachers in marginalized communities.

Special attention is placed on the high school-to-college transition, in line with the section in which our chapter is located, *Planting the Seeds to Foster College Access: Pillars and Resources of Support that Nurture College Preparation.* This research highlights the experiences of Latina/o/x students participating in a GYO program, aiming to prepare students for college and the teaching profession. Programs like these strive to build a pipeline into the teaching profession, wherein students from marginalized backgrounds return to their communities as teachers, as leaders, as agents of social change. This program is committed to increasing college preparedness and teacher diversity by engaging youth in addressing the issues they face. Following the insights of Pedro Noguera (2011), he calls on us to reject the question: how do we *motivate* students? And, instead, ask: how do we foster a *love for learning*? We argue one way to achieve this goal is by providing students the opportunities to exert their agency in transformative ways. The teaching profession offers a powerful platform through which one can exert their agency, enact social justice, and become the nepantlera/o/x teachers our communities need.

## Literature Review

Three intimately connected bodies of research inform how we approach this work. We explore the following herein: (1) *The Social Construction of Childhood*, where we problematize notions of childhood, exploring the social, political, and historical dynamics that undermine those who are constructed as "children"; (2) *Youth Participatory Action Research (YPAR)*, where we detail how YPAR offers opportunities for youth to deploy agency in meaningful ways through resistance, advocacy, and knowledge creation; and (3) *Teacher Preparation*, where we unpack scholarly work on increasing diversity, addressing the "teacher shortage," and how GYO programs fit into these broader efforts by nurturing college preparation, a key component of building a teacher pipeline. We draw from these scholarly works to explore how we might engender transformative academic spaces *for* and *with* future nepantlera/o/x teachers.

### *The Social Construction of Childhood*

In the United States, childhood is often taken for granted. Yet critical scrutiny reveals it is neither an organic process nor universal—it is socially constructed (Baquedano-López & Garrett, 2023). According to Cannella (2008), the notion of childhood emerged in the West during the 17th century, as a result of three historical discourses. The first, *dichotomous distinctions*, emerged via Western philosophy and science: Rene Descartes' separation of mind (i.e., individual) and matter (i.e., world of nature); dichotomous thinking during the Enlightenment and Modern periods; and psychological concepts (e.g., "normal"/"abnormal," "intelligent"/"slow"). The second, *individuals with reasoning capabilities and souls that must be saved*, emerged through an amalgamation of different discourses, from Greek philosophy on reason and mind to Charles Darwin's conception of children as independent organisms, to Christianity's concern for the individual soul. The third, *child as truth and predetermined reality constructed through positivist science*, emerged through theories of human development and natural law (i.e., universal rules of nature, objectivity, and the scientific method). The social construction of childhood, therefore, was not a single static event, but instead emerged as a consequence of various historical discourses (Cannella, 2008). These discourses constructed what we call "childhood," a category distinct from "adulthood," signifying the years between birth and 17 years old, and a "developmental stage" where "children" are conceptualized as incapable of reasoning, incapable of giving consent, and therefore, stripped of their right to vote under a liberal democracy (Brady, 2022).

Childhood, as an ontological experience, differs according to one's structural position. From its inception, childhood was a protected category reserved for upper-class, white males (Meiners, 2016). Simply consider the history of labor and exploitation, where racialized and impoverished groups were subjected to oppressive working conditions from an early age via slavery, industrialization, and agricultural work (Hindman, 2016). Today, agricultural work in the United States continues to rely on child labor, where children as young as 10 years old are legally permitted to work (Department of Labor, 2023), many of whom are Latina/o/x immigrants (Hindman, 2016). In education, youth of color are often perceived as older, having higher pain tolerance, and subjected to extreme racial violence (Brady, 2022; Rios, 2017). When children of color become adults, Meiners (2016) argues, a myriad of social processes render them "child-like," such as the mass incarceration of men of color, which severs their voting rights, as well as discourses and policies that construct women of color as property. Racialized bodies are, therefore, subjected to a paradoxical status as perpetual children while being denied their childhood.

### *Youth Participatory Action Research (YPAR)*

The construction of knowledge is typically done *for* children, *without* children in the process. Historically, those who are most affected by these decisions have the least say, especially in marginalized communities (Shedd, 2015). YPAR sets out to incorporate youth voices in the construction of knowledge, embracing a critical lens as we analyze social issues—that is, an analysis of social structures and the historical, political, and social dynamics shaping inequality (Mirra et al., 2015). YPAR employs a dialogical, problem-posing method (Freire, 2000), seeking to increase its analytical precision by engaging with youth and harnessing intergenerational knowledge. Youth take part in all phases, from research design to publication. Tapping into children's creative abilities, YPAR aims to imagine otherwise.

YPAR studies demonstrate children's capacity to become active agents in social change. This approach is employed by scholars and educators as a pedagogical strategy, research method, and as a form of praxis (Cammarota & Fine, 2010). As a pedagogical strategy, this method seeks to foster a critical consciousness among students by enabling them to understand social inequality and take action against it. As a research method, scholars center the voices of marginalized youth as they investigate issues affecting their communities. Researchers have employed YPAR within multiple contexts. Morrell (2004) examined how urban youth fostered academic learning spaces where literacy was responsive to their social conditions. Fernández's (2021) study on immigration and youth activism shows how Latina/o/x children developed a political consciousness early on as they attempted to navigate racialized discourses at home, at school, and in their community. As children reflected on their experiences, it became clear that Latina/o/x children actively resisted anti-immigrant discourses, as opposed to taking passive or apolitical stances (Fernández, 2021). Akom et al. (2016) illustrate how youth in Oakland, California engage critically with technology to meditate on ways of democratizing data, gathering local knowledge, and developing systems to identify access to healthy food. YPAR is deeply committed to social justice and turning theory into practice. Our study presents an opportunity to consider YPAR within the context of teacher pipeline programs.

### *Teacher Preparation*

Recently, scholars and policymakers alike have become increasingly concerned about the exodus of K-12 teachers (Davila Jr. et al., 2022). Compounding this national phenomenon is the widening racial gap between educators who teach in K-12 schools and students who attend them. Nearly 80% of K-12 teachers are white women (NCES, 2022). University initiatives and policy reforms are emerging across the United States to address these issues. Studies show that students of color benefit from having teachers of color by way of increased academic outcomes and healthier social identities (Bravo & Rodriguez-Mojica, 2021; Bristol & Martin-Fernandez, 2019; Fergus et al., 2020). Local, state, and federal governments are therefore implementing policies and initiatives to make it easier to become a teacher, sometimes by cutting standardized tests, other times by increasing financial support for future teachers.

GYO programs grew out of broader efforts to diversify and increase the number of K-12 educators. According to Unda (2023), GYO programs are becoming the most effective way of increasing diversity and recruiting students from high-need communities into the profession. GYO programs seek to recruit students—typically those in high school—to return to their communities as teachers (Gist, 2022). Nonetheless, as we discuss teacher preparation, it is important to caution against the assumption that teachers of color are superhumans capable of overcoming social inequality by virtue of their identity and lived experiences. We must seek to address both the social conditions in which students learn *and* the teachers who teach them (Davila Jr., Forthcoming; Philip & Brown, 2020). Teachers of color are vital in this process, as they are most likely to speak out against and dismantle structural inequality (Kohli, 2021). Few studies, however, examine the experiences of future Latina/o/x teachers, and even fewer examine the experiences of high school–level students who take part in GYO initiatives.

According to Gist and colleagues (2019), two types of GYO programs are prevalent in education discourse and policy. The first focuses on adults, many of whom already earned a bachelor's degree or work in a closely related field, allowing them to foster close ties with students and families in their community. The second focuses on K-12 students, mainly middle school and high school youth, as they prepare for college (Gist et al., 2019). We focus on the latter, specifically the high school-to-college transition, a key component of building a pipeline toward the teaching profession. Given the existing social, economic, and educational inequalities in U.S. society, educational opportunity is unevenly distributed, thereby limiting students' ability to pursue a teaching career (López, 2021). Nurturing college preparation is a way to address this issue. For us, "college preparation" includes and goes beyond the acquisition of traditional academic skillsets, such as formal writing, oral presentation, and research experience. Our conception of college preparation is informed by Conchas and Acevedo (2020), who emphasize the importance of critical consciousness development, allowing Latina/o/x students to tap into their *facultad* and become *nepantlera/o/xs* who resist oppression and transform their communities. Our chapter highlights a GYO program and students who exhibit that promise.

## Methodology

In accordance with YPAR (Mirra et al., 2015), the present research was a collaborative study among current and future educators at multiple levels—professorial, undergraduate, and high school. We held multiple dialogue sessions (Freire, 2000), wherein we discussed our research design, analysis of findings, and writing of this manuscript. We are all affiliated with the *Academy for Future Educators;* therefore we had unique access and built strong connections with students who wish to become teachers.

### *Data Collection*

During the 2023 *Academy for Future Educators* Summer Program, we announced this research opportunity in our opening remarks to high school summer fellows. Four accepted the invitation to take part in this study and obtained parental consent. Interviews were conducted shortly thereafter, each lasting approximately 30 minutes. We delved into three areas: (1) academic background, (2) educational inequality, and (3) imagining educational utopias. Their *testimonios,* that is, first-person narratives detailing how students experience and navigate inequality (Conchas & Acevedo, 2020), center youth voice in our data collection. Members of our research team, all of whom are co-authors of this chapter, conducted one-on-one interviews with participants. Semi-structured protocols were used, asking participants to discuss their academic experiences and explore alternatives to our current educational reality. For example, "How would you define academic success?" "Do you feel that social inequality and injustice has impacted you? How so?" and, "How would you describe your utopian education system?" Our participants include four Latina/o/x students, all of whom were 17 years old, rising seniors in high school, and pursuing the teaching profession. Three were Latina/o/x girls (Gloria, Lizet, and Laura) and one was a Latina/o/x boy (Mario). Lizet, Laura, and Mario were all Mexican descent, whereas Gloria's father was Salvadoran and her mother was Mexican. Lizet and Laura attended a public high school in a rural town, Gloria attended a private high school in a suburban community, and Mario attended a public high school in an urban city. All participants were assigned a pseudonym, and our research team then transcribed, cleaned, and analyzed interview data, following the procedure below.

### *Analysis*

We employed a qualitative discourse analytic approach in this study (Saldaña & Omasta, 2016). A critical perspective guided the development of codes to uncover logics and assumptions embedded in language and social structures. Saldaña and Omasta (2016) describes "code" as "a word or short phrase that symbolically assigns a summative, salient, essence-capturing, and/or evocative attribute for a portion of language-based or visual data" (p. 4). The analysis was organized into two coding cycles (Saldaña & Omasta, 2016). The first coding cycle was exploratory in nature with specific attention to the way students made sense of their identities, educational inequality, and transformative teaching practices. The second coding cycle organized the initial nine codes into three broader themes. We explore these in the following section.

To analyze our data, we organized a set of meetings. These meetings were organized by the second and third co-authors, who are undergraduate fellows in the *Academy for Future Educators*. Each meeting lasted approximately 1 hour. We invited participants to join, who are also high school fellows in the *Academy for Future Educators*. Participants had the opportunity to reflect on their responses, write notes, and engage in dialogue with our research team, ultimately writing and becoming co-authors of this chapter. In these meetings, we read interview transcripts, discussed findings, and developed arguments presented herein. We asked participants (i.e., high school fellows) to discuss their reactions, present objections, and build upon arguments. Our collaborative approach to data analysis brought together current and future educators at multiple levels—professorial, undergraduate, and high school—to achieve stronger analytical precision and center youth voice.

## Findings

Youth voices illuminate key issues and tensions as they prepare for college and for the teaching profession. Our findings are organized into three subsections:

(1) *Normalization of Inequality,* examining how students made sense of the way social structures are legitimated and reproduced; (2) *Teacher Care,* examining the way students conceptualized positive teacher-student relationships, especially with students from marginalized communities; and (3) *Imagining Utopias,* examining the way students discussed alternative education systems.

### *Normalization of Inequality*

A key element of critical consciousness development among youth is challenging what is otherwise deemed normal. Often, dominant ideologies along the lines of race, gender, and social class are taken for granted or perceived as "common sense," when in fact these ideological formations are socially constructed and intimately connected to structures of power. Their very essence enables them to reproduce over time, working against the interests of marginalized groups and shaping how they make sense of themselves and the world around them. Biko (2015) once argued, "the most potent weapon in the hands of the oppressor is the mind of the oppressed" (p. 68). Developing a critical awareness of social structures and how they operate is a necessary step toward social transformation, especially within the context of teacher preparation (Freire, 2000).

Youth in this study conveyed different stances in relation to social inequality. While some had already developed a critical consciousness, others were still trying to make sense of their social conditions, sometimes using dominant frames. In the following excerpt, Mario details how social context, particularly as youth are growing up, shapes how they make sense of inequality. He stated the following:

> I go to Seymour High School on the East Side. I would describe my academic journey or my academic life as very average ... there is a lot of violence and homelessness and very low-income struggles. When you come from higher income backgrounds, and you come from those areas where it's typically cleaner, it's typically safer, it reflects back on you. The environment you're in is going to be the environment you absorb and you get used to. So, for me, this is normalized, but others might think,

> "Oh my God, you live there? How could you live there? Do your parents not care?" But it's like, they do. They're just trying to get by.

Two social processes become evident as Mario unpacks the relationship between consciousness and context. First is the way social inequality has a normalizing effect, shaping the way students understand structures of opportunity. His use of the words "average" and "normalized," as well as phrases such as "it reflects back on you" and "you get used to" signal the way students are socialized to understand inequality in distinct ways, as a product of context. Second, he rejects the deficit discourse that Latina/o/x parents "do not care" and ostensibly live under these circumstances by choice. Within this space of nepantla, Mario is able to sit in the liminality of acknowledging both the economic limitations and his parents' strength. Indeed, his analysis suggests that choice and agency are limited in urban contexts.

Gloria flipped the normalization process on its head, illustrating how it worked in a different way and to her advantage. In the following excerpt, she details how the academic context at her private school normalized leadership, becoming an act of habit. She stated the following:

> The school I went to was really small. We were 60 girls per grade, and we all knew each other, so it didn't necessarily feel like leadership. It felt more like participating and it grew confidence in me. As I kept doing it, I realized, "Oh, look! I'm a leader in the community." It's something that I continue doing because once you start, you can't stop.

Gloria uses the pronoun "it" repeatedly, both as an index for her school and to emphasize the impact of this academic environment, a space that normalized leadership. She attributes her leadership ability to small class sizes, a phenomenon that is more common among schools serving upper-class students (Conchas & Rodriguez, 2007). Gloria, however, was one of few girls of color at her school. To gain admission, she endured a competitive application process. Since both of her parents were Latina/o/x immigrants, she applied for various scholarships for financial support. She was one of few students from marginalized backgrounds to have access to such a school, along with its unique opportunities for academic advancement.

Some youth, however, did not express a critical consciousness, akin to Gloria and Mario. Some appear to internalize dominant ideologies and use them to make sense of educational inequality. Consider the following responses:

> Maybe their parents didn't get a college degree, so maybe they don't see the importance of getting higher education. But I do know there's probably families that are like, "I want a better life for you." Even my parents want a better life for me. I would also say just their motivation to be there, because sometimes they feel like they're forced to be there. I guess you could say they just want to get out of high school and go on with their life.
>
> —Laura

> I also feel a big barrier is that a lot of our schools aren't performing well, so we have to encourage students to do well in school and actually stay in school because I know a lot of times our graduation rate hasn't been great this year. ... I know a lot of times I feel like a lot of the students that go to my high school try to make some goals. They make some goals, and then sometimes they feel like, "Oh, I don't think I'll be able to do it because I need this," or something along those lines. But in reality, they can do it. They need the motivation and encouragement from others, their parents, other students too, to be able to achieve those goals.
>
> —Lizet

Historical discourses based on individual logics (e.g., motivation) emerge in their responses, as they make sense of low academic performance at their school. As we consider these examples, it is important to note, however, that dominant ideologies are imposed upon people of color; students of color are not the originators of these discourses (Freire, 2000). This internalization of deficit thinking obscures the process by which contexts shape academic outcomes, and furthermore, the way unequal structures are legitimized. It is interesting to note that Lizet sheds light on the challenges experienced by students who may have an established goal, but she did not include a teacher as part of the "others" who can support students with achieving the goal. She could only imagine parents and peers being supportive. The various perspectives presented in this subsection reinforce the need for teacher preparation programs to create opportunities for future teachers to challenge social structures and prevailing discourses, thereby developing a critical consciousness.

### *Teacher Care*

Students drew from moments of suffering to meditate on teacher-student dynamics. Gloria and Mario emphasized the importance of having teachers who understand their background and experiences vis-a-vis marginalization. Valenzuela (2010) argued that critical care is necessary when working with students of color. Critical care displays an awareness of the social conditions that students experience and a commitment to social justice. Gloria and Mario stated the following:

> As students, we depend a lot on who we're being educated with. I feel like something for me that I lack a lot is representation in teachers. In my school specifically, there's no Latinx or Black educators. Having a diverse group of educators would help a variety of students succeed and feel like if there are people out there teaching, we can really be good students and continue pursuing higher education.
>
> —Gloria

> Every 1 in 30 teachers I had probably cared. I know that the education I've gotten is not the best compared to other people I've met. For example, [students in our summer program said] they're doing collaborative work, they're not doing lecture style. I feel like I never had that. I never had a support system in a teacher. I had to fend for myself. I do notice that I participate more in classes where I see myself in the teacher, when I know they've been in my position.
>
> —Mario

Both students were clear about the impact of teachers of color on their academic development. Their commentary echoes a vast body of research (Bristol & Martin-Fernandez, 2019; Gist, 2022; Phillip & Brown, 2020). Gloria was concerned about the dearth of teachers of color and how it negatively impacted students' ability to build strong relationships with educators at her school. Mario expressed a feeling of isolation, sharing that he could not depend on most teachers for support. The combination of these commentaries reinforces the argument presented by both Kim et al., (2022) and Conchas and Acevedo (2020), that it is insufficient to simply recruit more teachers; we must develop and recruit critically conscious educators.

Laura, on the other hand, had an inspirational experience in middle school, which ultimately shaped her determination to become a teacher. This experience prompted her to reciprocate and support other students in need. Laura stated the following:

> For eighth grade, my social studies teacher was an inspiration to me, just because I was seeing how he supported us as his students. And then I was also able to do that with some of my peers, who maybe struggled a bit or had a few questions.

Supportive teachers of color foster learning environments where other students are encouraged to pursue this profession. It is particularly important to note that both of her parents were also educators, and they, too, played key roles in the formation of her professional trajectory. Solorzano and Delgado Bernal (2001) discuss the importance of what they call *transformational role models* in the development of a critical consciousness, resistance, and social change. For them, resistance is not inherently transformative; resistance becomes transformative when it is informed by a commitment to social justice and a critique of structural inequality. Teachers of color play key roles in that process.

### *Imagining Utopias*

Our interviews carved a space for youth to consider ways of redressing inequality. Their task was to imagine a utopian education system, where inequality and injustice no longer exist. Inspired by speculative inquiry (Garcia &

Mirra, 2023), we sought to capture how youth imagined alternative, educational possibilities. We sought to understand issues resonating with students and the way youth delved into an imaginative space. When asked to imagine a utopian education system, Mario shared the following:

> I would say, first, it begins with eliminating gentrification and redlining. I definitely feel that the education system is, if you're Latinx, you go here; you're white, you go up in the suburbs. And I definitely feel you have to dismantle it first.

His commentary draws a connection between educational opportunity and residential segregation, a notable trend where Mario grew up. He proceeded to distinguish between the "east side" of his city (predominantly Latina/o/x) and a neighboring town (predominantly white), where differences in educational opportunity were remarkably evident. Mario argued, "I should be able to get the same education as someone 20 minutes away from me," attributing these geographic and academic differences to the creation of our school system. "I definitely feel it all started back when this country was first starting its educational system, where it was like, you go here, you go there." The link between education and segregation is well documented in scholarly research (Anyon, 2017; Lipman, 2013; Orfield & Eaton, 1996), a social phenomenon that Latina/o/x have contested (Solorzano & Delgado Bernal, 2001; Valencia, 2005). Mario calls for the end of gentrification, a social process that has profoundly impacted communities of color (Maharawal & McElroy, 2018; Ramírez, 2020). It is important to note that Mario offers a structural interpretation of educational inequality, delving beyond the academic sphere and drawing connections across multiple social structures. He places the onus on systems, not marginalized people.

For Lizet, youth voice arosed as a mechanism through which social justice could emerge. When asked to describe her utopian education system, she proposed a structural intervention wherein academic policy and practice required student input—a direct counter to existing procedure, where most often, adults, particularly white administrators, make decisions for and without the voices of youth of color (Shedd, 2015). Lizet stated the following:

> Making it better for students to let the school know about any issues they have and take them into account. Because I know there's been a couple of scandals at our school. I feel like the most recent one was an assistant principal that got fired from our school for saying something really bad. So, [I recommend they] take action and do anything that takes into consideration what students feel they need, because they're the ones at the school, they know what's going on.

Lizet's commentary positions youth voice as a powerful source of knowledge, particularly because youth themselves experience the processes educators and policy makers seek to address. She elevates children's experiential knowledge, positioning their subjectivity as an important perspective, as we strive towards a transformative education system. Her privileging of youth subjectivity challenges the more common, mainstream approaches to knowledge production that center around "experts" and "objectivity," who are typically affluent white adults (Mirra et al., 2015). Lizet envisions students not as *atravesada/o/xs*, but as *nepantlera/o/xs* because they serve as a bridge between their schooling contexts and the leadership who make decisions. Youth voice, and by extension youth subjectivity, serves as a bridge toward social justice, for they are the ones who experience and are impacted the most by education policy.

Laura, another student, emphasizes the importance of passionate teachers in her utopian education system. Her perspective on teaching was influenced by the academic context at her school, where a severe teacher shortage emerged. Her school proceeded to recruit temporary substitutes to teach classes for a prolonged period, having a negative impact on students' interest in content material and their ability to prepare for higher education. She emphasized the importance of quality teachers, not as those who raise test scores nor adhere to neoliberal conceptions of "good" teachers (Trujillo et al., 2017), but rather, teachers who genuinely care about students. Laura stated the following: "Just having teachers who are actually passionate about what they're doing and not just because they just want to get a paycheck."

Laura connected this statement to her deep concern about the teacher shortage at her school. "Last year, I was in a class and we had subs the entire year ... it sucked because we were just there. We weren't really doing much work." For Laura, passionate teachers—or, perhaps, the lack thereof in her situation—had a twofold impact on students: (1) she emphasized the importance of teachers who challenge students and how this pedagogical approach conveys care and passion for their profession, and (2) she argued that the presence (or absence) of passionate teachers affected whether students enjoyed content material. For Laura, having passionate teachers was a fundamental building block for a utopian education system.

Lastly, Gloria called for a different approach to grading, one that departed from contemporary efforts that insist on standardized testing and accountability (Au, 2022). Gloria, like the students featured in Jack's (2019) book *The Privileged Poor,* had access to unique educational opportunities, many of which students in urban communities cannot afford. These experiences shaped how Gloria envisioned a utopian education system. Gloria shared the following:

> My middle school didn't have any grades. We had something called, "progress reports," where a teacher wrote a page per student saying things they've done really great in the classroom and things they can improve. That helped me so much.

For her, grading should serve as a reflective process that fosters and inspires deeper learning. With such a practice, she would move from feeling like an atravesada in schooling and begin to understand how to navigate future education borderlands. She was wary about notions of competition—logics that are often promoted via standardized testing and accountability reforms (Au, 2022). Gloria recounted an experience in which she and her friends applied to the private high school she was attending. Initially, they were excited to pursue this next phase of their lives together, in hopes of attending the same school. Ultimately, she was the only one admitted. Gloria sought to reimagine a grading system that promoted student learning, and in doing so, envisaged an education system that could lift her community.

## Discussion

Despite increasing concerns about diversity and the exodus of K-12 teachers, few studies examine high school students participating in GYO initiatives—that is, teacher preparation programs seeking to recruit and train students to return to their communities as teachers (Unda, 2023). The present study examined four Latina/o/x youth from the *Academy for Future Educators,* a GYO program for rising high school seniors. This qualitative study investigated (1) how students might become active agents in the production of knowledge, (2) how students made sense of the social construction of merit, and (3) how students envisioned transformative academic spaces. Our findings detail promising practices and potential obstacles, as we improve efforts to prepare future teachers of color. Most importantly, youth remind us it is insufficient to simply recruit *more* teachers. We must recruit and train critically conscious teachers who take action as *nepantlera/o/xs* to transform the social conditions that sustain marginalization.

Three major findings emerged through our qualitative analysis. First, youth wrestled with the *normalization of inequality,* showing how they reflected upon and resisted dominant discourses, as well as the way dominant discourses were potentially internalized. Second, youth emphasized the importance of *teacher care,* delineating how "care" went beyond psychological notions of kindness and compassion, calling upon teachers to understand the marginalization of Latina/o/x students, in line with Valenzuela (2010). Last, youth were tasked with *imagining utopias,* where they delved into an imaginative space, addressing the myriad factors that shape educational inequality—gentrification, teaching, grades, and youth voice. Such utopias would represent a schooling experience that did not position students as *atravesada/o/xs,* but would be a welcoming experience that prepared them academically for higher education.

Students' lived experiences shaped their utopian visions. Their imagination was not a "view from nowhere" (p. 70), in the words of Nagel (1989), a proponent for positivist science. Their subjectivity, their knowledge, their experiences were central to how they imagined alternative education systems. We, as authors, were particularly interested in delving into a creative space, where youth could imagine a utopian education system, without the constraints of what Davila Jr. (2021) refers to as *discourses of practicality.* What emerged was counterintuitive. On the one hand, students presented necessary changes and encouraged educators and policymakers to consider structural interventions, such as ending gentrification and incorporating youth voice in the development of policy—a necessary detour from individual-level interventions blaming marginalized communities. On the other hand, we were surprised to find that even when students were queried to imagine a *utopian* system, some of their responses were still quite "practical." These findings present an opportunity for further dialogue, examining the way schooling limits creativity, and vice versa, how a critical education might augment youths' creative capacities.

Findings highlight the importance of honing students' ability to imagine otherwise, as done with any other academic skill set. Indeed, Conchas and Acevedo (2020) remind us that oppression is a double-edged sword, such that students who are rendered *atravesada/o/xs* are also those who have access to *la facultad*, enabling them to reimagine and resist oppressive structures, thereby becoming *nepantlera/o/xs* (Anzaldúa, 2012). Conchas and Acevedo (2020) also remind us that our current education system is fundamentally a colonial project. First, historically, public school officials conceptualized academic institutions as instruments of assimilation, largely influenced by Catholic church leaders. Second, the increasing presence of Mexican students led to the elimination of Spanish curricula and physical abuse. Third, school curricula in the United States is, for the most part, anglo-centric. Fourth, elected officials sought to create a segregated society, and by extension, a segregated education system, a historical fact Mario echoed during his interview.

The *Academy for Future Educators* seeks to contest these historical and contemporary processes. This teacher pipeline program aims to recruit youth, as early as high school, to prepare for college and enter the teaching profession. Given the existing social, economic, and educational inequalities, programs such as these are vital to supporting youth by providing key navigational and academic resources to succeed academically and professionally. Our conception of college preparedness is comprehensive, including traditional academic skillsets, but also going beyond and incorporating youth in the production of knowledge and inspiring them to effect social change. This program recruits and trains youth from urban contexts, with the goal of preparing students to return to their communities as teachers. Most importantly, the *Academy for Future Educators* seeks to cultivate *nepantlera/o/x* teachers who believe that another world is possible—and give birth to it.

## Conclusion

Historically, youth of color have played important roles in leading social change (Solorzano & Delgado Bernal, 2001). From the high school walkouts of the 1960s, to strikes for Chicana/o/x Studies in the 1990s, to calls for increased representation among K-12 teachers, youth of color are central in the transformation of academic institutions. Studies show, however, that youth of color are often rendered silent, marginal, or invisible (Freire, 2000; Rios, 2017; Shedd, 2015). The *Academy for Future Educators* seeks to address these issues by cultivating *nepantlera/o/x* teachers, not merely for the sake of redressing the "teacher shortage," but to empower members of marginalized communities to return home as teachers, as leaders, as agents for social change. Findings highlight the importance of promoting three key elements in GYO programs: (1) fostering a critical consciousness among youth, thereby preparing them to become educators who address key issues affecting their communities; (2) the importance of teacher care, and specifically, an awareness and attentiveness to the social conditions marginalized communities experience; and (3) providing opportunities for youth to delve into speculative inquiry, imagining new possibilities for the future of education.

The *Academy for Future Educators* broadens customary notions of college preparedness to foster *nepantlera/o/x* teachers. This program delves beyond traditional academic skillsets and seeks to prepare youth to become partners, in our efforts to promote social justice. Special emphasis is placed upon critical consciousness development, the production of knowledge, and imagining worlds where inequality and injustice no longer exist. Engaging youth in the production of knowledge calls on us to create these spaces in GYO programs and to integrate their voices in scholarly works, whether it is through special issues, academic journals, or scholarly books. We should strive to challenge the dichotomy between *students* and *scholars*, shifting toward *students as scholars*.

## References

Akom, A., Shah, A., Nakai, A., & Cruz, T. (2016). Youth participatory action research (YPAR) 2.0: How technological innovation and digital organizing sparked a food revolution in East Oakland. *International Journal of Qualitative Studies in Education, 29*(10), 1287–1307.

Anyon, J. (2017). What "counts" as educational policy? Notes toward a new paradigm. In A.R. Sadovnik, P.W. Cookson Jr., & S.F. Semel (Eds.), *Exploring education* (pp. 52–68). Routledge.

Anzaldúa, G. (2012). *Borderlands/la frontera: The new meztiza.* Aunt Lute Books.

Au, W. (2022). *Unequal by design: High-stakes testing and the standardization of inequality.* Routledge.

Baquedano-López, P., & Garrett, P. B. (2023). *On becoming bilingual: Children's experiences across homes, schools, and communities.* Taylor & Francis.

Biko, S. (2015). *I write what I like: Selected writings.* University of Chicago Press.

Brady, M. P. (2022). *Scales of captivity.* Duke University Press.

Bravo, M. A., & Rodriguez-Mojica, C. (2021). Bilingual teaching practices: Meeting the needs of Latina/o youth in secondary schools. *Journal of Leadership, Equity, and Research, 7*(2), n2.

Bristol, T. J., & Martin-Fernandez, J. (2019). The added value of Latinx and Black teachers for Latinx and Black students: Implications for policy. *Policy Insights from the Behavioral and Brain Sciences, 6*(2), 147–153.

Cammarota, J., & Fine, M. (2010). Youth participatory action research: A pedagogy for transformational resistance. In J. Cammarota & M. Fine (Eds.), *Revolutionizing education* (pp. 9-20). Routledge.

Cannella, G. S. (2008). *Deconstructing early childhood education: Social justice and revolution. Rethinking childhood.* Peter Lang Publishing.

Conchas, G. Q. (2012). *Streetsmart schoolsmart: Urban poverty and the education of adolescent boys.* Teachers College Press.

Conchas, G.Q., & Acevedo, N. (2020). *Chicana/o/x dream: Hope, resistance, and educational success.* Harvard Education Press.

Conchas, G. Q., & Rodriguez, L. F. (2007). *Small schools and urban youth: Using the power of school culture to engage students.* Corwin Press.

Davila Jr., O. (2021). Is structural change "practical"? Latino boys & imagining otherwise. *Journal of Leadership, Equity, and Research, 7*(2), 1–13.

Davila Jr., O. (Forthcoming). Teacher diversity as interest convergence? A cautionary note. *Labor Studies Journal.*

Davila Jr., O., Sinha, M., Rodriguez, T., Mariscal, K., Bravo, B., Garza, D., Mann-Wood, M., Alvarez, A., De La Lima, M., & Davis, L. (2022). From "teacher shortage" to resistance: A critical perspective on political discourse, education and imagining otherwise. *Teachers College Record.* https://journals.sagepub.com/pb-assets/cmscontent/TCZ/Commentaries%20Collection/2022%20Commentaries/From%20Teacher%20Shortage%20to%20Resistance-1668099865.pdf

Department of Labor. (2023). *State child labor laws applicable to agricultural employment.* https://www.dol.gov/agencies/whd/state/child-labor/agriculture#asterisk

Fergus, E., Noguera, P., & Martin, M. (2020). *Schooling for resilience: Improving the life trajectory of Black and Latino boys*. Harvard Education Press.

Fernández, J. S. (2021). *Growing up Latinx*. New York University Press.

Freire, P. (2000). *Pedagogy of the oppressed*. Bloomsbury Publishing.

Garcia, A., & Mirra, N. (2023). Other suns: Designing for racial equity through speculative education. *Journal of the Learning Sciences, 32*(1), 1–20.

Gist, C. D. (2022). Shifting dominant narratives of teacher development: New directions for expanding access to the educator workforce through grow your own programs. *Educational Researcher, 51*(1), 51–57.

Gist, C. D., Bianco, M., & Lynn, M. (2019). Examining grow your own programs across the teacher development continuum: Mining research on teachers of color and nontraditional educator pipelines. *Journal of Teacher Education, 70*(1), 13–25.

Hindman, H. D. (2016). *Child labor: An American history*. Routledge.

Jack, A. A. (2019). *The privileged poor: How elite colleges are failing disadvantaged students*. Harvard University Press.

Kim, A., Brewer, T. J., & Heilig, J. V. (2022). Planting toxic seeds in fertile soil: The knowledge acquisition, achievement, and behavioral beliefs inculcated into Teach For America corps members of color. *Handbook of Research on Teachers of Color and Indigenous Teachers*, 1039.

Kohli, R. (2021). *Teachers of color: Resisting racism and reclaiming education*. Harvard Education Press.

Lipman, P. (2013). *The new political economy of urban education: Neoliberalism, race, and the right to the city*. Taylor & Francis.

López, P. D. (2021). Latina/o/x teachers: History, policies, and politics. In E.G. Murillo, Jr., D. Delgado Bernal, D. Morales, L. Urrieta, Jr., E. R. Bybee, J.S. Muñoz, V.B. Saenz, D. Villanueva, M. Machado-Casas, & K. Espinoza (Eds.), *Handbook of Latinos and education* (pp. 124–134). Routledge.

Maharawal, M. M., & McElroy, E. (2018). The anti-eviction mapping project: Counter mapping and oral history toward bay area housing justice. *Annals of the American Association of Geographers, 108*(2), 380–389.

Meiners, E. R. (2016). *For the children?: Protecting innocence in a carceral state*. U of Minnesota Press.

Mirra, N., Garcia, A., & Morrell, E. (2015). *Doing youth participatory action research: Transforming inquiry with researchers, educators, and students*. Routledge.

Morrell E. (2004). *Becoming critical researchers: Literacy and empowerment of urban youth*. Peter Lang.

Nagel, T. (1989). *The view from nowhere*. Oxford University Press.

NCES. (2022). *Digest of education statistics*. Institute of Education Sciences. https://nces.ed.gov/programs/digest/

Noguera, P. (2011). *Walter N. Ridley distinguished lecture*. University of Virginia.

Orfield, G., & Eaton, S. E. (1996). *Dismantling desegregation. The quiet reversal of Brown v. Board of Education*. The New Press.

Philip, T. M., & Brown, A. L. (2020). We all want more teachers of color, right?: Concerns about the emergent consensus. *National Education Policy Center.*

Ramírez, M. M. (2020). City as borderland: Gentrification and the policing of Black and Latinx geographies in Oakland. *Environment and Planning D: Society and Space, 38*(1), 147–166.

Rios, V. M. (2017). *Human targets: Schools, police, and the criminalization of Latino youth*. University of Chicago Press.

Saldaña, J., & Omasta, M. (2016). *Qualitative research: Analyzing life*. Sage Publications.

Shedd, C. (2015). *Unequal city: Race, schools, and perceptions of injustice*. Russell Sage Foundation.

Solorzano, D. G., & Delgado Bernal, D. (2001). Examining transformational resistance through a critical race and LatCrit theory framework: Chicana and Chicano students in an urban context. *Urban Education, 36*(3), 308–342.

Trujillo, T., Scott, J., & Rivera, M. (2017). Follow the yellow brick road: Teach For America and the making of educational leaders. *American Journal of Education, 123*(3), 353–391.

Unda, M. D. C. (2023). The systematic exclusion of Latinx teachers in US public schools: A literature review. *Race Ethnicity and Education*, 1–21.

Valencia, R. R. (2005). The Mexican American struggle for equal educational opportunity in *Mendez v. Westminster*: Helping to pave the way for *Brown v. Board of Education*. *Teachers College Record, 107*(3), 389–423.

Valenzuela, A. (2010). *Subtractive schooling: US-Mexican youth and the politics of caring*. State University of New York Press.

CHAPTER 3

# Excerpt From "Arquitecta De Mis Sueños:

## Activating Students' Home Pedagogies in an Oakland 8th Grade Humanities Classroom"

*Jacey de la Torre*

### Introduction

THE NEED TO acknowledge the rich plural literacies that students collect from their home and community lives is well understood among progressives in education (New London Group, 1996). This recognition, however, only begins a more extensive process that seeks to mobilize students' epistemologies. Classrooms must serve as a space for students' various ways of knowing to meet and co-develop (Moje et al., 2004), particularly concerning the educator's potential to rekindle students' radical imaginations and how they "read the world" (Freire & Macedo, 1987) as tools for education.

As a graduate student, I sought to examine how my student teaching engaged students' diverse pedagogies of the home (Delgado Bernal, 2001). Through this inquiry, I sought to collate and catalyze students' home pedagogies and intergenerational knowledge as wellsprings for learning. In this chapter, I provide several key methods that I used to uplift Latina/o/x and Indigenous Mayan home pedagogies. I will describe the "River of Life" assignment I used in my *Indigenous Identities* unit, my attempts to foster a porous classroom of community-teacher dialogue, my incorporation of student feedback and other lessons learned because of this project, and finally, my attempts to bridge students' collective voices in their final product as an empowering narrative of Oakland's young Latina/o/x community. Honoring students' home knowledges may equip them with a distinct sense of voice and self, capable of navigating environments in higher education and making shrewd postsecondary decisions as stewards of their own stories.

## Bringing the Framework of *Atravesada/o/xs Nepantleando* into Focus

Gloria Anzaldúa's (1987) seminal Chicana feminist text is a bedrock of transdisciplinary thought and praxis. Delgado Bernal (2001) mobilizes Anzaldúa's borderlands theory in her work:

> A mestiza is literally a woman of mixed ancestry, especially of Native American, European, and African backgrounds. However, the term mestiza has come to mean a new Chicana consciousness that straddles cultures, races, languages, nations, sexualities, and spiritualities—that is, living with ambivalence while balancing opposing powers. [...] The concept of a mestiza consciousness has allowed me to better understand the lives of the students I interviewed and to organize and analyze my data in ways that are uncommon in the field of education. [...] I have operationalized a mestiza consciousness to include how a student balances, negotiates, and draws from her bilingualism, biculturalism, commitment to communities, and spiritualities in relationship to her education. (p. 627)

Delgado Bernal (2001) mobilizes the *concept* of being mestiza as a theoretical framework to understand identitarian hybridity. She explicitly charts how the term's use has shifted from a racial designation to a "new Chicana consciousness" that characterizes the interstitial spaces between hegemonic identities. This new use of the term becomes a tool to "better understand the lives of students," notably Delgado Bernal's Latina students navigating a college environment.

To exemplify this hybridity in her work, Anzaldúa deploys the ontology of the *nepantla*, which derives from the Nahuatl word often translated as that "in between" or uneasily categorizable according to the incomplete grammar that the West attempts to apply to the Latin American world. The Framework of *Atravesada/o/xs Nepantleando* (FAN) utilizes the concept of *nepantla* to characterize how Latina/o/x and Indigenous students approach the educational landscape obliquely (Conchas & Acevedo, 2020). In other words, Latina/o/x students, like all marginalized identities in the United States, must learn to develop a relationship to education that is necessarily *atravesada/o/x*: crosswise, disruptive, slanted, creative, *chingón*, new.

Other scholars have also gifted us language with which to locate students' needs and figured worlds (Hatt & Urrieta, 2020) within a particularly Indigenous frame of reference. For instance, discourse in Raza Studies and Latina/o/x scholarship calls for a *re-indigenizing* of classroom spaces, which may allow healing from intergenerational or historical trauma, as well as new ways to craft relation with one's community and school environment (Todd & Robert, 2018; Villanueva, 2013). These tools enable teachers to raise critical consciousness among their students, such that they can read the world through the word (Freire & Macedo, 1987) and come to know a reified sense of self within these worlds (Simpson, 2014).

Racialized and otherwise marginalized students' home pedagogies are not traditionally honored in higher education. Critical understanding of self-in-community readies students to be more powerful agents of their own worlds and possible futures, whether in higher education or in a different avenue within which young people can find meaning and success. This framework allows educators to render Latina/o/x students' educational experiences from an asset-based perspective, acknowledging the generativeness that comes from receiving the world in ways otherwise, beyond the hegemony of white Eurocentrism in academia. Culturally responsive teaching includes readying students to navigate higher education settings within which they might encounter hostility or ignorance toward their backgrounds and epistemologies. When educators are prepared to receive students' multiple sources of knowledge and wisdom, they can more holistically prepare students for the world ahead. In other words, students who have been given the space and time in their K-12 experience to determine their identity and voice would therefore develop a sense of higher preparation for further educational settings.

## Literature Review

In this chapter, the work is situated in a body of research that was a process of braiding together the several strands of my inquiry. One strand in this braid consists of the tools other scholars have used to bridge the home-school divide such that students can nourish the links uniting their worlds. Another strand finds itself in the goal of uplifting students' multilingualism. Finally, in a recursive visit to FAN, the last strand of theory is wielded in examining the spaces "in between" hegemonic categories of being and learning.

Delgado Bernal (2001) defined the *pedagogies of the home* as an array of "communication, practices and learning that occur in the home and community" (p. 624). Her initial study pertained to the condition of Chicana/Mexicana college students and how they recruited their home pedagogies as a means of interrupting dominant discourses in their college environments. These included bilingualism, biculturalism, syncretic spiritualities, and the students' commitment to return and contribute to their home communities. Delgado Bernal (2001) expounded:

> The pedagogies of the home extend the existing discourse on critical pedagogies by putting cultural knowledge and language at the forefront to better understand lessons from the home space and local communities. For example, because power and politics are at the center of all teaching and learning, the application of household knowledge to situations outside of the home becomes a creative process that interrupts the transmission of "official knowledge" and dominant ideologies. (p. 624)

Delgado Bernal (2001) also described the "critical raced-gendered epistemologies that offer unique ways of knowing and understanding the world based on the various raced and gendered experiences of people of color" (p. 107). This evolving conception of complex situated knowledge shaped by raced and gendered experience continues with Yosso's (2005) work on *community cultural wealth.* She defines community cultural wealth as "an array of knowledge, skills, abilities and contacts possessed and utilized by Communities of Color to survive and resist macro and micro-forms of oppression" (Yosso, 2005, p. 77). These types of wealth bolster those communities whose children have been previously alienated from academic communities, especially higher education; honoring the diverse knowledge held by students of color and working-class students opens a wider avenue to future opportunities for these students, including but not limited to college entry.

Yosso (2005) also names realms of knowledge or "capital" developed by marginalized communities as identity practices; familial capital included both pedagogies of the home (Delgado Bernal, 2001) and funds of knowledge (Moll et al., 1992). All students can benefit from bringing in outside funds of knowledge (Moll et al., 1992) into the classroom. Because those of minoritized communities are not traditionally represented in classrooms, honoring their discourses is particularly important. Yosso's different types of capital are interdependent. For example, linguistic and familial capital both concern the plural ways that students express themselves and their relationships with others through such systems as extended kinship networks and multimodal forms of communication.

In dialogue with home pedagogies is the New London Group's (1996) formation of *multiliteracies,* a pedagogy of multiliteracies that positions language as a representational tool constantly being remade by its users. The New London Group (1996) emphasizes the plurality of modern communication channels and focuses on democratizing modes of representation available to young people, our "designers of meaning [and] of social futures" (p. 65). This theorization suggests that all meaning-making is multimodal and that meanings relate to one another in a dynamic relationship.

A key component of this work is the burgeoning and rapidly evolving importance of digital literacies; young people are negotiating increasingly globalized relationships with technology, power, neoliberalism, and civic pluralism. New multimedia spaces can allow users to cultivate new, interconnected lifeworlds that resist the appropriation of community dynamics for corporate interests. The New London Group (1996) asserts with this that the boundaries between lifeworlds are porous and complex. A discourse of hybridity, then, "highlights the mechanisms of creativity and of culture-as-process" (The New

London Group, 1996, p. 82) that empower students to be their own storytellers. Equipped with this framework, Latina/o/x students may mobilize their multiliteracies for success within the K-12 classroom and towards greater college preparedness.

More insistence on hybridity can be found in scholarship that elevates students' complex relationships to multilingualism. García et al. (2017), in their seminal text, describe that language is something you "do," a "dynamic communicative process" (p. 1) wherein students can and do deploy their full linguistic repertoire in a space beyond the dominant spoken language. This process of synthesis and dynamism is generally referred to as translanguaging. This mechanism of language-making is evidence of FAN in action. When students have the depth of knowledge to treat linguistic borders as fluid, when they jump back and forth across the plural forms of speech that they use in their lives, a new way of knowing emerges that insists on a straddling of language: not one or the other, but both.

Another piece of the foundation on which my inquiry rests is the notion of the educational thirdspace. Moje et al. (2004) call for the "strategic integration" of diverse discourses in the classroom. The authors advocate for "the construction of 'third space' that merges the 'first space' of people's home, community, and peer networks with the 'second space' of the discourses they encounter in more formalized institutions such as work, school, or church" (Moje et al., 2004, p. 41).

The authors encourage the integration of funds of knowledge from outside the frame of school, drawing on the innate sociality and interdependency of funds of knowledge. This work rests on Bhabha's (1993) hybridity theory, or the sense of being "in-between" as a process energized by globalization, digitization, and interconnectedness of world and local systems. Soja's (1999) work on thirdspace further critiques the binaries of social and physical space, arguing that spatialization is a socio-political active process. Moje et al. (2004) animate these theories for use in the classroom, affirming that students' different discourses can and must be recruited as educational resources. A pedagogy that cultivates a sense of thirdspace, like the act of crossing over inherent to the FAN network, must then envision itself as more than the sum of its parts.

With these theoretical structures in mind, I now turn to the context and methods I deployed in my classroom to honor students' home pedagogies and epistemologies.

## Setting and Participants

In *Teaching to Transgress,* bell hooks (1994) writes that today's students "rightfully expect that [teachers] will not offer them information without addressing the connection between what they are learning and their overall life experiences" (19). These are guiding words for me: my teaching attempts to center the "connections between." I believe that every identity we hold is also a relationship to something else. Our interconnectedness binds us to one another, constitutes our life-worlds, and urges us to remember our responsibility towards the collective.

I was raised in a predominantly Sikh and Latina/o/x neighborhood in the California East Bay town of El Sobrante. My twin sister and I grew up low income, and the area's crime rate is 135% higher than the national average. In many ways, my home community mirrors aspects of the neighborhood where I teach. My mother is white and my father is a second-generation Mexican-American. My abuela Flora learned English and assimilated into American culture as a means of survival. She did not teach Spanish to her sons because she wanted to protect them from the same harsh treatment she received as a migrant woman in Los Angeles in the 1950s. My dad grew up with a minimal understanding of Spanish and a fragmented connection to his linguistic heritage; mine is similarly punctured with holes.

When I was in school, I developed proficiency in Spanish, built from the colorful snatches of the language that was used in my home community. As I develop my command of Spanish, I see this literacy as building a dual bridge: backward to the language ghosts of my history and forward to a horizon of expanded Chicanisma. My own punctured identity as a Spanish speaker is always present in my practices with students.

While in graduate school at UC Berkeley, I student-taught an eighth-grade humanities class at ASCEND TK-8 School in the predominantly Latina/o/x Fruitvale area of Oakland, California. My classroom as a student teacher formed the core of my study. This class consisted of 27 students and was equally split among boys (12) and girls (12), with an additional three nonbinary and trans-identifying students. Two of my students were Black, one being Afro Latina/o/x, with the remaining 25 identifying as non-Black Latina/o/x. Sixty percent of these students were second-generation Mexican Americans, 30% were second-generation Guatemalan Americans and Indigenous, and 10% were second-generation Honduran or Salvadoran American. Almost all students spoke some level of Spanish and were once considered emergent bilingual (EB). Most of the 8th graders who participated in this research had been at ASCEND since kindergarten and, at the time of the study, were officially designated as Reclassified Fluent English Proficient (RFEP).

The incipient community of Guatemalan families in Fruitvale speak mostly Mam, a Mayan language spoken by half a million people (Rancaño, 2021). On average, about a quarter of the students in my classroom identify as Indigenous Mayan and speak Mam, or their families speak it. Stavely (2019) detailed, "Indigenous languages like Mam are becoming increasingly common in the United States. Several thousand Mam speakers are estimated to now live in Oakland, adding to a larger Mayan community in the Bay Area." Kamiya (2016) with the organization Teacher Scholar Voices conducted a study on Mam-speaking families' desires for their children's education. The authors conclude, "we realized that the work of supporting our newcomer families is mostly about relationship building, listening, and education -- education that can flow both ways, between the school and the parents" (Kamiya, 2016, p. 3). This invitation to *atravesar* (cross) the boundaries that historically exist between power structures and Indigenous families is an act of empowerment; teachers can position families as the experts in their own experiences and knowledge, and educators can hold themselves accountable to listen to their needs.

## Findings

The results of my experiences in the classroom as a student teacher illuminate the need for a pedagogy that honors students' diverse ways of knowing. In their River of Life art projects, students demonstrated a hunger for integrating the multiple geographies and identities of their lives in multivocal, overlapping ways. My conversations with families and other local stakeholders also indicated a desire for teaching that honors the whole child and seeks to develop a student's voice as embedded within the context of their community and family networks. Finally, our class' final poetry project was successful in inviting students to articulate a nuanced self of academic and personal voice.

## *River of Life, Classroom of Storytellers*

One method with which I attempted to weave together students' home and classroom learning was my *Indigenous Identities and Storytelling* unit. Through this 6-week cycle, I implemented a host of tasks meant to meaningfully animate students' pedagogies of the home and Fruitvale community as bases for learning. A task demonstrative of this goal was the River of Life assignment, a 4-day art project. I began with a journal-writing prompt that asked students the following questions:

> What are the key *moments* that have had an impact on who you are today?
> Which are the most important *relationships* in your life?
> Which places marked important *transitions* in your life?

After students had spent some time reflecting on these questions, I continued, "What would your life look like if it were a River? How can you use *images* to symbolize important moments of your life on this River?" We spent three class periods making our Rivers. We did a gallery walk, some partnered shares, and a whole-class debrief on our final day. I asked students, "What did you hear that resonated with you? What kinds of stories do we share with one another? What stories make us different?" My goal with this project was to elevate a specifically Indigenous approach to artmaking; that is, encouraging students to think about both the interconnectedness of their Rivers, and of their shared identities as storytellers.

Students' final products stood as examples of aesthetic thinking and as representative of students' complex experiences and identities. Many students drew the Mexican flag or the Guatemalan flag alongside drawings of the Golden Gate Bridge, the OakTown tree, or the outline of the state of California. Some also drew their bedrooms, the outline of their apartment buildings, the *papel picado* that lines Fruitvale's International Boulevard during the annual *Día de Muertos* festival, and the orange-and-blue concrete sign outside of ASCEND itself. These rich combinations indicated the artists' plural national and regional affinities and attachments to space and place. One student, Manny, created a Tetris-like horizon of buildings on his River signifying his neighborhood in East Oakland. This was overlaid above three stripes of green, white, and red—the colors of the Mexican flag. This choice particularly exhibits the diasporic experience of borders reimagined and overlapping.

My work finds peerdom in Jonathan Rosa's seminar (2020), Latina/o/x Languages and Identities Beyond Borders, specifically concerning his expression that Latina/o/x identities are sometimes conceived of as separate from one another and sometimes subjects "laminate these identities [together]" (21:36). Rosa studied the multifaceted expressions of *Latinidad* among Puerto Rican and Mexican communities in Chicago and noted that Latina/o/x students across different communities express identity connected to place as well as ethnos. These students engaged in image making similar to that of my students, often shading the colors of the Mexican and Puerto Rican flags over symbols of Chicago in spray-painted artwork on murals, skateboards, and shoes. Rosa (2020) details that "diasporic realities and [...] remapping of borders is related to the remapping of [...] Mexicanness and Puerto Riconess" (25:30) in relation to one another. Similarly, my students' experiences with immigration and *Latinidad* engender a mosaic of national and cultural affinities.

Students' use of layers in their artwork to indicate their plural and coinciding identities speaks not only to their sense of geographical fluidity but also to their allegiance to the FAN approach. That is, students insisted on presenting their stories as multiple and co-constitutive rather than only communicating a singular aspect of themselves in their art. This plurality demonstrates students' rewiring of borders to render their own worlds more fully, which may reside comfortably in the "in between" among spaces. Through this connectedness, students may "cross" or defy the figurative borders and restrictive categories that striate their lives. The figures in their Rivers of Life illuminate that students map their identities to and through place to create hybrid images of belonging.

Students' other artistic choices for this project also communicated their layered conceptions of self. Many students used their Rivers to convey chronological accounts of their lives through symbols. One student, Marbin, uniquely divided his River into three parts: his past, present, and future. In his future section, Marbin drew a house he sees himself living in; another building that, in his words, "represents college and writing and things;" and a profile of the future adult he imagines himself to be. "I see Marbin's organization of his project demonstrating the first component of what the Downtown Brooklyn Arts Management Fellows describe as Robin D.G. Kelley's concept of Freedom Dreaming, that is, 'a tool that invites us to create the world we dream of by, first, visualizing the future we want to live in'" (Downtown Brooklyn Arts Management Fellows, 2021). The ordinariness of Marbin's envisionment doesn't detract from its power; rather, I believe we are called to see the fantastical in the everyday and the radical imaginary in our young peoples' visualizations. Furthermore, goals such as access to college and housing can indeed be seen as radical for children of color in the face of late capitalism and neoliberalism. In this and other artistic spaces, we can, and therefore must, co-conspire to connect shared visions of a livable world. Students may more readily carve paths to college and other future successes through rigorous academics, as well as through ample opportunities to engage in critical self-reflection and co-imagining possible futures.

Finally, the class time that we spent sharing our Rivers provided a space for rich translanguaging (García et al., 2017). When students shared what they had made with one another, I noticed that, as they began to explain the labels they attached to certain items or places, their language choices shifted to more fully surround the concepts they drew. For example, Lucas pointed to a sketch of a hospital and a house with a palm tree and recounted, "This is to show the city of Puerto Vallarta, *donde yo naciera y donde viniera mi papá. Todavía nuestra familia tiene conexión a la ciudad* [where I was born and where my father came from. Our family still has ties to the city]." Another student, Francisco, described a painting at his grandparents' house in Guatemala using Mam words *q'ij* (sun) and *xjaw* (moon) to talk about the symbols he made on his River. Other students utilized their plural language repertoires when their drawings represented a particular aspect of their culture, even without accompanying labels. For example, my student Sara described of the food she'd drawn, "I drew these two pieces of pan dulce, *específicamente las conchas rosa y amarilla, porque estos sabores son mis favoritos y el tipo que prefiero también* [especially the pink and yellow conchas, because those flavors are my favorite type of sweet bread]." The FAN structure is also present here through students' straddling across semantic and linguistic divisions: involving symbolization and visual representation in this task helped facilitate students' use of their full language resources when sharing and making meaning of what they'd drawn. Building on their extratextual cognitive resources was an effective scaffold in inviting students' translanguaging into our classroom.

An expansive application of this project may be a systemic responsibility. The school environment at large can take a role in framing students' lived experiences as assets for study (Paris & Alim, 2014). The home-school divide cannot be expected to be undivorced in one assignment. It is therefore our responsibility to do the work of *nepantleando,* or unseparating, these realms of student life that are typically siloed in normative discourses of K-12 schooling. The River of Life assignment allowed students to map and link the multiple arenas of their lives and usher in the more phantasmic, generative spaces of possible futures. If students have experience using their home knowledges and imaginations throughout other learning contexts, they will be accustomed to home-school engagement that deepens over time. That is, when students are equipped to *atravesar* (navigate) the many spaces of their lives, their learning and knowledges can become more fluid across contexts such as home life, extracurriculars, and opportunities for college and career preparation.

### *The Porous Classroom*

Central to the broader work of contextualizing and mobilizing students' local funds of knowledge is the notion that learning experiences must be fungible within and across traditional academic spaces. I want my classroom to be permeable and interact fluidly with the surrounding community in an ongoing ecosystem of exchange. This is a stance of social justice, not only within which educators are constantly committed to learning about the environment of their students, but through which students can begin to reconstruct the idea of classrooms themselves as sites of learning, belonging, and even liberation.

Part of this commitment to trans-community dialogue must be engagement with students' families. Teachers are called to ask for families' input and needs so as to develop a "grassroots" pedagogy (de los Ríos & Molina, 2020) that incorporates "students' lived histories, family cultural practices, and experiences" (p. 49). My communication with families aims to establish and maintain a bilateral channel of exchange. This focus in dialogue holds me accountable to families' offerings and expressions of their needs, which in turn connects me to the wealth of their funds of knowledge. Teachers must listen and respond proactively to families, and we are moreover urged to learn from the epistemologies made knowable through these conversations. Such work enables us to bridge the needs of families to their children's direct classroom experiences, resituating us in the FAN system's imperative to center the strands that tie together our students' lives.

In my practice, I communicate with families about their children's progress, their successes, areas of growth, and conduct several cycles of check-ins for focal students. My conversations with families have been impactful in reinforcing the importance of school-home dialogue as a form of support for focal students. As part of my research inquiry, I used these exchanges as a space to gain a fuller understanding of families' funds of knowledge.

One example of a family sharing their way of knowing with me was a conversation with my student Tina's *abuela*, Eldelmira, over the phone. She shared that Tina moved in with her *abuelos* and had been adjusting to the prolonged absences of her mother, who worked during the night. We discussed the regulatory activities that Tina was doing at her grandparents' house to keep her life structured in the wake of home instabilities. Eldelmira asserted:

> *Las rutinas son muy importantes para los jóvenes. En el hogar usamos las latas para quedarse Tina ocupada por poquito tiempo, para que aprenda las responsabilidades. Todo su comportamiento es sencilla pero también comprometida. Creo que tiene buen flujo entre el trabajo y el juego que la atende en el éxito escolar* [Routines are very important for kids. At home we use chores to keep Tina occupied for a bit of time so that she learns responsibility. She is easygoing but committed. I think she has a good flow between work and play, and this helps with her academic success].

This comment was impactful because it allowed me not just to better understand Tina and her home situation but to envision the interchange more wholly between her and other young people's lives as students and their responsibilities within their family economies. In this case, Tina's participation in the domestic work of her home compounded her overall sense of capability across the arenas of her life. In general, students' engagement in family tasks was constitutive of their home pedagogies and the articulation of these ways of knowing within other spheres of work, including but not limited to their identities as students. Another important piece was Eldelmira's affirmation that her granddaughter's participation in home tasks helps gave her life a needed routine and structure. Yosso's (2005) work on community cultural wealth was present in this conversation, during which familial capital channels directly into assets for learning. Yosso (2005) named the value of familial responsibilities in promoting a sense of duty to one's kinship and community networks. This sense of duty may then fold into a student's own practice in *nepantleando* and fusion of knowledges, through which they consider themselves part of a broader nexus of home and school worlds.

Another parent I spoke with expressed her hopes for her daughter, AJ, "*que su camino continúa a haber andado bien* [that she continues on her journey well]." This was part of a longer conversation we held about high school readiness, both academically and socioemotionally. This mother's words were particularly resonant for me because they captured the idea that one's school experience is a "*camino*," or an expedition through space and time. Student transitions into high school are of constant relevance for me as an eighth grade student teacher, and all middle school teacher-practitioners are called to consider the complex shifts and experiences through which students traffic as they pass from one school year to the next. More universally, all students' senses of self are in a constant state of becoming, and our time with them is a unique opportunity to impart tools with which to navigate their many and ongoing transformational processes of identity- and world-making. Through these passages or "*caminos*," teachers can unite, clarify, and strengthen young peoples' renderings of the world.

Flores (2018) speaks on the "importance of entering spaces as listeners and learners alongside students and families in order to cultivate relationships and transform classroom practices" (p. 60). This process of building strong relationships with families echoes the message of the Teacher Scholar Voices (Kamiya, 2016) study that concludes education must "flow both ways" between schools and the communities they serve (p. 3). Such flow would instantiate a potent educational thirdspace, an act of *atravesando,* that combines the resource and episteme of students' plural realms of life.

Another element of the porous classroom includes collaboration with the neighborhood's various nodes of service, business, and fellowship. After my second research cycle, I had only just begun to have full conversations with local entities about what meaningful partnership looks like. These include community-serving organizations in the Fruitvale neighborhood near our school, including 67 Sueños, Homies Empowerment, Radio B'alam, Hasta Muerte, and Wahpehpah's Kitchen. I am committed to mobilizing these dialogues as part of an expansive commitment to place consciousness in my teaching. Fischer (2020) described that place-conscious pedagogies "assume that individual and collective identities are complexly tied to the perceptual, sociological, ideological, political, and ecological dimensions of the local places we dwell" (p. 4). In crafting relationships with local organizations, I intend to amplify local funds of knowledge and "the readily available agency in communities" as a core component of learning (de los Ríos & Molina, 2020, p. 35). These connections allow students to create a *nepantla* network of community stakeholders that could assist them in endeavors beyond the classroom, college readiness being one such pathway out of many.

## Teaching as Bridge Building

I am hesitant to end my inquiry with any major sense of conclusion, except to say that dialoguing and collaboration will continue to be one spiraling component of which instruction is part. ASCEND follows an expeditionary learning model, centering opportunities for project-based learning. These culminate in an opportunity for students to showcase the products of their learning to the broader community. Towards the end of my research cycle, one of our administrators, Jeff Embleton, helped me develop my new *Indigenous American History and Futures* unit with several local organizations in mind as potential opportunities for transcommunity dialogue and learning. These include Planting Justice, the Sogorea Te' land trust, and the Intertribal Friendship House and Native American Health Center. Partnerships with these organizations may foster bridges for mutual learning and growth between our school and the local community.

Another way my research continues to live and grow is through the incorporation of student feedback. In exit tickets and conversations, I asked my students about their experiences with my *Indigenous Identities* unit and the other structures through which I primarily executed the methods for my inquiry. Notably, many students expressed their dislike toward small-group discussion, around which my and my co-teacher's instruction largely revolved. They had varying reasons for their opinion. One student, Carmen, said that they are more hesitant to speak than they are to write. This sentiment is representative of a cluster of students, who often refrain from oral participation in class due to shyness or confusion over material or both.

In helping students reach grade-level standards for oracy, I think of emotional scaffolding. Many teacher-practitioners whose work I've witnessed or studied speak on the importance of *formal* scaffolds, such as sentence starters and graphic organizers, or that of *informal* scaffolds, such as words of encouragement. I believe that the concurrence of *both* these elements is necessary if we are to holistically provide the supports students need. Even given all the tools to succeed at a task, students will be hesitant to use them if they do not feel socioemotionally confident to do so. I see encouragement less as a tool, though, and more as one integral component of the broader culture of learning and safety that I seek to cultivate in my classroom. Such work requires constant dialogue and (re)shaping of norms and is symptomatic of the porous classroom mentioned above that I aspire towards. Here, I am in conversation with other teacher-practitioners who re-orient their classroom as a site to revive the spirit (Todd & Robert, 2018) and promote a sense of belonging as a prerequisite for student success (Fischer, 2020).

A piece of feedback I received about one of our core activities, small-group discussions, also informed my practice. Some students were discouraged by its unswerving allegiance to the literary analysis of our unit texts. They expressed that the task of close reading, interpreting, and co-constructing meaning about a text began to feel redundant and repetitive throughout the year because they felt confident in their skill and were seeking different challenges in class. Other students expressed that they never felt very successful talking about texts in small-group discussions, and the unchanging format made them feel consistently overwhelmed. My conclusion is that literary analysis should not go out the window but that it could shift to *one of many* tools for responding to texts rather than the principal format. Students enjoyed the other ways offered to interact with text throughout my instruction, such as in the space I gave them to illustrate a scene from one of the unit poems and describe its importance; the assignment to respond to a symbol from one text by making and sharing one's own symbol that represents a similar idea; and the choice I gave students to assign a color or "vibe" to each poem as a way to explain its mood. In each of these tasks, analysis was present and positioned *alongside* other ways of demonstrating an understanding value abstract and aesthetic thinking.

This multidisciplinary approach once again seeks to nourish the FAN system, through which students can *mezclar y combinar* their diverse ways of cognition and problem-solving. When students are given the option to respond to a prompt multimodally, they can more deeply engage in an act of "crossing over" the categories of thought and learning traditionally isolated from one another in education. Here, those categories are abstract alongside analytical thinking, but opportunities for further multidisciplinary teaching abound.

## Toward a Shared Poetics of Oakland as the Path Forword

I responded to student feedback by pivoting away from a discussion-based final performance as an end to the unit, choosing instead to have students model the unit texts with their own writing. This choice built upon students' prior use of personal connections throughout the unit and addressed their preference to de-prioritize academic talk as a summative activity. In our 4-day final week of the unit, my class spent 3 days writing a poem or scene modeled after one of the unit texts. On the last day, students chose one of their poems to revise and share in an open mic.

In addition to the unit texts, Nick and I also introduced some poems from an anthology recently completed by Nick's former student, Carolina, for her senior portfolio at Oakland School of the Arts. Much of her work demonstrated themes mirrored by the poems we had studied, such as reverence towards elders and the connection between place and sense and self. This was a great opportunity to bridge former and current students at ASCEND in an intercommunity dialogue about their shared experiences. For instance, one of Carolina's poems about Fruitvale addressed the issue of gentrification: "I don't like when foreign hands touch Oakland." Some of my students responded with their poems expressing their love for their neighborhood in its full complexity. One of my students, Francisco, wrote in his poem "To Oakland":

> where you can see people have bad luck getting a job just waiting
> a city is like sweet as a candy and a city where i can smell raw food in the street
> [...] and where i still remember when i almost got hit by a drunk guy in his bicycle.

Another of my students, Lucas, titled his poem "Bay Area View":

> The sounds of burning tires and people shouting to each other breaking up
> And also people having dinner in peace and [...] talking about their day.

Finally, one of my students, Jaritza, wrote:

> The sounds of oakland are comforting
> like hearing one of your favorite songs
> you haven't heard in years.

These poems elicited students' intricate feelings toward their home, in which they illustrate the dyadic reality of living among struggle. These expressions exceed the simplistic descriptions with which low-income communities are often framed; instead, pain and pleasure of experience merge, or *nepantlear*, to create a mosaic of feelings. To me, these scripts move beyond surface-level connections to home and present a layeredness that challenges teachers to continue this act of linkage, of *atravesando*: we can thereby draw on students' rich funds of knowledge in ever-evolving ways. Finally, another student, Carmen, wrote a poem tracing their fortitude to family in a particularly resonant way:

> Poderosa latina, guerrera de mi madre.
> Soy como el cielo, clara y transparente.

Arquitecta de mis sueños.
[Strong Latina, warrior of my mother.
I am like the heavens, clear and strong.
Architect of my dreams.]

To me, this writing represents the kind of transformational articulations of self that teachers hope their instruction may elicit for all students. Within Carmen's words may reside Kelley's (2003) freedom dreaming, Yosso's (2005) aspirational capital, and Villanueva's (2013) narratives of hope.

By continuing to grant students the space to construct their own meaning in response to class material, I hope to help them engineer and enact their own *sueños*. Flores (2018) asserts the importance of writing as a process of regeneration: "It is the act of writing that provides a release in which we reconstruct our lived experiences and realities to construct new meanings. In this process of reconstruction, we begin to heal" (p. 3). In all, this instruction succeeded in nourishing students' use of their experiential knowledge by inviting them to develop and share stories about their worlds. Importantly, students' earlier River of Life assignment prepared them to surface the complex themes of home and belonging present in their poetry by way of storying and organizing their narratives in multiple ways throughout the unit.

The need for students to express their knowledge in ways other than speaking and writing about the literary elements of text is an issue that circumscribes my entire project. That is, honoring the spirit and epistemology of the home calls us to think of more expressive ways of talking about a text and teaching at large. Students' ways of knowing frequently include and exceed the scope of tasks offered to them in class. This means that teachers must think of ways to remain loosely allegiant to standards of writing, reading, and speaking so that students can access discourses of power (Delpit, 1988) while at the same time developing a curriculum that engages their multiliteracies in genuine depth. This can look like incorporating more opportunities for abstract thinking, as was successful in my unit. It can also look like using more multimedia content as texts worthy of analysis, to vary the means of students' response to material, and to reorganize the notion of what constitutes a valid rigorous text. In my unit, I made use of artwork and am now thinking about how to incorporate other media, such as music, film, infographics, and more. Such coupling of multimedia to more traditional learning materials is a move towards *atravesando* students' interests and classroom learning, honoring the diversity of modern literacies and straddling the edge between academic and cultural epistemologies.

## Conclusion

In this chapter, I outlined briefly existing frameworks for using student's home pedagogies for meaningful learning in the classroom. I discussed several methods with which I pursued my inquiry using both instruction and conversations beyond the classroom. What has emerged illustrates the need for radical fluidity within education. The porous classroom plants a seed of access to future classrooms and opportunity. Students who more fully develop their educational identities with all of the tools in their lives made available to them—the wisdom of their elders, the poetics of their neighborhoods, the internationalism of their families—bloom into more complete versions of the people they will grow up to be. These students necessarily become more prepared to succeed in higher education settings as stewards of their own stories. When we honor home pedagogies in our teaching, we allow students to develop a confident and capable academic identity, rich in its plurality and animated in its strength. These empowered students may then break down barriers in higher education by arriving at secondary institutions with a reified sense of self that can carry them through educational and institutional challenges.

We are thus called to destabilize the boundaries between classroom and non-classroom spaces, the previously siloed discourses of literary analysis and personal connection to text, considering which experiences are literary, and so much more. All of these strategies imagine teaching as a process of bridge building across the spaces that constitute our students' lives and the spirit that animates them. Our epistemologies constantly shift into new, complex landscapes of being and doing. It is with these movements in mind that, as educators, we can wrest new formations of our shared worlds.

## Reference

Anzaldúa, G. E. (1987). Borderlands/La Frontera: The New Mestiza. *San Francisco: Aunt Lute.*

Bhabha, H. K. (1993). Culture's in between. *Artforum International*, 32(1), 167-171.

Conchas, G. Q., & Acevedo, N. (2020). *The Chicana/o/x dream: Hope, resistance and educational success.* Harvard Education Press.

de los Ríos, C. V., & Molina, A. (2020). Literacies of refuge: "Pidiendo posada" as ritual of justice. *Journal of Literacy Research*, 52(1), 32–54. https://doi.org/10.1177/1086296X19897840.

Delgado Bernal, D. (2001). Learning and living pedagogies of the home: The mestiza consciousness of Chicana students. *International Journal of Qualitative Studies in Education*, 14(5), 623–639. https://doi.org/10.1080/09518390110059838

Delpit, L. D. (1988). The silenced dialogue: Power and pedagogy in educating other people's children. *Harvard Educational Review*, 58(3), 280. https://doi.org/10.17763/haer.58.3.c43481778r528qw4.

Downtown Brooklyn Arts Management Fellows. (2021). "Freedom dreaming: A call to imagine." *Freedom Dreaming Collective*, CUNY Academic Commons. https://freedomdreaming.commons.gc.cuny.edu/about/.

Fischer, S. (2020). Placemaking and the child reader: Toward a place-conscious framework for reader response research and pedagogy. *Journal of Language and Literacy Education*, 16(1), 1–25.

Flores, T. T. (2018). Cultivando la voz mujer: Latina adolescent girls and their mothers rewriting their pasts and imagining their futures. *Literacy Research: Theory, Method, and Practice*, 67(1), 211–227. https://doi.org/10.1177/2381336918786733.

Freire, P., & Macedo, D. (1987). Literacy: reading the word and the world. Praeger Press.

García, O., Johnson, S. I., Seltzer, K., & Valdés, G. (2017). *The translanguaging classroom: Leveraging student bilingualism for learning.* Caslon.

Hatt, B., & Urrieta Jr, L. (2020). George: Our Cultural Broker into the Figured World of Academia. In M. Sánchez & M. Billye Sankofa Waters (Eds.), *How we got here: The role of critical mentoring and social justice praxis* (pp. 32-41). Brill.

hooks, b. (1994). *Teaching to transgress.* Routledge.

Kamiya, M. (2016 Dec. 15). Education flows both ways: An inquiry into the needs of Mam speaking newcomer students. Lead by Learning. https://weleadbylearning.org/2016/12/15/education-flows-both-ways-an-inquiry-into-the-needs-of-mam-speaking-newcomer-students/.

Kelley, R. D. G. (2003). *Freedom dreams: The Black radical imagination (New ed.).* Beacon.

Moje, E. B., Ciechanowski, K. M., Kramer, K., Ellis, L., Carrillo, R., & Collazo, T. (2004). Working toward third space in content area literacy: An examination of everyday funds of knowledge and discourse. *Reading Research Quarterly, 39*(1), 38–70.

Moll, L. C., Amanti, C., Neff, D., & Gonzalez, N. (1992). Using approach. *Theory Into Practice, 31*(2).

Moll, L., Amanti, C., Neff, D., & Gonzalez, N. (2006). Funds of knowledge for teaching: Using a qualitative approach to connect homes and classrooms. In C. Amanti, L.C. Moll, & N. Gonzalez (Eds.), *Funds of knowledge* (pp. 131–141). Routledge.

New London Group. (1996). A pedagogy of multiliteracies: Designing social futures. *Harvard educational review, 66*(1), 60–92.

Paris, D., & Alim, H. S. (2014). What are we seeking to sustain through culturally sustaining pedagogy? A loving critique forward. *Harvard Educational Review, 84*(1), 85–100.

Rancaño, V. (2021). *How Mam speakers are helping 1,300 students in Oakland navigate remote learning*. KQED.

Rosa, J. (2020 Nov. 18). *Latinx languages and identities beyond borders* [Lecture]. Mellon Sawyer Seminar Series, Duke University.

Saldaña, J., & Omasta, M. (2016). *Qualitative research: Analyzing life*. Sage Publications.

Simpson, A. (2014). *Theorizing native studies*. Duke University Press.

Soja, E. (1999). Thirdspace: Expanding the scope of the geographical imagination. *Human Geography Today, 260*.

Stavely, Z. (2019). *In this Oakland classroom, students teach each other their home languages -- and learn acceptance*. Local News Matters Bay Area.

Todd, K. L., & Robert, V. (2018). Reviving the spirit by making the case for decolonial curricula. *Decolonial Pedagogy: Examining Sites of Resistance, Resurgence, and Renewal*, 57–72. https://doi.org/10.1007/978-3-030-01539-8_4.

Villanueva, S. T. (2013). Teaching as a healing craft: Decolonizing the classroom and creating spaces of hopeful resistance through Chicano-Indigenous pedagogical praxis. *The Urban Review, 45*, 23–40.

Yosso, T. J. (2005). Whose culture has capital? A critical race theory discussion of community cultural wealth. *Race Ethnicity and Education, 8*(1), 69–91.

CHAPTER 4

# Advancing An *Atravesada/o/xs Nepantlera* Summer Bridge Curriculum:

## Nurturing Latina/o/x Student Facultad in College Access and Transition

*Brianna R. Ramirez*

### Introduction

THIS CHAPTER EXPLORES how an introductory higher education and collegiate experience course component, of a more extensive summer bridge program for first-time freshmen and first-generation students before the start of their fall quarter at a Research 1 (R1) university, contributes to nurturing Latina/o/x student *facultad* and facilitating the activation and application of student *facultad* in the navigation of the new higher education context. The current chapter aims to build on previous scholarship that considers the summer bridge curriculum as a significant opportunity and opening for supporting Latina/o/x students and students of color in their college transition and success through an approach that recognizes students as holders of knowledge and rooted in advancing critical consciousness and navigation of higher education contexts (Puente & Ramirez, 2021, 2023). To do so, this chapter explores an Introduction to Higher Education and College Experience course that is offered as part of a summer bridge program that serves incoming first-generation, low-income, or students of color at an R1 institution in southern California. Students who participate in this summer bridge program complete two university-level courses for academic credit and attend various events and workshops that introduce them to campus resources and strategies to support their academic, social, and emotional well-being while in college. This chapter centers on the development of student *facultad* in an Introduction to Higher Education and College Experience course for supporting navigation of higher education as *atravesada/o/xs*. In exploring the course curriculum and outcomes through a Framework of *Atravesada/o/xs Nepantleando*, this chapter makes visible the curricular strands that advanced an *atravesada/o/xs nepantleando* pedagogical orientation for a higher education curriculum that intentionally and thoughtfully supported Latina/o/x students in honing and strengthening their capacity to see and navigate how inequities function and shape opportunity structures and experiences for students of color and first-generation college students. This chapter argues that a summer bridge curriculum that explicitly teaches about the histories and contemporaries of racism and intersectional marginalities in higher education before the start of a student's first quarter can support the strengthening and development of Latina/o/x student *facultad*, which in turn supports *atravesada/o/xs* in their strategic navigation of this new context.

## Literature Review

Summer bridge programming is one institutional approach to supporting students in their access and transition to college during the "bridge" period in the summer before the start of their first quarter/semester at the institution (U.S. Department of Education, 2015). This section provides an overview of the summer bridge literature, including the traditional deficit and developmental approach of summer bridge programs, diverse summer bridge curricular strands, and an understanding of the outcomes and impact of summer bridge programs on college access and retention.

### *Developmental and Deficit Approach in Summer Bridge*

Summer bridge programs have traditionally been framed as interventions in the college access and transition processes of first-time freshmen or transfer students who are considered "lacking" and "underprepared" for college (Kallison & Stader, 2012; U.S. Department of Education, 2015). Most summer bridge programs function as remedial or developmental interventions designed to reduce the need for developmental coursework (Sablan, 2014). Rooted in the achievement gap (Ladson-Billings, 2006) argument that college access and transition can be challenging for "academically underprepared students," developmental summer bridge programs often aim to address the presumed gaps in knowledge and skills necessary for accessing and navigating college successfully (U.S. Department of Education, 2015). Many summer bridge programs focus on engaging students from historically marginalized backgrounds, including first-generation students, students of color, and students from low-resource schooling contexts, who are typically framed as lacking the necessary preparation to succeed in college-level courses (Kallison & Stader, 2012). Therefore, summer bridge programs aim to remediate the education accessible to historically marginalized students by providing fundamental content knowledge, information, resources, and navigational strategies considered completely absent in their communities. Not surprisingly, these programs, rooted in a developmental approach, aim to prioritize academic knowledge over social and emotional dimensions of the transition (Barnett et al., 2012), intending to attend to the academic "deficits" students from historically marginalized communities are carrying to higher education. The focus on remediation approach in summer bridge programs for addressing the educational disparities and gaps experienced by historically marginalized students upholds deficit assumptions and beliefs about the very students these programs are intended to equitably serve.

### *Summer Bridge Curriculum*

Overall, summer bridge programs aim to support college readiness and transition (Sablan, 2014; U.S. Department of Education, 2015), yet these efforts' central strands, approach, and implementation vary. The curriculum of summer bridge programs varies across programs, institutions, and the student population the programs intend to serve (U.S. Department of Education, 2016). The U.S. Department of Education (2016) describes summer bridge programs as typically 2 to 4 weeks that include some attention to four curricular strands: (1) orientation to college life and resources, (2) academic advising, (3) training in skills necessary for college success, and/or (4) accelerated academic coursework. Some programs aim to prioritize math, reading, and writing skills through coursework, some center college preparation that attends to the emotional and psychological dimensions of the transition (U.S. Department of Education, 2015), and others aim to teach about college knowledge and college expectations (Barnett et al., 2012). There are also summer bridge programs with a curriculum that advances a discipline's content knowledge, such as Science, Technology, Engineering, and Mathematics (STEM)-centered programs supporting STEM pathways for underrepresented students (Ashley et al., 2017). The approach or mission of the program also shapes the curriculum. Programs rooted in a remediation goal often prioritize academic knowledge over social and emotional dimensions of the transition for historically marginalized students, such as focusing on fundamental math and writing skills, along with study skills, test taking, and learning styles, to attend to the academic "deficits" students from historically marginalized communities are carrying to higher education (Barnett et al., 2012). Puente and Ramirez (2021, 2023) consider how the summer bridge curriculum can move beyond remedial or developmental programming to address the "educational debt" owed to students of color from historical and contemporary sociopolitical contexts and systems instead of positioning students as deficit through a lens that prioritizes the achievement gap (Ladson-Billings, 2006) at the core of these programs. Puente and Ramirez (2021, 2023) argue that summer bridge programs aiming to serve students of color through a race and intersectional equity lens can be an intentional space for centering a curriculum that nurtures student intersecting identities and critical understanding of the higher education context, which can support student transition and navigation rooted in the racialized identities of students. Scholars argue that these are necessary to justly serve and prepare students of color to access and transition to college (Puente & Ramirez, 2021, 2023).

### *Outcomes*

Though the impact and effect of summer bridge programs on student achievement vary, potentially positive impacts have been quantitatively found (U.S. Department of Education, 2016). Research has identified positive impacts of summer bridge programs on student retention (Cabrera et al., 2013), grade point average (GPA) (Pascarella & Terenzini, 2005; Strayhorn, 2011), and academic skills (Strayhorn, 2011). Attending a summer bridge program positively affected the postsecondary attainment of underrepresented minority (URM) students (Murphy et al., 2010). Scholars have also begun to explore the impacts of summer bridge programming beyond traditional norms and operationalizations of success in the transition to college. For example, Strayhorn (2011) found that for underrepresented college students, summer bridge programming can also contribute to supporting students in forming positive beliefs about their academic skills and abilities within a context where underrepresented students often feel inferior or lack of belonging. Additionally, Puente and Ramirez (2021) argue that summer bridge programs can also support Latina/o/x students to understand and reclaim their community history with educational inequities, cultivate a campus community, and negotiate their racial and cultural identities in their new college environment that can support strategic and successful negotiations of the campus racial climate.

## Theoretical Framework

This chapter applies a Framework of *Atravesada/o/xs Nepantleando* (FAN) to explore how an introductory critical race higher education and college experience course can facilitate and strengthen Latina/o/x student *facultad* and navigation of an R1 and predominately white institutional context. FAN situates Latina/o/x students as holders of *facultad*, or as Gloria Anzaldúa defines, a "sixth sense" or embodied knowledge that is activated, awakened, and carried by people who are marginalized within systems and structures of oppression. *La facultad* emerges within the marginalized body as a mode of survival and protection and stems from a deep, intimate, and structural understanding of power and inequity in society (Keating, 2022). FAN argues that Latina/o/x students are holders of *facultad* due to their *atravesada/o/xs* position within U.S. society and U.S. educational systems. The *facultad* that students hold, carry, and create supports them in negotiating and navigating the higher education context as *atravesada/o/xs,* perpetual outsiders in higher education and constantly straddling the liminality. Acevedo-Gil (2019) coined college-going *facultad* to name the experience and practice through which Latina/o/x students filter and understand college information and resources through their intersectional identities, experiences, and contexts to anticipate and support the navigation of challenges and obstacles that they may experience as *atravesada/o/xs* in higher education contexts.

Applying FAN in this chapter facilitates redefining college access by positioning access within the intersecting systems of oppression that shape Latina/o/x student educational opportunity structures and experiences. Additionally, FAN is utilized to unapologetically position student and community histories, experiences, and knowledge systems as central to shaping Latina/o/x college access and negotiations. In doing so, FAN supports a rejection of traditional college knowledge that positions Latina/o/x students as lacking critical college information, resources, and capital and instead reframes Latina/o/x students as holders of *atravesada/o/xs* college-*conocimiento* (Acevedo-Gil, 2019), critical and embodied knowledge that is necessary for *atravesando* to college. Through FAN, this chapter makes visible how a summer bridge course that centers the histories and experiences of students of color in higher education can facilitate the strengthening and activation of *facultad* within higher education through explicit support in situating and connecting their intersectional realities and experiences within the history, climate, and resources about their new higher education context. Therefore FAN facilitates the exploration and theorization of a summer bridge curriculum that is rooted in supporting *atravesada/o/xs* in negotiating the white supremacist, heteropatriarchal, and colonial histories and contemporaries that underlie higher education (Wilder, 2013) through nurturing and activating their embodied knowledge systems within their college access and transition.

## Methods

This chapter braids together the experiences of Latina/o/x students who have previously completed the higher education course as part of the summer bridge program and my pedagogical testimonio (Prieto & Villenas, 2012; The Latina Feminist Group, 2001) as an instructor for this course, previous teaching assistant for this course, and co-researcher on a study exploring summer bridge programming. The method section includes an overview of the summer bridge program, followed by insight into this research's data collection and analysis processes.

The summer bridge program is a free, 5-week program that serves incoming first-year students at the R1 institution in California. Students submit a formal application for the program in spring with priority admission for first-generation and students from historically underserved populations. The program aims to support students in strengthening their academic skills, confidence, and belonging and building community at their new campus through seminars, workshops, activities, courses, and an optional residential component. Summer bridge students are assigned to a peer mentorship group, a small group of participants led and facilitated by a peer mentor, a current student at their university, and summer bridge alumni. Peer mentors are accessible to students during the summer and the first academic year. Students in the summer bridge program can earn up to eight units of college credit by completing two courses of the preselected summer bridge offerings. The higher education course I am centering in this chapter, American Higher Education and Collegiate Experience, is one of the courses offered each year. The American Higher Education and Collegiate Experience course is designed to facilitate critical thinking about equity and justice in higher education, exploring the purpose of higher education through a historical and contemporary lens.

The Latina/o/x student voice highlighted in this chapter is part of a larger study of the summer bridge curriculum, experience, and impact on first-year experience at the R1 conducted with the summer 2018 cohort. In 2018, the program included 292 majority students of color, as reflected in the following racial/ethnic demographics: 56% Latina/o/x, 27% Asian, 11% Black, 4% white, and 2% other racial/ethnic identified or not disclosed. Students were all residents of California, with San Diego County, Los Angeles County, and Riverside County among the most represented among the student participants. Data for this larger study included 34 one-on-one semi-structured interviews with students of color who completed the program, including Black, Latina/o/x, and Asian American students, seven identity-based focus groups with three to six students each, including Black, Latina/o/x, Southeast Asian, LGBTQ+, men of color, women of color, and students of color in STEM, and a series of observations of the summer bridge courses and programming. Students who completed the summer bridge program in the summer of 2018 were invited to participate in the data collection through in-class announcements made by the research team during the last week of the summer bridge program and through a series of recruitment emails during and post program completion. The recruitment announcements and emails invited students to participate in an individual interview if they identified as a student of color and to participate in a focus group if they identified with any of the identity-based groups. All interviews and focus group data were transcribed for data analysis. This chapter draws from the 24 Latina/o/x students who participated in individual interviews and 6 students in the Latina/o/x focus groups in this larger qualitative study co-led by a collective of Chicana/o/x education scholars and graduate students. The Latina/o/x students whose voices are centered in this chapter are first-generation college students, many from low-income and immigrant backgrounds, and majoring in various disciplines.

My pedagogical *testimonio* (Prieto & Villenas, 2012) makes visible my reflections and learning from engaging with the course as a critical race feminista Chicana educator in many roles, including an instructor (summers 2022, 2023), previous teaching assistant for the course (2019–2021), and co-researcher for the larger summer bridge research project (2018–2020). I began documenting my pedagogical testimonio in the summer of 2022 through written reflections and voice memos that capture a retrospective account of my experience as a researcher and teaching assistant and my present experience while teaching the course. The intersection of these experiences informs my intent of making visible the power and possibility for cultivating student *facultad* through racial and intersectional justice-centered higher education courses as part of the summer bridge and transition curriculum.

This course, and therefore this chapter or any writing about the course curriculum, reflects a more extended history of critical and just educators and instructional assistants who have taught this course and have unapologetically engaged in a race/ethnicity-centric and critical race theory analysis and teaching of higher education. I recognize the undeniable mark, labor, and contribution of previous instructors and teaching assistants in the curriculum for this course and in my pedagogical journey and learning. The course is rooted in a vision for racial and intersectional justice in education laid out by previous instructors. As an instructor and previously as a teaching assistant, I hope my efforts continue to move this intended legacy forward. As a critical race and Chicana/Latina feminist scholar and educator, I strive to strengthen the curriculum and pedagogy in this introductory course to reflect the intersection of race, gender, sexuality, and nativism, along with the explicit teaching of making visible the hidden curriculum of higher education that functions against our students.

Data analysis for this chapter aimed to make visible the layers of the summer bridge curriculum that nurtured student *facultad*. The data analyzed for this chapter included 24 Latina/o/x student interview transcriptions, one Latina/o/x focus group transcription from the 2018 program, five written pedagogical reflections from 2022–2023, and two transcribed voice memos when I taught the course in the summers of 2022 and 2023. With the intent of making visible the curricular components of this summer bridge course, the data were analyzed first through holistic coding (Saldaña, 2013), which supported the "chunking" of the various forms of data in this study to identify broader topics or strands. Holistic coding is an appropriate first-cycle coding method guided by a researcher's general idea of what they aim to investigate (Saldaña, 2013). A list of holistic codes encompassing the various data forms was then further developed into curricular themes through focused coding (Saldaña, 2013). The themes from the analysis are presented in the findings section as the core curricular strands.

## Findings

Through insight from student experience and insight from my pedagogical *testimonio*, this chapter makes visible how the higher education course in the summer bridge curriculum can facilitate the strengthening of Latina/o/x student *facultad* within their new higher education context during the summer at the start of college. In this findings section, I highlight four central curricular strands that are braided through the course with examples from student data to demonstrate how the course nurtured student capacity to see and understand how power and marginality shape opportunities and experiences of Latina/o/x students and students of color in higher education. In this section, I make visible how student engagement with each course curricular strand supported student *nepantleando*, strategic navigation as *atravesada/o/xs* in college.

The four curricular strands that support strengthening Latina/o/x student *facultad* include: (1) strengthening our shared language to name, understand, and discuss issues of race, racism, and intersectionality in higher education; (2) making visible the history and lineage of U.S. universities and the institutional history of the campus students will attend; (3) centering campus racial climate and the experiences of Latina/o/x and students of color broadly and at the specific institution; and (4) advancing the strategic navigation and resistance of Latina/o/x and students of color in higher education. These course strands are situated within larger bodies of literature and, importantly, the institutional history, contemporary student experiences, and resources and supports of the specific campus students are entering. The findings demonstrate how a course can nurture Latina/o/x students' capacity to understand how power and systems function in higher education and at this campus and how students activated and applied course learning and experience to understand and navigate the college campus as *atravesada/o/xs*.

## First Curricular Strand: *Strengthening Shared Language to Name Issues of Race, Racism, and Intersectionality in Higher Education*

A core dimension of the introductory higher education course that students complete as part of the summer bridge program centers on advancing a shared language for understanding and discussing issues of race, racism, and intersectionality in higher education. This curricular strand is engaged in the course through an unapologetic centering on race and intersectional justice. Historically, this higher education course has been taught through a critical race orientation that centers a race, racism, and intersectional lens and approach to education and education justice (Delgado & Stefanic, 2000). Throughout the course, we engage with the Combahee River Collective (1977) and Kimberle Crenshaw's (1989) intersectionality framework as central theories, perspectives, and concepts for framing a race and intersectional justice approach in all the themes and topics we discuss. Students are invited to position themselves within the systems we are exploring and to reflect on how they experience identity, systems, and marginalities. This invitation is intended to uplift the experience and knowledge students hold and have created about how systems of marginality exist and function in their daily lives. In the focus group data, an incoming Latina undergraduate, Martha, highlighted her learning from taking this course during summer bridge:

> Some of the things that we learned in [the course], things that always felt, like microaggressions and stuff, but I never had words for it, or I never knew that that was an actual thing everyone goes through, so even learning that it's an actual thing, just that alone was reassuring that oh, I am not just feeling these things, you know, that they're real. I thought that was reassuring, I also liked how the course kind of touched upon a multitude of underserved and underrepresented communities and not just a singular one or two. Obviously, within this program, there are people of all backgrounds, so it kind of gave everybody a chance to find something to which they could relate and also learn something new about their peers. I liked that.

Martha shows that the course supported her in reflecting on their own experiences and in naming and speaking about her experiences in connection to course concepts and theories as she shared that "things [she] always felt ... but ... never had the words for it." Martha holds *facultad,* a deep and intimate knowledge of inequities and marginalization rooted in her experiences and embodiments. Importantly, having a shared language to name, discuss, and reflect on how power systematically and structurally functions against students of color and diverse populations supported students in connecting their experiences with students from different marginalized backgrounds, a powerful lesson as students began their college trajectory. This curricular strand supports students in bridging their *facultad,* the embodied knowledge and sensitivity for recognizing that power exists in U.S. society that stems from their lived experiences to the context of education. Critical pedagogue Paulo Freire argues and demonstrates how the capacity to "name" one's world is a necessity of critical consciousness, solidarity, and learning.

### Second Curricular Stand: *Making Visible the History and Lineage of U.S. Universities and the Institutional History of the Campus*

Braided throughout this course is the curricular strand of making visible the historical context of the contemporary forms of racism and marginality that students from racialized backgrounds experience in higher education. This strand is contextualized within a more extensive scope of U.S. higher education and the institutional history of the specific campus students attend. For example, in the summers of 2022 and 2023, we engaged in learning from the work of Craig Steven Wilder (2013), reading excerpts from *Ebony and Ivy*, a core text through which Wilder tracked and made visible the historical racist and colonial roots of the first universities in the United States. Coupled with this reading and discussion, we also critically analyzed enrollment and graduation data at the institution, disaggregated by race/ethnicity, gender, financial aid recipients, and first-generation college student status. This historical and contemporary connection serves as a core introduction to the course to make the lineage and connections between the past and the student's transition to the university. Denise, an undocumented Latina student, shared in a plática that through taking the course during a previous summer, she described, "there were a lot of things that were mentioned [in the course] that kind of made me realize why it's so hard for people who are minorities to be here or to receive a higher education overall." Denise points to the course-building awareness about the historical structural and systemic inequities that shape higher education access and opportunity for generations of historically marginalized communities. Similarly, Anthony, a Latino student in a physical science discipline, described that the course supported his understanding of the racial/ethnic student composition and navigating culture shock at the campus. He shared:

> [The course] definitely did help with the culture shock that everybody talks about, coming into a big university. 'Cause I know that for me, I don't see many Latino students, especially in my classes, but I know that they're there. When I took [the course], we looked at the numbers of

> students by race at this campus and also ways to challenge that mindset of I'm the only one, so it kind of helps me think like, I do belong here, like don't belittle yourself, and you're not the only one, but you're like the only one in this class, but you know there are people in other spaces here, so you're not the only one.

Anthony highlighted that explicit analysis and discussion of the campus history and demographic data made visible the underrepresentation of Latina/o/x students and students of color that he would then experience as the only one or one of the Latina/o/x students in his courses. However, this learning also supported Anthony in recognizing from the data that there was a larger Latina/o/x student presence on campus than reflected in his courses, a powerful reminder to Anthony that supported him in combating the structural racism in access and opportunity reflected in the underrepresentation of Latina/o/x students on college campuses. Anthony shows that students mobilize knowledge about the historical and institutional contexts in their strategic navigation and negotiations as *atravesada/o/xs* in higher education.

### Third Curricular Strand: *Centering Campus Racial Climate and The Experiences of Latina/o/x and Students of Color Broadly and at the Specific Institution*

A third dimension of the course curriculum builds on our learning of higher education's historical racist and colonial roots with explicit learning and discussion of the campus racial climate experienced by Latina/o/x students and students of color at the institution students attend. To support a theoretical exploration of student contemporary experiences, we engage with campus racial climate literature (Harper & Hurtado, 2007; Hurtado, 1992; Hurtado & Carter, 1997) as a lens to explore recent and contemporary experiences of students of color on campus. This includes analyzing the recent demands written by the Black Student Union (BSU) on campus and engaging with recent literature on the experiences of different historically marginalized groups in their transition and navigation of higher education. By including diverse experiences within higher education, the intention is to support students in seeing themselves reflected or connected within the readings this week. Students are invited to bring their lived experience and knowledge about societal inequities to their new context in higher education by positioning themselves and their current college transition within campus racial climate literature. Veronica, a Latina student in a social science discipline, shared the following:

> I think there were many things that we covered [in the course] that you usually don't cover in other settings, So, like institutional racism, I didn't know that was a thing, microaggressions, and just everything that has to do with being in a higher education setting as a minority overall. I grew up in a community that was just minorities, so I went to school with many minorities. You would rarely see anyone that was a higher class than you. So, for me, I didn't necessarily know how to talk about or recognize microaggressions or institutional racism because we were all the same basically, but I know they exist and that they impact me ... now that I am in college, I see and feel the whole, like feeling inferior to others because, there are even people who are probably the same race/ethnicity as you, but they grew up in a higher class. They don't relate to what you went through, even though you kind of come from the same background in a way.

Veronica described that she explored and engaged with the course material rooted in her lived experience growing up in a racially segregated and low-income community, attending low-resourced schools shaped and informed her transition to college, and she navigated a context and climate that is so different from her community. Veronica's experience points to the course serving as a bridge connecting her critical reflection and understanding of her lived experience to the new climate she is navigating in higher education. It was evident in Veronica's experience that through learning and exploring the contemporary racial climate at the university and recent literature on this topic, her sensitivity and critical understanding of inequities in her own life and of educational opportunity structures, her *facultad* was strengthened and applied to understanding how these systems produce and create student *atravesada/o/xs* in higher education and shape their everyday experience in college.

**Fourth Curricular Strand:** ***Advancing Strategic Navigation and Resistance of Latina/o/x and Students of Color in Higher Education***

The fourth curricular component that supported the bridging of Latina/o/x student *facultad* to higher education in this course is the explicit learning about navigation and resistance of Latina/o/x and students of color in higher education. For example, in the summer of 2023, we read "The Campus Underground Railroad: Strategies of Resistance, Care, and Courage within University Cultural Centers (Jenkins et al., 2021) from *Plantation Politics and Campus Rebellion* (Williams et al., 2021) that situates campus cultural centers, programs, and spaces as to politicize the existence, role, and supports available specifically on campus. Coupled with this reading, students learned from alumni of the campus and alumni of the summer bridge program who served as guest speakers and shared their experiences engaging specific spaces, resources, and supports on campus in their journey to graduating from the campus. For example, in the summer of 2022, a queer Latino student who at the time was enrolled in a higher education counseling master's program served as a guest speaker, and in the summer of 2023, an undocumented Chicana student at the time the first year of their doctoral program facilitated a class session. The course presented opportunities to learn and hear about strategies for navigating the campus from students who experience higher education as *atravesada/o/xs* at the intersection of systems. This curricular component also included explicit learning about resistance in education. For this unit, we explored and applied the transformational resistance model (Hannegan-Martinez et al., 2022) and analyzed archival materials from the university library that documented examples of student activism on campus.

Learning about agency and resistance in higher education from the perspective of students of color and students at the intersection of marginalized systems can empower and further strengthen student agency. Abigail, a Latina student, shared her experience in taking the course during a previous summer bridge program:

> I feel like if a situation ever comes up, I know the words to defend myself or to defend my friend who's also a minority. So, in a way [the course] educated me and it's also going to help me in the future if anything ever happens to me.

Abigail highlighted that the course strengthened her capacity to advocate for herself and others by developing "the words to defend myself or to defend my friend." Abigail made visible that she now held the "words" to advocate for herself, expressing her knowledge and practice of discussing history, data, and facts about inequities in higher education. She situated this knowledge and "words" as a tool to leverage in her navigation and negotiation in higher education. This curricular strand supports students in recognizing the long history of student agency and resistance in higher education and invites students to reflect on their role, contribution, and agency as they begin their college journey as *atravesada/o/xs*. Powerfully, Abigail pointed to students activating learning from the course to protect, defend, and advocate for themselves and other students from marginalized backgrounds, an important lesson they take with them on their college journey.

## Advancing an *Atravesada/o/x Nepantlera* Summer Bridge Curriculum

The Latina/o/x student experience centered in this chapter makes visible the impact of a summer bridge course and curriculum they engaged with before their first year in college. Braided together with insight about key curricular strands of the Introduction to Higher Education and College Experience course rooted in my experience engaging with this course as instructor, teaching assistant, and co-researcher, this chapter demonstrates how a summer bridge course intentionally situated within advancing student learning and consciousness of the racial and intersectional oppressive histories and contemporaries in higher education, specifically at the institution students are entering, can facilitate making the hidden curriculum of higher education visible to students and be enacted by Latina/o/x students in their navigation of higher education. Previous studies found that summer bridge can positively impact college transition and traditional markers of success (i.e., GPA) for students from historically marginalized backgrounds (Cabrera et al., 2013; Pascarella & Terenzini, 2005; Strayhorn, 2011). However, summer bridge efforts often draw from a remedial and deficit approach that positions students and their communities as lacking critical college knowledge (Tornatzky et al., 2002) about the transition to college. Scholars argue that this remedial and deficit paradigm positions the summer bridge curriculum as filling a role of depositing knowledge and resources into students and communities before the start of their semester/quarter in college without critical interrogation or teaching of the institutionalized racist and oppressive systems that produce these inequities (Puente & Ramirez, 2021). Ultimately, rooted in racist and marginalized ideologies about communities, a curriculum that is rooted in this deficit and remedial lens limits the possibilities of summer bridge justly serving Latina/o/x and students of color.

This chapter builds on scholarship that situates summer bridge as a critical opportunity to nurture critical understanding and exploration of intersectional identities, systems, and histories that shape the contemporary experiences of Latina/o/x students in higher education (Puente & Ramirez, 2021, 2023). By considering student *facultad* (Acevedo-Gil, 2019; Conchas & Acevedo, 2020), the embodied knowledge, and lived experience navigating within and against systems and structures of marginality in education, this chapter re-positions students as holders and carriers of knowledge (Delgado Bernal, 2002) about power, marginality, and navigation. This chapter demonstrates how an Introduction to Higher Education and College Experience course completed by students as part of their summer bridge experience can support and facilitate Latina/o/x students in strengthening and activating their *facultad* within their transition to higher education.

Scholars have explored *facultad* within higher education to make visible how Latina/o/x students navigate and negotiate higher education contexts at the intersection of various systems of marginality (Acevedo-Gil, 2019; Conchas & Acevedo, 2020; Muñoz, 2018). Muñoz (2018) considered the process of strengthening and activating *facultad* within higher education by exploring how undocumented college student activists strengthen their critical legal consciousness through their lived experience and negotiations within higher education. Acevedo-Gil's (2019) college-going *facultad* identified the process through which Latina/o/x students anticipate challenges as *atravesada/o/xs* in higher education through a practice of engaging, understanding, and making meaning of college information through their lived realities and intersectional systems they experience. College-going *facultad* is an embodied practice and system of knowing that Latina/o/x students hold, carry, and enact to strategize and navigate challenges and obstacles that will experience as students who experience educational spaces in the United States on the margins (Acevedo-Gil, 2019; Conchas & Acevedo, 2020). This chapter establishes that an *atravesada/o/xs nepantlera* summer bridge curriculum, a summer bridge effort rooted in the explicit interruption and teaching about the historical and contemporary marginalities that shape processes, practices, and experiences that produce student *atravesada/o/xs* in higher education, can support students in positioning and activating their *facultad* and support student preparation for the negotiations, navigation, and challenges they will encounter in college. Therefore, summer bridge can cultivate space for activating, strengthening, and awakening Latina/o/x student *facultad* as a vital tool for student success, navigation, and resistance.

## Implications

This research argues that opportunities for students to explicitly bridge and situate their *facultad* to a higher education context at the start of their college trajectory are meaningful as Latina/o/x students experience the college transition as *nepantleras*, constantly navigating, straddling, and negotiating their racial and gendered identities and systems with their new college student contexts (Ramirez et al., 2023). Higher education institutions can advance an *atravesada/o/xs nepantlera* summer bridge curriculum through nurturing and supporting Latina/o/x student access and transition through cultivating spaces of learning and community that recognize the practices and systems of knowing students bring with them and intentionally support students to strengthen and position this *facultad* within how racism and intersectional oppressions exist, are upheld, and produced within higher education.

An *atravesada/o/xs nepantlera* summer bridge curriculum requires institutions to *expand and invest in summer bridge efforts that intentionally and exclusively serve Latina/o/x students and students of color*. As many institutions explore and strive to become Hispanic-serving institutions, this research argues that serving Latina/o/x students requires a summer bridge curriculum and programming that explicitly attends to serving Latina/o/x students and centers the nuanced experience of Latina/o/x students and students of color in higher education. Students need spaces and opportunities to build confidence, belonging, and community as they start college that feels comfortable, inviting, and relevant to their experience. Summer bridge curriculum should facilitate the activation of student facultad within higher education as a core strategy for negotiating, navigating, and thriving in higher education.

*Nurturing student facultad will require summer bridge facilitators to engage in an epistemological shift away from traditional, Eurocentric, and developmental summer bridge approaches and revisiting how these ideological beliefs are embedded in all facets of a summer bridge curriculum.* This shift requires a deep interrogation of how Latina/o/x students and students of color have traditionally been positioned and engaged in summer bridge efforts and generally in higher education. Facilitating an *atravesada/o/xs nepantlera* summer bridge curriculum, which is often guided through instructors, staff, faculty, peer mentors, and folks in various other roles, requires the capacity to recognize and potential to nurture student embodied knowledge.

Furthermore, *an atravesada/o/xs nepantlera summer bridge curriculum must awaken, nurture, and strengthen student facultad through a racialized and intersectional atravesada/o/x centered curriculum.* The goal of a summer bridge curriculum rooted in serving Latina/o/x students and students of color in college access and transition that recognizes and nurtures student facultad is to facilitate and create space for students to strengthen their college-*conocimiento* (Acevedo-Gil, 2019), critical and embodied knowledge that is necessary for *atravesando* to college as racialized and marginalized students. This chapter explored the curriculum strands of a specific course taught within a summer bridge program to highlight that learning about Latina/o/x students and students of color knowledge, agency, and resistance, historically and in the contemporary, can awaken, nurture, and position student *facultad* within higher education.

## Conclusion

This chapter explored summer bridge programming and curriculum as a critical opportunity for supporting Latina/o/x college access and transition. This chapter offers *atravesada/o/xs nepantlera* summer bridge curriculum to deconstruct and reimagine the possibilities for summer bridge that are rooted in the racialized and marginalized identities and systems that students navigate in their access and transition to college. Through analysis of the curricular strands of a summer bridge course, this chapter argues that an *atravesada/o/xs nepantlera* summer bridge curriculum, a summer bridge curriculum that facilitates student learning and reflection with the racialized and intersectional *atravesada/o/x* student experience and history in higher education, could support an awakening, strengthening, and application of Latina/o/x student *facultad* within their new higher education context.

Student experiences in this chapter point to *atravesada/o/xs* activating and drawing from their *facultad* for surviving, negotiating, and navigating the racist and oppressive higher education systems and climate during their first year in college. The analysis shared in this chapter centers on exploring one course that forms just one component of a larger summer bridge program. Further examination can make visible how an *atravesada/o/xs nepantlera* summer bridge curriculum is possible within other dimensions of course design and coursework and within the various components of a program to support the creation and alignment of a summer bridge program curriculum that aims to justly serve and is accountable to supporting Latina/o/x students in access and transition to college.

## Reference

Acevedo-Gil, N. (2019). College-going facultad: Latinx students anticipating postsecondary institutional obstacles. *Journal of Latinos and Education, 18*(2), 107–125.

Ashley, M., Cooper, K. M., Cala, J. M., & Brownell, S. E. (2017). Building better bridges into STEM: A synthesis of 25 years of literature on STEM summer bridge programs. *CBE—Life Sciences Education, 16*(4).

Barnett, E. A., Bork, R. H., Mayer, A. K., Pretlow, J., Washington, H. D., & Weiss, M. J. (2012). Bridging the gap: An impact study of eight developmental summer bridge programs in Texas. *National Center for Postsecondary Research*.

Cabrera, N. L., Miner D. D., & Milem J. F. (2013). Can a summer bridge program impact first-year persistence and performance? A case student of the new start summer program. *Research in Higher Education, 54*, 482–490.

Combahee River Collective. (1977). *A Black feminist statement* (pp. 269-277). https://careprogram.ucla.edu/education/readings/Combahee1977

Conchas, G. Q., & Acevedo, N. (2020). The Chicana/o/x Dream: Hope, Resistance and Educational Success. Harvard Education Press.

Crenshaw, Kimberlé. (1989). Demarginalizing the intersection of race and sex: A Black feminist critique of antidiscrimination doctrine, feminist theory, and antiracist politics. *University of Chicago Legal Forum 1*(8), 139-167.

Delgado, R., & Stefancic, J. (Eds.). (2000). *Critical race theory: The cutting edge*. Temple University Press.

Delgado Bernal, D. (2002). Critical race theory, Latino critical theory, and critical raced-gendered epistemologies: Recognizing Students of Color as holders and creators of knowledge. *Qualitative Inquiry, 8*(1), 105–126.

Hannegan-Martinez, S., Mendoza Avina, S., Delgado Bernal, D., & Solorzano, D. G. (2022). (Re)Imagining transformational resistance: Seeds of resistance and pedagogical ruptures. *Urban Education*, 00420859221092973.

Harper, S. R., & Hurtado, S. (2007). Nine themes in campus racial climates and implications for institutional transformation. *New Directions for Student Services, 2007*(120), 7–24.

Hurtado, S. (1992). The campus racial climate: Contexts of conflict. *The Journal of Higher Education, 63*(5), 539–569.

Hurtado, S., & Carter, D. F. (1997). Effects of college transition and perceptions of the campus racial climate on Latino college students' sense of belonging. *Sociology of Education*, 324–345.

Jenkins, T.S., Conerly, R., Hypolite, L.I., & Patton, L.D. (2021). The campus underground railroad: Strategies of resistance, care, and courage within university cultural centers. In B.C. Williams, D.D. Squire, & F.A. Tuitt (Eds.). *Plantation politics and campus rebellions: Power, diversity, and the emancipatory struggle in higher education* (pp. 199-224). SUNY Press.

Kallison, J. M., & Stader, D. L. (2012). Effectiveness of summer bridge programs in enhancing college readiness. *Community College Journal of Research and Practice, 36*, 340–357.

Keating, A. (2022). *The Anzaldúan theory handbook*. Duke University Press.

Ladson-Billings, G. (2006). From the achievement gap to the education debt: Understanding achievement in US schools. *Educational Researcher, 35*(7), 3–12.

The Latina Feminist Group. (2001). *Telling to live: Latina feminist testimonios*. Duke University Press.

Muñoz, S. M. (2018). Unpacking legality through La Facultad and cultural citizenship: Critical and legal consciousness formation for politicized Latinx undocumented youth activists. *Equity & Excellence in Education, 51*(1), 78–91.

Murphy, T. E., Gaughan, M., Hume, R., & Moore, S. G. (2010). College graduation rates for minority students in a selective technical university: Will participation in a summer bridge program contribute to success? *Educational Evaluation and Policy Analysis, 32*, 70–83.

Pascarella E. T., & Terenzini, P. T. (2005). *How college affects students: A third decade of research*. Jossey-Bass.

Prieto, L., & Villenas, S. A. (2012). Pedagogies from Nepantla: Testimonio, Chicana/Latina feminisms and teacher education classrooms. *Equity & Excellence in Education, 45*(3), 411–429.

Puente, M., & Ramirez, B. R. (2021). Relearning self, recentering comunidad, and reidentifying within academia: A culturally relevant approach to summer bridge programs for incoming Latinx undergraduate students. *About Campus, 25*(6), 23-28.

Puente, M., & Ramirez, B. R. (2023). Summer bridge as a counterspace: Redefining postsecondary success for students of color. *Journal of Student Affairs Research and Practice*, 1-14.

Ramirez, B. R., Puente, M., & Contreras, F. (2023). Navigating the university as nepantleras: The college transition experiences of Chicana/Latina undergraduate students. *Journal of Diversity in Higher Education, 16*(5), 1–13.

Sablan, J. R. (2014). The challenge of summer bridge programs. *American Behavioral Scientist, 58*(8), 1035–1050.

Saldaña, J. (2013). *The coding manual for qualitative researchers.* Sage.

Strayhorn, T. L. (2011). Bridging the pipeline: Increasing underrepresented students' preparation for college through a summer bridge program. *American Behavioral Scientist, 55*(2), 142–159.

Tornatzky, L. G., Cutler, R., & Lee, J. (2002). College knowledge: What Latino parents need to know and why they don't know it (ED469295). ERIC. https://eric.ed.gov/?id=ED469295

U.S. Department of Education. (2015). *Developmental Summer Bridge Programs. What Works Clearinghouse Intervention Report.*

U.S. Department of Education (2016). *Summer Bridge Programs. What works Clearinghouse Intervention Report.*

Wilder, C. S. (2013). *Ebony and ivy: Race, slavery, and the troubled history of America's universities.* Bloomsbury Publishing USA.

Williams, B. C., Squire, D. D., & Tuitt, F. A. (Eds.). (2021). *Plantation politics and campus rebellions: Power, diversity, and the emancipatory struggle in higher education.* State University of New York Press.

CHAPTER 5

# The Ambivalent Experiences of Undocumented Students as *Atravesada/o/xs Neplantleando* in STEM at a Community College During the COVID-19 Pandemic:

## Practical Lessons for the Cultivation of College Readiness in Higher Education

*Luis M. Andrade*

### Introduction

When the COVID-19 pandemic began in 2020, early studies found that while the entire world faced health risks, COVID-19 had a disproportionately negative effect on communities of color, LGBTQ+ populations, and other minoritized communities (Liu & Modir, 2020; Salerno et al., 2020). Black, Latina/o/x, and Indigenous populations had the highest cases of infections and deaths, and communities of color showed higher signs of depression and mental health difficulties than white and other communities (Liu & Modir, 2020). Fortuna et al.,

(2020) argued that such minoritized communities "are the same communities already experiencing the toxic stress of poverty, crime, unemployment, racism, and discrimination" (p. 1).

Additional studies revealed that the COVID-19 pandemic disproportionately negatively affected the stress levels in undocumented and migrant communities due to a combination of unemployment, health disparities, and risks of deportation (Endale et al., 2020; Liu & Modir, 2020). Despite governmental responses to assist American citizens, such as emergency relief federal aid, and educational institutions' piecemeal attempts (e.g., financial aid and student resources), studies revealed that undocumented populations in general were not included in such interventions (Montiel et al., 2022). The pandemic had a negative effect on undocumented students' socioemotional states, too, because they worried about their and their family's health and economic stability, and they reported a lack of assistance or validating instruction at school (Andrade, 2021c).

Despite the existent research, less is known about the experiences of students navigating Science, Technology, Engineering, and Mathematics (STEM) fields in community colleges during the pandemic to cultivate their college readiness. As Aurin et al. (2021) illustrated, "According to a 2018 U.S Census Bureau Survey, there are approximately 454,000 undocumented college students ... Largely absent from existing research, however, is a focus on undocumented students in STEM" (para. 1–2). Such research is important because undocumented students often enroll in community colleges due to their affordability, closeness to home, and accessibility (Valenzuela et al., 2015). Hence, there is an exigency to understand the identities and needs of undocumented students in STEM to create curricular and institutional support for them, especially in community colleges (Aurin et al., 2021; Flores, 2011; Valenzuela et al., 2015).

Grounded in the Framework of *Atravesada/o/xs Nepantleando* (FAN) (Conchas & Acevedo, 2020), this study draws from *testimonios* of 14 undocumented Latina/o/x students majoring in distinct STEM fields at a community college. The study aims to understand their experiences and generate a list of recommendations for higher education leadership to cultivate college readiness and better address their needs during the pandemic and beyond. FAN is fitting and helpful in the present study due to its centralization of student voices and survival mechanisms when exploring undocumented students' intersectional experiences and knowledge to transform their communities and educational institutions. The study will first provide a brief literature review about barriers that undocumented students face and systems of support that help them thrive, an explanation of FAN, the use of *testimonios* as the core methodology, and the *testimonios* of students' ambivalent experiences—the simultaneous interplay between positive and negative experiences—as they inhabited states as *atravesada/o/xs nepantleando* in STEM during the pandemic. The study ends with the practical recommendations for higher education leadership.

## Barriers and Support Systems for Undocumented Students

Researchers have extensively documented the barriers that undocumented students face in higher education, including financial difficulties, a lack of support, and fears of deportation (Perez et al., 2009, 2010; Teranishi et al., 2015). Additional studies found that undocumented students faced negative interactions with faculty or staff on their campuses and campus climates that did not affirm undocumented students (Abrego, 2006; Perez, 2010; Suárez-Orozco & López Hernández, 2020). In community college contexts, Terriquez (2015) showed that undocumented students faced financial strain, stress, and mental or other health problems, and additional obstacles.

Researchers have noted that undocumented students face unique psychological stressors and psychological trauma (Enriquez et al., 2021) that impede the attainment of higher education degrees (Fernandez, 2018). One stressor is the perpetuation of ideologies of "deservingness" by educational institutions, politicians, media, and society (Anguiano & Nájera, 2015). The ideology of deservingness intersects notions of "illegality," meritocracy, and dichotomies of good versus bad migrants and perpetuates the marginalization of undocumented students, nonstudents, and families (Anguiano & Nájera, 2015; Conchas & Acevedo, 2020; Enriquez et al., 2019). The COVID-19 pandemic exacerbated undocumented students' stress, too, because of their preexisting economic vulnerabilities, competition over jobs, and limited access to health care or other resources (Endale et al., 2020; Enriquez et al., 2021). In a study of 109 undocumented students, researchers found that the participants faced "high clinical levels of anxiety and depression," stress, and suicidal ideation during the pandemic (Goodman et al., 2020, p. 34). Ongoing anti-immigration policies, police brutality in the United States, and inflexible or insensitive faculty expectations also added to their negative psychological states (Andrade, 2021c; Montiel et al., 2022).

Other research pinpoints systems that may cultivate college readiness and support. For instance, financial aid services are of utmost importance because a lack of federal financial aid has negatively affected undocumented students' well-being and success (Diaz-Strong et al., 2011; Weissman, 2019). As such, researchers recommend that institutions must find ways to provide scholarships, grants, and money to students without requiring Social Security numbers or risking their legal livelihoods (Jaimes Pérez, 2014). Additional studies show the importance of counselors who understand undocumented students' identities and needs (Tapia-Fuselier, 2019), undocumented student resource centers and spaces (Tapia-Fuselier, 2021), professional development for faculty, staff, and leadership (Nienhusser & Espino, 2017), changes in curriculum to validate students and minimize microaggressions (Andrade, 2021b; Nienhusser et al., 2016), and support for student clubs and organizations, mental health services, and advocacy for students (Valenzuela et al., 2015). The present study furthers the research on systems of support for undocumented STEM students during and beyond the pandemic.

## *Atravesada/o/xs Nepantleando* in Theoretical Perspective

The previous literature review identifies barriers and systems of support that coincide with Conchas and Acevedo's (2020) FAN presuppositions that students inhabit identities as *atravesada/o/xs* in and outside of school but can positively navigate such spaces' *nepantleando* if there are support systems for them to build bridges for themselves and others. At the core of Conchas and Acevedo's (2020) FAN is "feminist scholarship in the field of education that has interweaved Anzaldúan concepts, such as *atravesada/o/x* (transgressor), *nepantla* (in-between), *la facultad* (ability to see beneath the surface), and *nepantlera/o/x* (individuals who navigate in-between spaces)" (p. 2). The FAN is essentially committed to several goals:

1. Identifying the nature of and how policies or institutions marginalize students and place them in positions as *atravesada/o/xs,*
2. Explaining how students critically recognize oppressive conditions via distinct *facultades* to positively resist and protest while living and traversing distinct spaces (*nepantleando*), and
3. Identifying systems of support that activate students' productive *nepantleando.*

While engaging in distinct *facultades,* or understandings of the underlying oppressive conditions they encounter, *atravesada/o/xs* navigate in-between states, a *nepantla/o/x* way of living, that help them navigate such conditions to eventually enact pragmatic liberatory actions. As such, FAN "engage asset-based and interdisciplinary perspectives to highlight the various strategies that Chicana/o/x students use to foster hope, resistance, and success in the education system" (Conchas & Acevedo, 2020, p. 12).

To achieve their first goal, Conchas and Acevedo (2020) provide examples of distinct policies throughout history and their logics that make students live in limbo and precarious states. For example, policies have long failed Chicana/o/x students by misunderstanding their needs, criminalizing them, especially Latino males, or perpetuating xenophobic, anti-immigration, or heteronormative sentiments. In the case of immigration policies, the government has denied undocumented Latina/o/x student's paths to citizenship, and this has negatively affected their well-being and academic success. Moreover, policies that are racist, gendered, and classist have marginalized and perpetuated coloniality that does not account for the complexities, intersectional identities, and histories of students. As such, Conchas and Acevedo (2020) illustrate that students inhabit the state of *atravesada/o/xs.*

Conchas and Acevedo (2020) then turn to understand how students engage in *la facultad* as they inhabit *nepantla* to resist and "subvert systems of coloniality and oppression in the U.S. educational system to achieve success" (p. 21). To engage in *la facultad* is to be constantly aware of surroundings, to look below the surfaces of educational terrains, and, consequently, to move from such a critical consciousness to resistance and collective empowerment. For example, the authors provide different case studies that exemplify how students at 4-year universities or community colleges, student parents, or students who have a disability while majoring in STEM fields resisted and found educational pathways "to support their families and become an example for future generations" (Conchas & Acevedo, 2020, p. 13). *La facultad* enables students to tap into their agency and identify support systems that help them build bridges, become hopeful, and collaborate with others—this is Conchas and Acevedo's third goal of identifying systems of support that facilitate students' productive *nepantleando.* As examples, students' testimonios reveal that special programs, such as MESA, working with peers, faculty support, school mentors, and family are sources that positively inform or empower students to become productive *nepantlera/o/xs* to persist and succeed. Lastly, the case studies' findings debunk deficit mindsets held by faculty and administrators, which view students as deficient, unskilled, or in stereotypical ways (e.g., students as criminals).

Despite the existing research and FAN findings, there is a dearth of research about undocumented students' experiences in STEM (Aurin et al., 2021), which makes the application of FAN to understand undocumented students' experiences in STEM during the pandemic timely and urgent. The remainder of this study discusses *testimonios* as the main methodology, the findings, and recommendations for higher education leadership.

## Methodology

The present study utilizes *testimonios* as the core methodology. *Testimonios* emerge from a tradition of feminist and critical research that centers students' voices, civic engagement, and resistance to oppressive educational systems (Conchas & Acevedo, 2020; Pérez Huber, 2009). *Testimonios* challenge Eurocentric, gendered, colonialist, and racist dimensions of Western academic spaces as they focus on social justice and attention to previously silenced or excluded voices in distinct institutions, including educational institutions (Delgado Bernal et al., 2012). *Testimonios* may also challenge traditionally Eurocentric paradigms because they do not rely on quantitative approaches, which tend to reduce findings to statistics or numerical data; on the other hand, *testimonios* depend on intimate, personal relationships between researchers and participants to identify the unquantifiable, lived experiences of people. Pérez

Huber (2009) views testimonio as "a verbal journey of a witness who speaks to reveal the racial, classed, gendered, and nativist injustices they have suffered as a means of healing, empowerment, and advocacy for a more humane present and future" (p. 644).

### *Data Collection and Recruitment*

One way of capturing *testimonios* is through interviews that are conducive "to understand [students'] realities within a larger context of structural and systematic inequality–within and beyond educational institutions" (Pérez Huber, 2009, p. 649). To that end, after receiving Institutional Review Board approval, I sought to recruit students who self-identified as undocumented, majoring in STEM, and over the age of 18 to interview them. Procedurally, a dean who oversees an undocumented students program provided me with two lists of undocumented students in STEM and their emails because I have worked with the undocumented student program for many years. The first list included 85 students and the second list included 20 students. I proceeded to email students on both lists to solicit participation in the late summer and early fall seasons in 2023. I also asked STEM faculty members to share a flier with students asking them to participate in the study.

I recruited 14 Latina/o/x students (see Table 5.1) and used one-on-one interviews that took approximately 1 hour each. During the interviews, I used a questionnaire with open-ended questions that allowed them to speak about their origin stories, the reasons why they selected STEM majors, and how they felt navigating such fields during the pandemic. While some researchers may interview students for extended periods of time several times to gain rich *testimonios* (Conchas & Acevedo, 2020), the 1-hour duration of interviews in the present study was sufficient to reach thematic saturation or enough consistency and repetition in descriptions, to gain enough insight to fulfill the purpose. Thirteen interviews occurred via Zoom and one student sent me written responses to my questions.

**Table 5.1** *Description of Participants*

| Pseudonym | Gender | Age | Country of Origin | Ethnicity | DACA Recipient? | Major |
|---|---|---|---|---|---|---|
| Cherry | Female | 20 | Mexico | Hispanic/ Latinx | No | Aerospace Engineering |
| Santiago | Male | 32 | El Salvador | Hispanic/ Latinx | No | Biochemistry |
| Mati | Female | 24 | Mexico | Hispanic/ Latinx | No | Biology |
| Rosa | Woman | 25 | El Salvador | Hispanic/ Latinx | No | Chemistry |
| Melanie | Female | 20 | Mexico | Hispanic/ Latinx | No | Computer Information Systems |
| Cafe | Female | 22 | Mexico | Hispanic/ Latinx | Yes | Computer Science |
| Jose | Male | 20 | Mexico | Hispanic/ Latinx | No | Computer Science |
| Luis | Male | 30 | Mexico | Zapotec | Yes | Computer Science |
| Moon | Female | 25 | El Salvador | Hispanic/ Latinx | No | Computer Science |
| Tlaloc | Male | 21 | Mexico | Hispanic/ Latinx | Yes | Computer Science |
| Olivia | Female | 33 | El Salvador | Hispanic/ Latinx | Yes | Computer Science & Computer Programming |
| Jacob | Male | 26 | Mexico | Hispanic/ Latinx | No | Computer Programming |
| Vanessa | Female | 21 | Mexico | Hispanic/ Latinx | No | Math |
| Renata | Female | 20 | Guatemala | Hispanic/ Latinx | No | Mechanical Engineering |

### *Setting and Sample*

The participants in the present study were selected from a community college in an urban city of Southern California that is a Hispanic-Serving Institution and has a predominantly Latina/o/x student body. At the time of the study, the school transitioned to offer on-ground courses as the state of California relaxed COVID-19 rules, including indoor mask mandates.

Figure 5.1 lists the participants and uses pseudonyms to safeguard their identities. Nine students self-identified as Female/Woman and five students as Male. The sample includes students from Mexico, El Salvador, and Guatemala. Fourteen students self-identified as Hispanic/Latina/o/x and one self-identified as Zapotec. The students' majors are alphabetized under the Major column.

### *Testimonio Themes*

After transcribing all interviews, I sought predominant themes in students' *testimonios* by closely reading all of the statements many times. This was a process that included looking for repeated descriptions and words that create certain categories (Pérez Huber, 2009). Echoing Pérez Huber's (2009) approach to analyzing *testimonios*, I sought "thematic categories that emerged from the data" (p. 647), such as constant references to support services, including the undocumented student program, or descriptions about gained skills, complex, intersectional difficulties, feelings of loneliness, and other complementary tellings. I looked for and identified saturation or the point in which students said similar things or described experiences in consistent ways. As such, I created a final list of saturated common themes by quantifying students' responses to show predominance; such quantification is reflected in the *testimonio* findings.

### *Researcher Positionality*

When analyzing *testimonios*, constant critical reflexivity and genuine honesty are vital to do justice to participants' voices (Creswell & Miller, 2000; Pérez Huber, 2009). Therefore, it is important to share my positionality. My desire to be fully transparent and honest comes from my own history as a formerly undocumented student and member of a mixed-status family. In other research, I have discussed the ways that my upbringing helped me develop a critical *nepantlera/o/x* consciousness while navigating higher education institutions and balancing the pressures of home and the sociopolitical oppressive landscapes on my journey to the professoriate (Andrade, 2021a). The emergence of a *nepantlera/o/x* consciousness energizes my desire for racial equity in my research, at my site of employment, and beyond. It is also important to disclose that I have worked with, interviewed, mentored, and published studies about undocumented students for over a decade. My positionality and advocacy show a commitment to the communities of undocumented students in schools, a "prolonged engagement in the field" (Creswell & Miller, 2000, p. 127), which is important for trust and positive rapport with participants, as well as fidelity to report the findings in an ethical and credible way.

## Students' Ambivalent *Testimonios*

For the purposes of clarity and practicality, this section lists positive and negative experiences that students reflected in their *testimonios*. Despite this organization, my goal is to show that a separation into strictly positive or negative *testimonios* is not entirely clear-cut because almost all students described tugs-and-pulls between good or bad experiences, or nuanced ambivalence in their experiences. Ambivalence means that while some students had very positive descriptions of their experiences in STEM, their *testimonios* also included some negative elements. The same is true for some *testimonios* that had largely negative descriptions of their experiences—they, too, identified some positive aspects of their experiences. Hence, reading the ambivalence in the following *testimonios* may be bemusing or perplexing at times, but it is a reflection of modes of living that *atravesada/o/xs nepantleando* inhabit.

### *Testimonios of Positive Experiences in STEM During the Pandemic*

Eight students' *testimonios* revealed largely positive experiences with some degrees of ambivalence while they navigated STEM majors. The reasons for such experiences differed.

#### *Support services at school.*

Several students explained positive experiences because they received important support services from the school. As Vanessa explained:

> As an undocumented student in STEM, I would say my experience has mainly been positive. For starters, [the school] provides a lot of support for its undocumented community from [an undocumented student program] with lots of resources, to free legal services, to our own [undocumented student program] therapist. The main problem being an undocumented STEM student has been the uncertainty the future holds. Many times, I find myself questioning whether I'll be able to make the most of my degree, let alone stay in this country.

Similarly, Olivia illustrated:

> So right now, at the school level, it seems good. Like I have access to the same thing that the other students have, like ... tutoring, and I can do internships and I'm fortunate that I have DACA ... I'm really able to get paid for my internships where I work ... I think it'll be hard and it'll be different once I'm outside of school, I think that's when it will affect me more. When I might not be able to work in a field that I got my degree in.

Vanessa and Olivia's *testimonios* suggested that they had good experiences due to the services provided to them, but they both showed a degree of ambivalence when they revealed that they were afraid of their future careers because of their status. It is important to note that Olivia was one of the few students who had a DACA permit during the pandemic, while other students did not (see Figure 5.1). Benuto et al. (2018) found that, while DACA was helpful to many undocumented students, some students eventually felt liminal feelings of nonbelonging when they realized the truly limited benefits of the permit. Moon also stated:

> Normally, they don't have a lot ... for computer science ... However, the [STEM] program has a specific tutoring center and where you can get help any time. So that makes me feel like I have more support ... and also the counseling. They have counseling.

Moon's *testimonio* showed ambivalence because it spotlighted the importance of tutoring and counseling provided by the STEM program, but these services were not found outside the program. In all, the *testimonios* coincided with research that identifies special programs as important sites that cultivate college readiness and relationships with counselors and tutors (Conchas & Acevedo, 2020; Tapia-Fuselier, 2019, 2021; Valenzuela et al., 2015) and undocumented students' fear of their futures in STEM because of their status (Aurin et al., 2021).

*Gaining useful skills and personal growth.*

Other students reported gaining useful skills or personal growth in difficult STEM courses. For example, Luis explained:

> I would say, it's been challenging ... But also, on the other and the flip side, I think it's been as a student in STEM, ... it's allowed me to change how I think, change how I approach problem-solving. And so, the STEM classes that I took were, yes, challenging, but they were ... laboratories where I got to practice ... critical thinking and problem-solving skills through a variety of exercises ... Yeah, that's been my overall experience: challenging but very rewarding.

Jacob illustrated:

> When I first started I was very optimistic because ... I was like, 'I can do whatever I want to,' but once I started failing classes, that discouraged me, but I feel like when I was going to school, there was the STEM lab that I really appreciate, because I've made a lot of connections there with like people who who are able to help me like my chemistry classes. I remember all the tutors ... Obviously the classes are really, really harder ... I just felt like I wasn't prepared mentally to like study like my study habits were bad, so I had to deal with that as well. But once I got the hang of it, I, you know, like I was able to deal with it.

Similarly, Renata described, "It's been very challenging but amazing. It's been, you know, I've gone through a lot of things. Sometimes I'm scared to speak up, so I just don't do it and I figure it out myself. I've become a better person and everything." Ambivalence arose in Luis, Jacob, and Renata's statements when they discussed the increased difficulty of their courses and they struggled because of the online modalities, failing classes, or fears of speaking up, yet each of the students gained useful skills and personal growth. They each saw a bright side, despite their struggles.

Luis, Jacob, and Renata's *testimonios* align with Conchas and Acevedo's (2020) assertion that Latina/o/x students carry or develop skills and assets that help them navigate challenging sites, particularly when there are support systems in place for them. Moreover, the *testimonios* align with the findings in my earlier studies about undocumented community college students (Andrade, 2021b, 2021d), which showed that, after Donald J. Trump's presidential victory in 2016, students became hyper-vigilant and developed *conocimientos* about spaces on campus that were conducive for their self-growth and empowerment. My findings revealed that students developed a spatial awareness about sites that validated them (e.g., clubs or special programs) *or* invalidated them, including classrooms, which are important for their college readiness.

### *Testimonios of Negative Experiences in STEM During the Pandemic*

Six students reported largely negative experiences with some degree of ambivalence. The reasons for such experiences differed.

#### *Complex, intersectional reasons.*

When describing their negative experiences in STEM, some students listed complex, intersectional reasons why they felt that way. For example, Santiago explained:

> Huge nightmare because there have been so many things that I could qualify for as an undocumented student and I can't because I don't have a social number ... [A]lso technology-wise as well, ... [because] I cannot buy like a good computer because we don't have money. We have to prioritize bills and food. You know, things we cannot afford, textbooks because the STEM textbooks are expensive ... It's truly hard because you're not dealing with, like, you know, normal classes ... They get harder

> and harder as I go along ... It feels like going up the hill, and like never-ending, you know, like pulling a rock up the hill.

Similarly, Rosa illustrated,

> It's a bit difficult. It is quite an expensive and time-intensive degree. I don't know if I actually truly developed the time management skills necessary or the financial flexibility for it. Things like technology, books, access codes, and materials add up.

Lastly, Jose described,

> My experience being an undocumented student in STEM would have to be tough because it hasn't been easy trying to manage these difficult courses while trying to balance a part-time job and having time to myself.

The latter *testimonios* revealed financial, technological, academic, and personal reasons why they faced negative experiences in STEM.

Santiago, Rosa, and Jose's *testimonios* showed degrees of ambivalence when the students later identified positive systems of support that helped them thrive and their college readiness. For example, Santiago appreciated the financial support given to him due to the federal emergency relief funds. Santiago explained, "After Biden came into [office], I started to apply to COVID-19 relief programs [at the school], but they were first-time first serve. They covered a couple of bills." Santiago also noted that "[the school] also had Every Table meals that I apply for and ... they delivered those at the time and it was huge ... because we were also dealing with food issues." Jose also illustrated, "They ... gave out the emergency grants I believe every semester which would be up to like $1,600," and Rosa appreciated the food distribution. She stated, "I don't quite remember any stand outs, other than the fact that groceries were at some point still being distributed." Rosa went on to describe, "Also the [undocumented student] program informed us that we could apply for emergency funds, or something like that." In all, Santiago, Rosa, and Jose's *testimonios* revealed ambivalence due to the support they eventually received, despite their overall negative experiences in STEM.

*Unequal opportunities.*

Another reason why students described negative experiences in STEM was because they felt that they did not have the same opportunities as other students. For example, Cherry explained:

> It's been hard because sometimes we do have a STEM lab in [school], and sometimes I'm there and like I try to make conversation with other people and like they just tell me, like, 'Oh, yeah, I got an internship at this place. I'm gonna start working there.' So, it makes me feel some type of way because my options are limited unfortunately ... Sometimes when I try to apply for scholarships, it's mostly people who have residency, our citizens.

Similarly, Café illustrated,

> I'm not consciously thinking about it, but then I meet other people on campus. We do come from like really different backgrounds, and like, like, more importantly, they have papers, and I don't ... that's the only time that I get like reminded like that, "Oh, yeah, like, like, oh, they're getting the Pell grant. I'm not."

Cherry's statement reveals some ambivalence because, although she was aware of opportunities that she could not access, she did mention having access to the STEM lab that offers tutoring and support for students. Café showed some degree of ambivalence when she mentioned, "The only ones that did help were the [undocumented student program] and EOPS. We still had our regular meetings for EOPS like every semester. ... The [undocumented student program] just reaching out to us." Cherry and Café's *testimonios*, as well as the *testimonios* describing complex, intersectional reasons for the student's negative experiences, are supported by research that suggests students' recognition of endless barriers that they uniquely face in higher education, such as financial difficulties, invalidating campus climates, and requirements, such as Social Security numbers, that are exclusionary (Andrade, 2021c; Jaimes Pérez, 2014; Perez et al., 2009).

*Feeling lonely in STEM.*

Moreover, students discussed feeling lonely in STEM. For example, Tlaloc explained, "I would say, like individual, lonely, I guess, because ... from when I started to now, apparently, I haven't met anyone else that was undocumented in my field or in my classes. ... I've been living my whole life like this, and ... I'm used to it." Fortunately, Tlaloc later added:

> I do remember seeing resources even before that. I saw like, uh, resources for mental health and stuff like that. It's awesome. But I never took advantage [...] because I've learned to deal ... with stuff by myself ... I just don't take advantage, because and I still have this mentality from my community/family and I know it, I know it's kind of harmful. So, it's just to myself.

In his *testimonio,* Tlaloc revealed ambivalence because, although he felt lonely, he did hear about mental health services on campus. Unfortunately, he did not ask for mental health support because of a cultural stigma against men seeking such assistance. Moreover, Mati described:

> Overall, I think, ... it has been okay ... The, my main focus, when I do go in the classroom would be, you know, just learning and passing the class and I don't really think about, 'Oh, my God, I'm undocumented and in this STEM class.' No. I do think that STEM doesn't really have a lot of a lot of connection with undocumented students. I don't really find a lot of things that have that connect those 2 in school specifically.

Mati's *testimonio* captured ambivalence as she described having an "okay" experience in STEM, not seeing her undocumented status as a hindrance in STEM, but also noticing that the STEM program did not offer any specific help or outreach to undocumented students. Tlaloc and Mati's *testimonios* suggested that STEM courses or the program did not create opportunities for undocumented students to meet or did not advertise sites where they could connect with undocumented students. The feelings of loneliness are unsurprising because, as Valenzuela et al. (2015) found, institutions infrequently openly embrace or advocate on behalf of students, which adds to students' secrecy and isolation.

## Discussion and Practical Recommendations for Higher Education Leadership

The present study found that undocumented students inhabited ambivalent states as *atravesada/o/xs nepantleando* because they experienced tugs-and-pulls between positive and negative experiences as they navigated different STEM majors during the pandemic. Student participants revealed multifaceted ambivalence because some of the *testimonios* that reflected positive experiences also included negative dimensions and while other *testimonios* revealed negative experiences, they later pinpointed positive dimensions. For instance, while some students positively identified support services at school, they feared for their futures or did not find similar supports outside of their STEM fields, and while some students gained useful academic and personal skills, they still had difficulty navigating the arising difficulty of their courses and online modalities. Moreover, the students who described complex, intersectional reasons for their negative experiences, perceptions of unequal opportunities, and feelings of loneliness, simultaneously alluded to positive supports, such as financial aid, meal distribution, the undocumented student program, the STEM lap, and mental health services.

The concept of ambivalence was not surprising because, as Anzaldúa (2007) described, *atravesada/o/xs* often live in borderlands—physically, emotionally, and psychically—where they may feel a sense of dislocation or ambiguity. To live in the education borderlands (Conchas & Acevedo, 2020) means that students experience times of satisfaction or marginalization and distinct, complex, or contradictory states in distinct colonial landscapes. As Anzaldúa (2007) noted, "The ambivalence from the clash of voices results in mental and emotional states of perplexity. Internal strife results in insecurity and indecisiveness" (p. 78). Unfortunately, inhabiting states as *atravesada/o/xs* can be daunting because, as Benuto et al. (2018) explain, liminality, particularly due to undocumented status, can be overwhelming and stressful.

Fortunately, as Anzaldúa (2007) and Conchas and Acevedo (2020) theorize, *nepantlera/o/xs* develop active *facultades* and *conocimiento* of the intricate contours, shades, and cracks in their surroundings to cope and survive. *Atravesada/o/xs* develop a productive sense of *nepantleando*, the ability to transgress and build bridges for themselves and others, especially when there are support systems that foster their college readiness and success. As such, the *testimonios* in this chapter alluded to support systems that higher education leadership must continuously implement and support, including, but not limited to the STEM program, undocumented student program/club, counselors, financial aid, mental health, tutoring, and other services, such as technology, food, and more to help them thrive in STEM.

The question then becomes, how can institutions and the institutional agents within them minimize the potentially overwhelming ambivalent states that undocumented STEM students may experience during the pandemic and beyond? Research acknowledges the importance of culturally responsive special programs, pedagogy, and institutional support to help undocumented students feel a sense of belonging (Pérez et al., 2010; Suárez-Orozco et al., 2015), but the *testimonios* in this present study reveal unique and nuanced recommendations for higher education leadership to help undocumented students in STEM. The following recommendations are optimal.

### *Advertise financial aid and resources for undocumented students in STEM*

Several *testimonios* revealed a need for financial aid and other material resources during and beyond the pandemic. Because financial security is a top priority, educational institutions must intentionally advertise financial aid and other resources that will help STEM students finance their academics, textbooks, technological, nutritional, or other needs. The good news is that certain states, such as California, provide financial aid for undocumented students, but students are often unaware of or misinformed about the application processes. Therefore, as Jaimes Pérez (2014) explains, schools should provide and professionally develop counselors and financial aid technicians who may help undocumented students navigate application processes. Moreover, educators should tell students that such financial aid or resources will not legally jeopardize their well-being, and schools should find ways to "remove requirements for Social Security numbers [for students] to receive institution-sponsored scholarships and financial aid" (Jaimes Pérez, 2014, p. 32). Ultimately, faculty, staff, and administrators should advertise such assistance to all undocumented students and STEM students to remedy culturally invalidating climates.

### *Create and advertise support for undocumented students in the STEM program*

*Testimonios* frequently identified the STEM program as an important site for counseling, tutoring, and other services for them. Unfortunately, some students did not view the STEM program as conducive to connecting with other undocumented students, and other students were simply unaware of these services. Therefore, the STEM program staff should promote intentional communiques that affirm and validate undocumented students to improve their sense of belonging, lessen feelings of loneliness, and help them refine their skills and assets as they navigate STEM majors. Moreover, the STEM program can connect students with other extracurricular activities, such as the undocumented student club that several students mentioned, or professional networks that can help them find internships, scholarships, and career pathways to mitigate students' fears of the future. As research has shown, students collaborated with counselors or other institutional agents in special programs or clubs designed for them to cope with their anxieties and stress, as well as to succeed academically (Conchas & Acevedo, 2020; Perez et al., 2009, 2010). Generally, STEM faculty and administrators should advertise the STEM program and undocumented student club in courses and across campus.

### *Foment and promote professional development for STEM faculty*

Although special programs and financial and other material assistance are important for undocumented students' college readiness, there is an ongoing need to foment and promote professional development for STEM faculty. To be precise, all faculty, especially STEM faculty, need to learn about the complex, intersectional identities of students and the unique difficulties they face inside and outside of the classroom and in their career pathways to accommodate their needs or to show empathy during challenging sociopolitical times, such as the pandemic. Given that students face intersectional barriers, such as fears about their futures because of their status, technological difficulties, financial strain, textbook inaccessibility, and the increasing difficulty of courses, faculty, then, could direct students to available resources on campus, particularly financial aid, and collaborate with administrators or staff to help students access technology, textbooks, food, or other resources to succeed. Additionally, past research has shown that faculty communication plays a key role in showing positive validation when they use empathetic language in emails and classrooms (Andrade, 2021c). Such language may use encouraging messages, flexibility, immediacy, and compassion. Syllabi can also include language that affirms undocumented students and encourages them to speak to professors when they face overwhelming stress related to their status and liminal states in the country. Suárez-Orozco and López Hernández (2020) found that having at least one faculty or staff member to talk with may decrease anxiety in undocumented students. Hence, constant reminders of these positive affirmations and flexibility throughout the semester are key to creating comforting and culturally affirming spaces that are conducive to the student's college readiness. In all, undocumented students have a sharp ability—*facultades* and *conocimientos*—to recognize when faculty are aware and genuine in their attempts to validate their identities and needs. As such, faculty continuously play a key role in strengthening the bridges that students create for their college readiness and aspirations during and beyond the pandemic.

## Conclusion

To foster college readiness, community college leadership, staff, and faculty must learn about undocumented STEM students' experiences as *atravesada/o/xs nepantleando* and their ambivalent states, particularly the overwhelming nature of inhabiting such positionalities. Learning about these states is important to recognize the circumstances and racism that undocumented students face, particularly the ways that oppressive immigration policies intersect with stressors from the pandemic, financial security, employment, and socioemotional well-being of students, and to develop culturally responsive interventions. *Testimonios* from the present study shed light on sites where students feel (in) validated, supported, or understood (Andrade, 2021b). In particular, STEM labs, tutoring, counseling, undocumented student programs, other special programs, financial aid, and mental health, were some of the supports that students described positively. Yet more needs to be done because students still felt uncertain about their futures, did not find supports outside of their STEM classes or program, did not connect with other undocumented students in STEM, felt lonely, or declared ongoing complex, intersectional barriers.

The good news is that the *testimonios* shed light on the possibility of creating or maximizing the success of preexisting structural interventions, such as continual support and sustainability of undocumented student centers/programs, STEM labs with tutoring, financial aid, sustenance, and other supports, such as legal and mental health services. Beyond the existence of these supports, however, is the need for administrators, staff, and faculty to continuously advertise the supports in STEM classes and sites, as well as other areas, such as the library, counseling centers, and online to ensure that students do not miss these opportunities. The ongoing and expansive dispersal of supports designed for STEM students need specific promotion for and to undocumented students to avoid exclusion or perceptions that they do not have equal opportunity to services, generally. Lastly, there are some barriers, such as limitations to DACA and undocumented status that need federal resolve; yet schools may create coalitions with surrounding communities and state governments to address some of the immediate barriers that STEM students face, such as financial troubles, and to pressure the federal government to create immigration reform and support for undocumented communities (Jaimes Pérez, 2014). The ultimate goal, as Gonzales et al. (2013) state, is to help "them to identify legally permissible options for education, community participation, civic engagement, and continued belonging [that] can play an important role in reducing anxiety" (p. 19).

The ambivalent *testimonios* in the present study revealed that students were active *atravesada/o/xs nepantleando* confronting obstacles in STEM fields during the pandemic while resisting failure and building bridges for themselves and others to succeed. From the *testimonios* emerged useful recommendations for higher education leadership to address their unique needs. While these *testimonios* are powerful, future scholars may further apply FAN to a larger sample of Latina/o/x students from diverse nationalities, mixed races, ages, institutional types (4-year, public, private, or graduate institutions), or that self-identify as different genders. Future studies may further support the present findings that, despite their experiences as *atravesada/o/xs*, undocumented students carry and gain knowledge that STEM fields and institutions should adopt to become more culturally responsive to student needs.

## Reference

Abrego, L. J. (2006). "I can't go to college because I don't have papers": Incorporation patterns of Latino undocumented youth. *Latino Studies*, 4(3), 212–231.

Andrade, L. M. (2021a). Re-membering the "Mexican Flu" pandemic: A Nepantlerx Criticism and autohistoria. *Border-Lines, XIII.*

Andrade, L. M. (2021b). "The war still continues," Part II: The importance of positive validation for undocumented students one year after Trump's presidential victory. *Journal of Hispanic Higher Education*, 20(1), 3–16.

Andrade, L. M. (2021c). "We still keep going": The multiplicitous socioemotional states & stressors of undocumented students during the COVID-19 pandemic. *Journal of Hispanic Higher Education*, 15381927211000220.

Andrade, L. M. (2021d). "We've lived in a constant state of fear": On Anzaldúa's Coyolxauhqui Imperative and undocumented students' path to conocimiento. *Border-Lines, XIII*, 9–36.

Anguiano, C. A., & Gutiérrez Nájera, L. (2015). Paradox of performing exceptionalism: Complicating the deserving/underserving binary of undocumented youth attending elite institutions. *AMAE Journal*, 9(2), 45–56.

Anzaldúa, G. (2007). *Borderlands/la frontera: The new mestiza* (3rd ed.). Aunt Lute Books.

Aurin, K., Dominguez, M., Cota, E. K., Castano, E., Gonzalez, F., & Laureano, A. (2021). Undocumented at Cal: Is UC Berkeley failing to support undocumented STEM students? *Institute for Research on Labor and Employment*. https://irle.berkeley.edu/wp-content/uploads/2021/01/Is-UC-Berkeley-Failing-to-Support-Undocumented-STEM-Students.pdf

Benuto, L. T., Casas, J. B., Cummings, C., & Newlands, R. (2018). Undocumented, to DACAmented, to DACAlimited: Narratives of Latino students with DACA status. *Hispanic Journal of Behavioral Sciences*, 40(3), 259–278.

Conchas, G. Q., & Acevedo, N. (2020). *The Chicana/o/x dream: Hope, resistance, and educational success*. Harvard Education Press.

Creswell, J. W., & Miller, D. L. (2000). Determining validity in qualitative inquiry. *Theory Into Practice, 39*(3), 124–130.

Delgado Bernal, D., Burciaga, R., & Flores Carmona, J. (2012). Chicana/Latina testimonios: Mapping the methodological, pedagogical, and political. *Equity & Excellence in Education, 45*(3), 363–372.

Diaz-Strong, D., Gómez, C., Luna-Duarte, M. E., & Meiners, E. R. (2011). Purged: Undocumented students, financial aid policies, and access to higher education. *Journal of Hispanic Higher Education, 10*(2), 107–119.

Endale, T., St Jean, N., & Birman, D. (2020). COVID-19 and refugee and immigrant youth: A community-based mental health perspective. *Psychological Trauma: Theory, Research, Practice, and Policy, 12*(S1), S225. https://doi.org/10.1037/tra0000875

Enriquez, L. E., Rosales, W. E., Chavarria, K., Morales Hernandez, M., & Valadez, M. (2021). COVID on campus: Assessing the impact of the pandemic on undocumented college students. *Aera Open, 7*(1), 23328584211033576. https://doi.org/10.1177/23328584211033576

Fernandez, J. (2018). Undocumented Latino students pursuing degrees in STEM disciplines: Attitudes, perceptions, teacher support, and future views. *Journal of Latinos and Education, 17*(4), 344–357.

Flores, G. M. (2011). Latino/as in the hard sciences: Increasing Latina/o participation in science, technology, engineering and math (STEM) related fields. *Latino Studies, 9*, 327–335.

Fortuna, L. R., Tolou-Shams, M., Robles-Ramamurthy, B., & Porche, M. V. (2020). Inequity and the disproportionate impact of COVID-19 on communities of color in the United States: The need for a trauma-informed social justice response. *Psychological Trauma: Theory, Research, Practice, and Policy, 12*(5), 443–445. https://doi.org/10.1037/tra0000889

Gonzales, R. G., Suárez-Orozco, C., & Dedios-Sanguineti, M. C. (2013). No place to belong: Contextualizing concepts of mental health among undocumented immigrant youth in the United States. *American Behavioral Scientist, 57*(8), 1174–1199.

Goodman, J., Wang, S. X., Guadarrama Ornelas, R. A., & Hernandez Santana, M. (2020). Mental health of undocumented college students during the COVID-19 pandemic. *MedRxiv, 2020-09*, 1–43.

Jaimes Pérez, Z. (2014, December). *Removing barriers to higher education for undocumented students.* America Progress. https://www.americanprogress.org/wp-content/uploads/sites/2/2014/12/UndocHigherEd-report2.pdf

Liu, S. R., & Modir, S. (2020). The outbreak that was always here: Racial trauma in the context of COVID-19 and implications for mental health providers. *Psychological Trauma: Theory, Research, Practice, and Policy, 12*(5), 439.

Montiel, G. I., Torres-Hernandez, T., Vazquez, R., Tiburcio, A., & Zavala, F. (2022). "It wasn't only the pandemic:" A collaborative autoethnography of Latinx women in higher education navigating the COVID-19 pandemic in rapidly shifting immigration contexts. *Journal of Latinos and Education, 21*(3), 266–276.

Nienhusser, H. K., & Espino, M. M. (2017). Incorporating Undocumented/DACA-mented status competency into higher education institutional agents' practice. *Journal of Student Affairs Research and Practice, 54*(1), 1–14.

Nienhusser, H. K., Vega, B. E., & Saavedra Carquin, M. C. (2016). Undocumented students' experiences with microaggressions during their college choice process. *Teachers College Record, 111*(2), 1–33.

Perez, W. (2010). Higher education access for undocumented students: Recommendations for counseling professionals. *Journal of College Admission, 206*, 32–35.

Perez, W., Espinoza, R., Ramos, K., Coronado, H. M., & Cortes, R. (2009). Academic resilience among undocumented Latino students. *Hispanic Journal of Behavioral Sciences, 31*(2), 149–181.

Perez, W., Espinoza, R., Ramos, K., Coronado, H., & Cortes, R. (2010). Civic engagement patterns of undocumented Mexican students. *Journal of Hispanic Higher Education, 9*(3), 245–265.

Pérez Huber, L. (2009). Disrupting apartheid of knowledge: Testimonio as methodology in Latina/o critical race research in education. *International Journal of Qualitative Studies in Education, 22*(6), 639–654.

Salerno, J. P., Williams, N. D., & Gattamorta, K. A. (2020). LGBTQ populations: Psychologically vulnerable communities in the COVID-19 pandemic. *Psychological Trauma: Theory, Research, Practice, and Policy, 12*(S1), S239–S242. https://doi.org/10.1037/tra0000837

Suárez-Orozco, C., & López Hernández, G. L. (2020). "Waking up every day with the worry": A mixed-methods study of anxiety in undocumented Latinx college students. *Frontiers in Psychiatry, 11*, 1–14.

Suárez-Orozco, C., Katsiaficas, D., Birchall, O., Alcantar, C. M., Hernandez, E., Garcia, Y., Michikyan, M., Cerda, J., & Teranishi, R. T. (2015). Undocumented undergraduates on college campuses: Understanding their challenges and assets and what it takes to make an undocufriendly campus. *Harvard Educational Review, 85*(3), 427–463.

Tapia-Fuselier, N. (2019). Undocumented students, community colleges, and the urgent call for undocu-competence. *Journal of Student Affairs, 28*, 145-152.

Tapia-Fuselier, N. (2021). Enhancing institutional undocu-competence through establishing undocumented student resource centers: A student-encompassed approach. *Journal of College Access, 6*(2), 132–145.

Teranishi, R., Suárez-Orozco, C., & Suárez Orozco, M. (2015). *In the shadows of the ivory tower: Undocumented undergraduates and the liminal state of immigration reform*. The Institute for Immigration, Globalization, and Education at UCLA.

Terriquez, V. (2015). Dreams delayed: Barriers to degree completion among undocumented community college students. *Journal of Ethnic and Migration Studies, 41*(8), 1302–1323.

Valenzuela, J. I., Perez, W., Perez, I., Montiel, G. I., & Chaparro, G. (2015). Undocumented students at the community college: Creating institutional capacity. *New Directions for Community Colleges, 2015*(172), 87–96.

Weissman, S. (2019). *Undocumented students struggle to afford college*. Diverse Education. https://www.diverseeducation.com/students/article/15105490/undocumented-students-struggle-to-afford-college

CHAPTER 6

# Cultivating Equitable Outcomes for Latina/o/x Students:

## Examining the Implications of Implementing A.B. 705

*Audrey Baca Lopez and Victor DeAlba*

### Introduction

The California Community College (CCC) system has served as a critical pathway for social mobility among Latina/o/x and other Black, Indigenous, People of Color (BIPOC) students. More than 1.9 million students are enrolled in the CCC system, which is the largest system of higher education in the United States (California Community Colleges Chancellor's Office, 2022). Over 92% of the 116 campuses are designated as Hispanic-Serving Institutions (HSIs), making it a predominately Hispanic-Serving Institution System (Cuellar et al., 2023).

Latina/o/x students in California have faced significant barriers within this educational system due to disparate developmental education course placement (Rodríguez et al., 2018). Through educational reform efforts, California Legislatures have aimed to create more equitable pathways for Latina/o/xs and other BIPOC students. Among these reforms is California Assembly Bill 705, which required every California Community College to "maximize the probability" that entering students enroll and complete transfer-level English or mathematics within a 1-year time frame and within a 3-year time frame for students enrolled in an English as a Second Language course by the Fall Semester of 2019 (A.B. 705, 2017). This legislative bill can operate as a pillar for college readiness, equity, and access for Latina/o/x students in the CCC system who intend to earn an associate degree or transfer, as they are often delayed by developmental courses.

Developmental education has a documented history of creating barriers to transfer and completion, particularly for Latina/o/xs and other BIPOC students (Contreras & Contreras, 2015). For instance, in 2016, a Public Policy Institute of California (PPIC) study found that 87% of Latina/o/x and African American CCC students were placed into at least one developmental math or English class. There is significant scholarship that demonstrates how remedial course placement creates additional barriers and limits completion rates, especially among BIPOC students (Hern et al., 2020). Another study, The State of Higher Education for Latina/o/x in California, found that community colleges neglected to support more than 50% of Latina/o/x students in their educational goals (of attaining a credential or transferring) (The Campaign for College Opportunity, 2018a). The same report cited that transfer is taking longer to achieve—2% of Latina/o/x students attain transfer in 2 years, and a dismal 31% of Latina/o/x students attain transfer within 6 years (The Campaign for College Opportunity, 2018a).

For the purpose of this chapter, "equity refers to a heightened focus on groups experiencing disproportionate impact to remediate disparities in their experiences and outcomes" (Byrd, 2017, p. 1). While A.B. 705 is only one legislative piece of California's developmental reform efforts, this chapter focuses on the implementation of A.B. 705 because of its transformative framework that has implications for Latina/o/x student success. Research that explores initiatives like this one are critical to understanding how Latina/o/x students, and other underrepresented student populations, can achieve their intended educational goals (Rodríguez et al., 2018); moreover, at the time of the study, no other research had yet been conducted at the research site on the implementation of A.B. 705. This work offers a lens, from those educational leaders charged with enacting compliance to A.B. 705, to view the perceived implications for equitable outcomes for Latina/o/x students based on the organizational changes related to implementation efforts.

This chapter begins with a brief discussion of Hispanic-Serving Community Colleges, a review of transfer and completion for Latina/o/x students, and an overview of A.B. 705, a recent reform effort intended to be a pillar for college readiness, access, and equity. This chapter continues by addressing the theoretical framework, introducing the purpose, and describing the research methodology for this study. Findings are presented, followed by the implications and discussion.

## The Context of College Readiness for Latina/o/x Students

The varied history of exclusion and oppression of Latina/o/x students in California has created barriers to college and career readiness. Students and community advocates have placed pressure on policymakers to implement educational reforms that address these disparities. Among these reforms is the development of an HSI designation, which incentivizes institutions to provide expanded support to Latina/o/x students. The CCC system has taken the lead with a majority of its campuses being designated as HSIs (Cuellar et al., 2023). Additionally, the CCC system has contributed to the educational mobility of Latina/o/x students by providing them with a pathway to transfer to 4-year universities. In this section, we discuss the context surrounding HSIs and transfer and completion as it relates to college readiness for Latina/o/x students.

### *Hispanic-Serving Community Colleges*

The U.S. Department of Education (2023) defines an HSI as an eligible higher education institution that has an enrollment of undergraduate full-time equivalent (FTE) students of which at least 25% are Hispanic. In CCC, Latina/o/xs make up 47% of students, and 107 of the 116 campuses are designated as HSIs (California Community Colleges Chancellor's Office, 2022; Cuellar et al., 2023). HSIs, unlike Tribal Colleges and Universities and Historically Black Colleges and Universities, originated as predominantly white institutions and became HSIs because they are situated in areas where there have been increases in Hispanic births and immigration (Hurtado & Ruiz Alvarado, 2015) and increases in Latina/o/x college-going rates (Contreras, 2019).

Although the federal definition of HSIs only lists two requirements for the designation, HSIs should thoroughly examine their systems, processes, and policies that create excessive delays or obstacles for students and seek to dismantle them (Garcia, 2019). Another important and necessary aspect of understanding the academic and nonacademic experiences of Latina/o/x students is to listen to and incorporate student voice, especially with regard to the transfer pipeline (Del Real Viramontes & Vasquez, 2023). For HSIs to be relevant to Latina/o/x student populations, they must commit to hiring administration, faculty, and staff who reflect the demographics of the student population (Boualoy Dayton et al., 2004). Diverse faculty and staff, who can empathize with the challenges of being a first-generation, minoritized student, play a major role in mitigating ethnic and racial disparities in degree completion (Boualoy Dayton et al., 2004). Though many Latina/o/x students attend Hispanic-Serving Community Colleges, findings are conflicted about whether completion rates for Latina/o/x students are higher at HSIs versus non-HSIs due to various factors (Núñez et al., 2015). Scholars assert that further research is needed to gain a deeper insight into how HSIs serve their critical mass of Latina/o/x students (Contreras & Contreras, 2015; Garcia, 2019; Núñez et al., 2015).

### *Transfer and Completion for Latina/o/x Students*

Many education scholars have agreed that community college is one of the most significant pathways for Latina/o/x students to transfer and obtain a bachelor's degree. Abrica and Rivas (2017), whose research focused mainly on community college completion and transfer, emphasized the importance of HSIs and community colleges as a bridge to later degree attainment. More than 1.9 million students are enrolled in the CCC system (California Community Colleges Chancellor's Office, 2022), which is at least twice as many students as the University of California and California State University systems combined. Despite the significant number of Latina/o/x students attending the CCC system, they continue to face barriers when it comes to transferring and completing their degrees; understanding both pre- and post-transfer patterns, conditions, and experiences for Latina/o/x students is a crucial component (Contreras-Garcia, 2023). This suggests that much work must still be done to better identify and close completion gaps for Latina/o/x.

One of the reasons identified for lower completion rates has been disproportionate placement into remedial English and math courses. Scholars have pointed out that when developmental courses are made available, colleges continue to disproportionately enroll Latina/o/x students in them, despite recent A.B. 705 legislation (Hern et al., 2020). Conversely, students can complete transfer-level coursework at higher rates with support, guidance, and mentorship (The Campaign for College Opportunity, 2018a). Validation and care are enormously essential to persistence and completion rates for BIPOC students (Wood & Harris, 2017).

## A.B. 705 as a Pillar for College Readiness, Access, and Equity

Although the CCC system has provided pathways for educational mobility for Latina/o/x students, systemic inequities that disproportionately impact Latina/o/x students and other BIPOC students continue to permeate within this educational system. As a result, California legislators have proposed educational reforms that seek to address the shortfalls within CCC. Perhaps the most prominent legislative move is California Assembly Bill 705 (2017), which took effect on January 1, 2018.

This legislation can be characterized as a foundational pillar for promoting college readiness, access, and equity due to its intentional approach to reducing disparity through the use of multiple measures for college course placement (A.B. 705, 2017). This law is an intentional shift to close equity gaps, facilitate degree completion, and increase academic transfer at community colleges in California (Foundation for California Community Colleges, 2017). Considering that Latina/o/x students were more likely placed into remedial courses due to placement practices that relied on high-stakes placement tests (Acevedo-Gil et al., 2014), equity concerns were among the main reasons for the shift to embrace the use of multiple measures for placement (A.B. 705, 2017).

The goal of A.B. 705 is to not cause added delay by placing students into remedial courses. Scholars have noted that Latina/o/x students have a greater tendency to enroll part-time, which lengthens the time for degree completion (Contreras & Contreras, 2015). Numerous scholars have argued that standardized assessments alone are not effective for student placement (Henson & Hern,

2014; Hodara et al., 2012; Rodríguez, 2014; Scott-Clayton et al., 2014). To improve student completion of transfer-level math and English requirements, researchers recommend that students: (1) register for compressed courses; (2) engage in integrated developmental courses; (3) participate in corequisite courses; and (4) enroll directly in college-level classes, among other options (Acevedo-Gil et al., 2014; Center for the Analysis of Postsecondary Readiness, 2018). These suggestions require campuses to have one or more of these options available for students. Recent scholarship has outlined the benefits of students enrolling directly into transfer-level math and English courses, with co-requisite supports if needed, as a way to close completion gaps for Latina/o/x and Black students who have access to these options (Hern et al., 2020). With the enactment of A.B. 705, the California Community College System strives to close equity gaps and increase degree completion rates.

CCC system leaders stressed the potential effects of A.B. 705 and urged top-level campus administrators and academic senate presidents to see how "these changes represent an opportunity to close achievement gaps and explore new strategies to move students more swiftly toward their goals as part of a guided pathways framework" (Hope & Bruno, 2017, p. 2). The key changes brought by A.B. 705 within the CCC system create opportunities to reconsider how community colleges have historically pushed out and left out students of color (Acevedo-Gil, 2018; Clark, 1960, 1980). The restructuring of developmental education pathways and the shift to prioritizing access and success is pivotal to creating more equitable outcomes for students of color, especially for the high population of Latina/o/x students enrolled in the CCC system.

## Framework

The theoretical framework guiding this chapter is based on organizational change theory (Kezar, 2014), research that re-imagines organizational theories from a critical paradigm (Gonzales et al., 2018), and considers the Framework of *Atravesada/o/xs Nepantleando* (FAN) to examine ways Latina/o/x students navigating the inequities of the educational system (Conchas & Acevedo, 2020). Many scholars in the field privilege critical race theory as a theoretical framework for equity, Hispanic-Serving Institution, and Minority-Serving

Institution research (Acevedo-Gil et al., 2015; Jones, 2013; Salas, 2014; Suárez-Orozco et al., 2015). However, Kezar (2014) and Gonzales and colleagues (2018) offered a suitable lens for considering how the change process occurs in educational institutions and how the critical paradigm can be used to re-imagine how colleges change to implement legislative reforms.

Kezar (2014) recognized change as "those intentional acts where a particular leader drives or implements a new direction" (p. xii). The change process includes consideration of the type of change, the context for change, and the role of agency/leadership. Type, context, and agency inform the approach (or theories to apply) to the change initiative. Kezar (2014) used the term *change agent* to imply anyone can create change. Change is a multilevel process since leadership (and change) happens at every level. Change theory includes first-order and second-order change. The type of change influences the approach, or strategies, used to institute the change.

Likewise, Gonzales and colleagues (2018) used a critical paradigm to offer a different perspective to foreground justice. These scholars envisioned higher education institutions as spaces where diverse people and communities converge to foster a socially just world. Gonzales and colleagues (2018) prioritize four main issues, which include: (1) Labor in/justice, like the exploitation of emotional labor; (2) Intersectional justice, associated with people in academia who may be marginalized or minoritized in multiple ways; (3) Reparative justice, which considers educational institutions as tools of colonization and prioritizes repatriations; and (4) Epistemic in/justice, the concept that society is dominated by paternalistic, white male rules that limit who is valued as a knower and producer of knowledge.

The notion of emotional labor is particularly significant to this research. Emotion and emotional labor are "a form of labor compelled by organizational norms and rules" (Gonzales & Rincones, 2013, p. 2). Miller (2001) argued that even suppressing is an emotional act; other scholars note that emotional labor can generate dissonance and dissatisfaction, which affects a person even when away from work (Fisk & Friesen, 2012; Hochschild, 1983).

Critical organizational theory invites change agents and researchers to conduct transformational educational research, which only comes from re-imagining "higher education as *more than* a place where people come to be credentialed and graduated, *more than* a place where faculty and staff simply process programs and grants just as they process students" (Gonzales et al., 2018, p. 507). To better prioritize social justice and equity, researchers must embrace radically different lenses other than the traditional views that have dominated the literature and previously influenced the work of higher education institutions (Gonzales et al., 2018). The change agents in this particular study are the participants themselves, the staff, faculty, and administrators, as they hold the power to enact change, for the better or worse.

Finally, FAN helps to guide this chapter. FAN provides a lens for understanding the ways in which Latina/o/xs resist the barriers that are created within educational spaces when they are labeled as *atravesada/o/xs* or "outsiders" due to deficit-based stereotypes (Conchas & Acevedo, 2020). Even though Latina/o/xs make up a significant portion of the CCC student population, they still need to navigate within this educational system as *atravesada/o/xs* due to the disparate nature of remedial course placement and inequitable practices and policies. Utilizing FAN as a lens for examining the implications of implementing A.B. 705 can help us understand the impact and role of Latina/o/xs before, during, and after the legislation was enacted.

## Navigating the Implementation of A.B. 705

The case study data used for this chapter is part of a comprehensive and previously published article and dissertation study (Baca, 2019; Baca Lopez, 2022). The research was conducted at Nepantla College (pseudonym), a Hispanic-Serving Community College. The student population at Nepantla College was diverse; however, it is significant to note that the majority (over 70%) of the student population identified as Hispanic or Latina/o/x. Not only was the research site a Hispanic-Serving Institution, but it also served a high percentage of Latina/o/x students. The faculty and administration, however, did not reflect this demographic. Conversely, a majority (over 70%) of the faculty and administration of Nepantla College identified as white. The study included 11 participants (faculty, staff, and administration) who were tasked with implementing A.B. 705 at the college. The participant positions ranged from faculty to administration to supplemental support staff, with four administrators, six full-time faculty members, and one supplemental support staff member. To maintain confidentiality, participants were given pseudonyms.

This study included multiple data collection methods, such as semi-structured interviews, document collection and analysis, physical artifact collection, and observations (Merriam & Tisdell, 2016). Participants were interviewed at a time and location determined by the participant, both in person and via Zoom (a web conferencing service). The semi-structured interviews ranged from 35 to 60 minutes, conducted during a single session. The interviews with participants provide clarity into initiative implementation, especially at Minority Serving Institutions (MSIs) and for students of color (Jones & Assalone, 2016). Document collection included the campus equity plan, organizational websites, committee agendas and minutes, and professional development proposals. All documents provided insight into organizational changes related to the implementation of A.B. 705. Each data type aided in triangulating the policy implementation phenomenon (Yin, 2009). Observation occurred at an Equity Committee meeting, including general campus observations, to help answer the research question. Detailed field notes and a reflective journal were kept to navigate subjective researcher observations and identify key correlations between interviews, artifacts, and observations (Gonzales & Rincones, 2013). Brochures, flyers, and pictures of the research site gave insight into the change processes and campus culture. Artifacts, like student newspapers, the Fall 2018 and Spring 2019 class schedules, and the 2018-19 Course Catalog supported participant accounts and verified findings.

Data were analyzed by applying a deductive approach with predetermined codes formed from the research question and theoretical framework (Saldaña, 2016; Stake, 1995). Additional emergent codes (Saldaña, 2016) were added during the data analysis process to expose new meanings about the case (Stake, 1995).

### *Positionality*

All writing is influenced by the researcher's experiences, values, and biases (Creswell, 2013); it is key to explaining our positionality to readers. Thus, we are explicit in aspects of our identity that have shaped our role as researchers and scholars including our experiences in the education system and the development of our critical worldview.

*Audrey Baca Lopez.*

I am a multiethnic, Latina-mami-scholar. I have worked for over 20 years in K-12 schools, community colleges, and in the California State University system serving students who have been historically underserved and marginalized. As a first-generation student, I obtained my bachelor's and master's degrees from California State Polytechnic University, Pomona. I consistently worked two part-time jobs to pay for expenses while attending school full-time. I benefited from Pell Grants to fund most of my undergraduate schooling and took out loans to pay for my graduate coursework. I chose to obtain my doctorate in educational leadership from California State University, San Bernardino because it prioritized social justice, equity, and educational transformation. While it was an affordable way for me to further my professional learning and build a network in higher education, as a Latina, I was drawn to the Latina/o/x representation in the doctoral program's leadership and faculty (at the time—Drs. Nancy Acevedo, Edna Martinez, and Louie Rodriguez).

Although I persisted through California's public higher education system, I know I am one of few who have navigated this pipeline. Approximately 0.3% of Latinas earn a doctorate degree (Pérez Huber et al., 2015). I am invested in learning about how educational reform efforts, like A.B. 705, are impacting Latina/o/x students, particularly at the community college level, because it is a gateway for so many to further education.

*Victor DeAlba.*

I am an educated Chicano and the proud son of two immigrant parents. I grew up in a low-income and monolingual Spanish-speaking household, which often led to deficit-based stereotypes and barriers to accessing educational opportunities, a lack of knowledge on how to access resources, and unfamiliarity with how to navigate the U.S. schooling system. Despite these educational barriers, I obtained my associate's degree from Allan Hancock College and my bachelor's degree from the University of California, Los Angeles. Throughout my educational journey, I have largely relied on the Pell Grant and other private, state, and federal scholarships to cover my expenses. I am currently a Ph.D. candidate in the Educational Leadership Program at the Pennsylvania State University with a research focus on Latina/o/x student engagement and student voice. These lived experiences coupled with my academic background now serve as the foundation for my unique insight into how I navigate higher education and conceptualize educational leadership, and it contributes to my overall interest in addressing historical inequities among Latina/o/x students and amplifying their voices in educational scholarship and practice.

## The Implications of Implementing A.B. 705

The findings from this study show that the process of implementing A.B. 705 prompted staff at Nepantla College to conduct an in-depth analysis of institutional policies and educational practices. Through that process, they were able to identify how to address the academic needs of Latina/o/x students. The findings from this study have been organized into three key themes, which underscore the shifts towards more equitable institutional processes. These three themes also provide a glimpse into the ever-changing landscape of support and curriculum reform aimed at enhancing college readiness for Latina/o/x and other BIPOC students. Although there is a continuous need for improvement, these findings demonstrate how A.B. 705 is not just a legislative mandate, but rather, can also serve as a transformative pillar for the foundations upon which college readiness, access, and equity are built within the CCC system.

### *Institutional Commitment to Equity and Access*

Within this theme, we found that Nepantla College developed an institutional commitment to equity and access as an essential foundation for fostering college readiness, success, and completion among Latina/o/x students. Jayden, a participant in the study, detailed that Nepantla College's mission statement evolved over time to be more inclusive and how institutional documents influenced equity-focused changes, such as the campus equity plan (also known as the Integrated Plan). These steps taken by Nepantla College are in alignment with scholarly recommendations to become Hispanic-serving, and not just Hispanic-enrolling institutions (Garcia, 2019; Malcom-Piqueux & Bensimon, 2015). Other findings in this theme revealed that the 2017-19 Integrated Plan (Basic Skills Initiative, Student Equity, and Student Success and Support Program) was a foundation for the college's response to A.B. 705. This institutional document is required by all California Community Colleges as an accountability tool for promoting student success and equity.

In 2017, CCC instituted the Integrated Plan reporting, which merged the planning process of three different initiatives: the Basic Skills Initiative (which supported developmental education), Student Equity Program (which ensured equal educational opportunities by developing goals and activities to address disparities), and Student Success and Support Program (which focused on access and completion). This information clarified that Nepantla College used the Integrated Plan to drive equity efforts at the research site and how campus initiatives outlined in the plan aligned with the intent of A.B. 705 to support equitable outcomes for students.

Latina/o/x students were identified in the college's Integrated Plan as the largest target group because over 70% of the student population identified as Hispanic/Latino. Activities—such as the summer bridge program, Early Alert and intrusive counseling, and professional development with On Course and Reading Apprenticeship—served as elements of the college's response to A.B. 705 and existed before the legislation was enacted. Additionally, the Integrated Plan is tied to federal funding that supports activities and goals outlined in the plan. While the Integrated Plan is a required document, the findings indicated that the campus administration had already begun to intentionally prioritize equitable outcomes for students. This underscores the institutions' dedication to dismantling historical barriers to access and success and adopting policies that prioritize the educational needs and experiences of Latina/o/xs and other BIPOC students—such as those embodied in A.B. 705. This theme demonstrated the need to incorporate equity explicitly into institutional planning and practices as part of the commitment to equity and Hispanic-servingness (Felix & Fernandez Castro, 2018; Garcia, 2019).

### *Removing Institutional Barriers to Foster College Readiness and Broker Power to Students*

Within this theme, we found that the removal of institutional barriers helped to enhance college readiness and address issues of inequity. For example, discontinuing the use of the ACCUPLACER placement test and offering transfer-level math pathways, like social statistics courses, created a positive trajectory for equitable outcomes for students. These findings demonstrate what Nepantla College did to remove barriers, like offering a two-semester sequence for students to complete transfer-level English within 1 year and creating a self-guided placement survey to use instead of a placement exam. There were many positive implications for student equity related to the college's A.B. 705 implementation, which greatly influenced the majority of the Latina/o/x student population at Nepantla College. Alex, an administrator involved with placement and counseling, explained the students were empowered by being able to register directly in transfer-level coursework. Nelky, a top-level administrator, shared that A.B. 705 allowed for increased opportunity related to student completion. For instance, Nelky noted that more students were able to take contextualized math and quantitative reasoning courses that were more aligned with their majors, like a social statistics course for humanities and liberal arts majors. The college even planned to hire additional social statistics faculty (full-time and part-time) to support the increased demand for those courses. Other departments, like the business department, considered establishing a new math/quantitative reasoning curriculum in response to A.B. 705. Using multiple measures to determine placement and allowing students to enroll directly in transfer-level courses acknowledges the diverse backgrounds and strengths of Latina/o/x students and gives them the opportunity to complete their academic goals in reasonable time. Such changes aligned with FAN because the changes included resources to foster transfer and completion for Latina/o/x students, allowing them to engage the community college systems as *nepantlera/o/xs*.

### *Enacting La Facultad to Navigate Threats to Equitable Outcomes*

In this third and final theme, we outline perceived threats to equity. These threats consisted of fixed mindsets, inequitable practices, and deficit perspectives. Furthermore, findings revealed that acts of sabotage, implicit biases, and race-neutral and color-blind (Bonilla-Silva, 2014) or color-evasive (Annamma et al., 2017) approaches to understanding equity-placed equitable student outcomes at risk. These findings illuminated the role legislative changes take in promoting equitable reforms while also exposing inequitable practices and deficit-based mindsets that still endure in higher education. The demographics of the student population, mainly Latina/o/x, contrasted with the demographics of the faculty and administration, the majority of whom were white.

These findings connect back to the roles of faculty, staff, and administrators and that they can facilitate an environment where students feel like are *atravesada/o/xs* or can navigate as *nepantlera/o/xs* (Conchas & Acevedo, 2020). Scholars propose that validation and positive student engagement with faculty, counselors, staff, and administration are vital, especially for BIPOC students (Osei-Kofi & Rendon, 2005; Wood & Harris, 2017). This concept resonated in a story that Rae, an administrator, disclosed:

> We were sitting at the academic senate and ... [the] math department chair was giving an update on [the self-guided placement survey] for students ... one of the faculty members asked, "And what are you doing for as far as helping the students be successful in math?" And another one of [the math] faculty ... spoke up in front of the whole academic senate and said, "There's nothing in A.B. 705 that says that we have to work on students being successful." That caused quite a stir in the academic senate meeting, but that's exactly how [the] math faculty feel. They are not responsible for student success. That's what they believe.

Rae's testimony portrayed a vivid picture of the math department's culture. This example demonstrated systemic injustice for diverse student populations, which in this instance, stressed the limited views of responsibility that math faculty had for student success at Nepantla College. While not all the faculty held deficit views, several participants confirmed the math department, and some math faculty were major barriers to student success. Per a top-level administrator at the research site, the deficit-based perceptions from faculty and administration likely had negative effects on completion and persistence rates in transfer-level math courses and in the several levels of developmental math courses the department offered.

This example was also indicative of the emotional labor incurred by faculty, staff, and administrators as part of the A.B. 705 implementation throughout the college. In other words, there were implications for faculty who were invested in fostering student success by having to navigate a hostile environment fostered by deficit-based perspectives. On the other hand, the same can be said for the faculty, staff, and administration who experienced high levels of emotional labor as part of the change process, including those who resisted A.B. 705 changes. In another incident, identified by Tanner, who is an administrator, inequitable practices surfaced in a plan by the math department:

> Basically, what the plan is at this point is, because people are placing themselves directly into college level math, so the math [faculty] who are teaching have made a public commitment to make sure and fail as many of those students as they possibly can just to prove that A.B. 705 is a terrible idea.

Both Tanner and Jayden, a faculty member in the school of math and science, corroborated the existence of this plan at the research site. While many on the campus were in favor of the legislation, time and again, the interview data exposed problems of practice within the math department's pedagogies and deficit mindsets. Moreover, Jayden described threats to equitable outcomes related to implicit biases: "I've never heard anyone in my department use the word 'equity' or 'equitable.' I have heard them say, 'Well, of course our numbers are low, look at our demographic.'" Latina/o/x students represented the largest demographic at Nepantla College. This comment demonstrated the implicit (or explicit) bias that existed among some faculty and showed how the department "never" used language to address equity. The comment aligned with faculty viewing Latina/o/x students as *atravesada/o/xs* in the community college context.

Race-neutral and color-evasive approaches to understanding equity threaten equitable outcomes for BIPOC students (Annamma et al., 2017). Being color-neutral,[1] or not "seeing" a person by their skin color, affords white people a way to convey resentment towards BIPOC (Bonilla-Silva, 2014). Bonilla-Silva (2014) posits that color-neutralism is employed to "criticize [minorities'] morality, values, and work ethic" (p. 4). Equally, meritocratic ideologies, or views that people should be privileged and selected based on their abilities, also appeared in participant responses. The problem with meritocracy is that it does not take systemic inequities into consideration. Rae, an administrator, claimed:

> The push is, the reason why we need to get rid of the lower-level math classes and English classes, is, because we're putting up roadblocks for students of color, and that, that's a problem and we need to change that. So, what we're in one way, and I'm just going to be honest here, what we're suggesting is students of color can't do the work of students who are white. What's the issue there? We need to be really careful there.

Rae at first acknowledged the need for reform and stated that below transfer-level courses are barriers for BIPOC students, but also identified the requirements of A.B. 705 as a "push." The reference to "push" seemed to be referring to the fact that A.B. 705 was an external mandate legislated by the state and is, therefore "pushed" upon the college. Then, Rae shifted into notions of meritocracy with "what we're suggesting is students of color can't do the work of students that are white." This comment conveyed that A.B. 705 represented less of a means to promote access and equity and more of a way to upend meritocracy, suggesting that students of color need to earn transfer-level coursework. This sentiment was contrary to the intent of A.B. 705, which articulated that students' high school grades should be used as the primary means of placement in English and math, as these grades have been proven to be far more reliable at indicating student performance in college (Bahr et al., 2019).

Initiatives such as A.B. 705, though aimed at increasing access and equitable outcomes, are not always executed with an equity mindset by the individuals working directly with students. A.B. 705 could not mandate practitioners to change their values and beliefs. During the interview, Rae contemplated the worth of a community college degree:

> All students need to rise to the level of college level content. What are we giving a degree for at any college or university if we're not expecting students to learn a certain level of content of material? So, for the HSI students, I don't see HSI students any different than any of my other

> students. I don't see Black students any different than white students as far as this goes.

In this quote, Rae displayed a belief in high expectations as a standard for education, concerned primarily with the rigor of the content students should grasp to earn a degree. This belief is not misplaced; yet, maintaining color-evasive views makes it challenging for Rae to acknowledge the systemic barriers that exist for BIPOC. Rae does not even refer to the students as Latina/o/x, Hispanic, or Latina/o/x; Rae only refers to them as HSI students. Rae does use the terms Black and white though. Throughout the interview, Rae did not mention any factors that could have influenced existing systemic inequities. To restate, the administration holds an influential role in change initiatives. Rae's views of student success and equity influence policies and practices; they have direct repercussions for student outcomes (Bonilla-Silva, 2014; Wood & Harris, 2017).

While deficit and color-evasive ideologies can impact equitable outcomes for students, so can the high levels of emotional labor that change agents experience during the change process. Change and external mandates brought on by A.B. 705 incited emotional labor in the faculty, staff, and administration interviewed. Emotional labor has the potential to yield dissonance and dissatisfaction within an individual, which can influence a person in other aspects of life, even outside of work (Fisk & Friesen, 2012; Hochschild, 1983). Frustration, lack of communication, and breakdowns in the shared governance process contributed to dissension among faculty, staff, and administration. Overall, these findings illustrated the emotional labor involved in confronting deep-seated assumptions and values during this second order change process (Kezar, 2014).

Emotional labor manifested in many participant responses and was illustrated in different ways related to A.B. 705 reforms. Tanner, an administrator, identified, "Mostly the curriculum, where it needs to be done, is in the math area and again, there's a great deal of resistance there." Tanner corroborated the idea of resistance in certain areas of the campus, which was reported by numerous participants. As the campus was in its first semester of compliance with A.B. 705, some participants reported feeling frustrated at the lack of ownership to implement changes. Jaime, a faculty member, articulated the dilemma:

> It's hard to kind of do what the administration is asking, when the dean is saying, "Okay, you should be working on this," which makes kind of some sense to me. Okay, the law is the law. And then on the other hand ... faculty who again, a lot of them have been here for years, think the students are stupid, don't want to basically do any work, or don't want to have to change anything. So, that makes it hard, trying to get people to change who don't want to change.

Jaime stressed the challenges of implementing A.B. 705 where the administration, or the institutional change agents in power, is urging implementation, but some faculty reject change. This resistance to change suggests the emotional labor experienced during reform efforts. Likewise, Jaime's assertions problematized how some faculty still hold deficit views of students, resist changing their mindsets of student capabilities, and still, others lack the motivation to change.

In facing these threats to equitable outcomes, Latina/o/x students have navigated these systemic inequities by enacting *la facultad* or critical consciousness (Conchas & Acevedo, 2020). Despite the positive intentions of A.B. 705, Latina/o/x students and campus allies have continued to work tirelessly to pressure institutions to dismantle the existing barriers that prevent them from being able to excel. Through the Framework of *Atravesada/o/xs Nepantleando*, it becomes evident how Latina/o/x students have been able to enact their *facultad* as a form of resistance against these inequitable structures, thereby navigating their educational pathways with their communities as support (Conchas & Acevedo, 2020). This highlights the intersection between legislative action and collective resistance in the pursuit of educational equity and college readiness.

## Discussion and Conclusion

The findings from this study reveal that California Assembly Bill 705 can emerge as a pillar for fostering college readiness, equity, and access by encouraging institutions to critically evaluate and reform existing policies and approaches that perpetuate inequities. This legislative mandate challenged California Community Colleges to intervene on systemic barriers that have historically delayed or derailed the educational mobility of Latina/o/x and other BIPOC students. Although Latina/o/x students continued to resist the barriers and excel prior to the enactment of A.B. 705, the use of multiple measures to determine course placement has pushed the CCC system toward a more level playing field. Through the lens of the Framework of *Atravesada /o/xs Nepantleando,* this shift can be seen as brokering institutional resources and power for Latina/o/x students to more efficiently navigate through their educational journeys by eliminating mechanisms that stand in their way and promoting expanded supports. A.B. 705 acknowledges historical injustices and requires that institutions take action to address them. By doing so, this validates the lived experiences and assets of Latina/o/x students, empowering them to use those experiences as a form of capital to succeed in California's higher education system.

The three main themes—Institutional Commitment to Equity and Access, Removing Institutional Barriers to Foster College Readiness and Empower Students, and Enacting *La Facultad* to Navigate Threats to Equitable Outcomes—allow us to see the considerable benefits that the implementation of A.B. 705 has for Latina/o/xs and other BIPOC students. In the process of implementing A.B. 705, staff at Nepantla College were urged to revisit existing institutional documents, such as the mission statement, to evaluate their potential for equitable and inclusive outcomes for students. Though the campus did not include its HSI status in its revised mission, which would be a next step for prioritizing equity, it did attempt to address the diversity of the students it served (Malcom-Piqueux & Bensimon, 2015). The foundations of the college's response to A.B. 705 were built upon actions outlined in the campus' Integrated Plan. For instance, the research site identified several initiatives that aligned with the goals of A.B. 705 to increase equitable outcomes for students. The most powerful initiative was the campus' summer/winter bridge program. Having an established bridge or promise program that provides wraparound services can greatly influence positive equitable outcomes.

Faculty and staff who were involved in the bridge program seemed intrinsically motivated to do the work and committed to supporting BIPOC students. Researchers emphasize the importance of retaining staff and faculty who are equity-minded, especially at Minority Serving Institutions (Conrad & Gasman, 2015). Nelky, a top-level administrator, confirmed that other measures identified in the Integrated Plan such as the use of Early Alert, intrusive counseling, and professional development for faculty with On Course and Reading Apprenticeship contributed to the positive outcomes for Latina/o/x students on campus (personal communication, March 2019). Campus equity plans should be examined to see how campuses can leverage existing equity initiatives to further improve their implementation of AB 705 or even prioritize equity in other education reforms.

Additionally, as part of its response to A.B. 705, Nepantla College began offering alternative transfer-level math pathways like social statistics courses, which opened new pathways for students. This action, in combination with discontinuing the use of a single assessment for placement into transfer-level math and English courses, presents a positive outlook for equitable outcomes for Latina/o/x students. The positive effects attributed to Nepantla's flexibility in modifying admissions and counseling pathways to increase student enrollment directly into transfer-level coursework contrasted with deficit perspectives, colorblind ideologies, and high levels of emotional labor, which held potentially negative consequences for student success and retention rates.

The threats to equitable outcomes, such as implicit biases, deficit perspectives, and especially the lack of ownership exhibited by faculty in the math department, could be detrimental to student success. Validation and positive student engagement are integral for student success, whereas the clear defiance exhibited by math faculty to support student success, and limited accountability by the department leadership, posed a major challenge for other change agents on campus who prioritized equitable access. However, despite institutional inequities, scholars propose that forms of marginalization like this can be recognized by Latina/o/x students and used instead as a way to develop *la facultad* to navigate educational systems (Conchas & Acevedo, 2020).

Ideas of meritocracy and color-evasive ideologies do little to confront the issues of race and equity on any campus, let alone at a Hispanic-Serving Institution, such as Nepantla. While the campus student population was predominantly Latina/o/x, the majority of the faculty and administration were white (The Campaign for College Opportunity, 2018b). Negative assumptions and limited ability to see student potential contradict the intent of the bill to close equity gaps. Research demonstrates that administration, faculty, and staff should reflect the student population and the fact that faculty diversity plays a key role in countering ethnic and racial disparities in student degree completion (Boualoy Dayton et al., 2004).

Understanding the experiences of Latina/o/x students as they navigate these institutions framed as *atravesada/o/xs* can help us intervene on some of these threats to equitable outcomes. A.B. 705 requires change agents and the institution to evaluate values, culture, beliefs, and assumptions (Kezar, 2014). This led to a significant amount of emotional labor as indicated in the findings. Feelings of stress, frustration, confusion, and dissent were prevalent in participant responses. Emotional labor that participants experienced could have been reduced with several actions by (1) providing further guidance on policies, expectations, and procedures; (2) increasing communication on shared governance practices; and (3) allowing additional time for sensemaking. Collaboration is important to ensure equity lies at the center of reform efforts.

The results presented in this chapter revealed positive implications attributed to prioritizing equity in institutional documents and removing institutional barriers. Conversely, the findings also exposed underlying problems of practice that persist in higher education.

## Endnote

[1] While Bonilla-Silva (2014) uses the term "color-blindness," we use color-neutral to avoid reproducing ableist language.

## References

A.B. 705, Irwin. Seymour-Campbell Student Success Act of 2012: matriculation: assessment, CA. Stat. § 745-78213 (Cal. 2017). https://leginfo.legislature.ca.gov/faces/billTextClient.xhtml?bill_id=201720180AB705

Abrica, E., & Rivas, M. (2017). Chicanas in IR: Data-driven advocacy for Latinx students from institutional research contexts in the community college. *Association of Mexican American Educators Journal*, 11(2), 43–64. https://doi.org/10.24974/amae.11.2.349

Acevedo-Gil, N. (2018). Latinas/os navigating the labyrinth: Persistence in community college developmental education. In A.J. de los Santos, L. I. Rendon, G. Francisco Keller, A. Acereda, E. Mara Bensimon, & R. J. Tannenbaum (Eds.),

*New directions: Assessment and preparation of Hispanic college students* (pp. 179–200). Bilingual Press.

Acevedo-Gil, N., Santos, R., Alonso, L., & Solórzano, D. (2015). Latinas/os in community college developmental education: Increasing moments of academic and interpersonal validation. *Journal of Hispanic Higher Education, 14*(2), 101–127. https://doi.org/10.1177/1538192715572893

Acevedo-Gil, N., Santos, R., & Solórzano, D. (2014). Examining a rupture in the Latina/o college pipeline: Developmental education in California Community College system. *Perspectivas: Issues in Higher Education Practice and Policy, 3*, 1–20.

Annamma, S. A., Jackson, D. D., & Morrison, D. (2017). Conceptualizing color-evasiveness: Using dis/ability critical race theory to expand a color-blind racial ideology in education and society. *Race Ethnicity and Education, 20*(2), 147–162. https://doi.org/10.1080/13613324.2016.1248837

Baca, A. (2019). *"Now let us shift": A case study of developmental education reform in a Hispanic Serving community college* (Publication No. 850) [Doctoral dissertation, California State University, San Bernardino]. CSUSB ScholarWorks. https://scholarworks.lib.csusb.edu/etd/850/

Baca Lopez, A. (2022). Implementing AB 705: Implications for equitable outcomes of Latinx students. *Journal of Leadership, Equity, and Research, 8*(2). https://journals.sfu.ca/cvj/index.php/cvj/article/view/217

Bahr, P., Fagioli, L., Hetts, J., Hayward, C., Willett, T., Lamoree, D., Newell, M., Sorey, K., & Baker, R. (2019). Improving placement accuracy in California's community colleges using multiple measures of high school achievement. *Community College Review, 47*(2), 178–211. https://doi.org/10.1177/0091552119840705

Bonilla-Silva, E. (2014). *Racism without racists: Color-blind racism and the persistence of racial inequality in the United States.* Rowman & Littlefield Publishers.

Boualoy Dayton, N., Gonzalez-Vasquez, C. R., & Plum, C. (2004). Hispanic-serving institutions through the eyes of students and administrators. *New Directions for Student Services, 105*, 29–40. https://doi.org/10.1002/ss.114

Byrd, T. L. (2017). *Successful African American community college student athletes' perceptions of factors of academic success.* University of San Francisco.

California Community Colleges Chancellor's Office. (2022). *Key Facts | California Community Colleges Chancellor's Office.* https://www.cccco.edu/About-Us/Key-Facts

The Campaign for College Opportunity. (2018a). *The state of higher education for Latinx in California.* https://collegecampaign.org/wp-content/uploads/2019/10/State-ofHigher-Ed-Latinx-Report-2018.pdf

The Campaign for College Opportunity. (2018b). *Left out: How exclusion in California's colleges and universities hurts our values, our students, and our economy.* https://files.acrobat.com/a/preview/da371fb2-ae1c-41ca-a126-7bbd4695696e

Center for the Analysis of Postsecondary Readiness. (2018, February). *Early findings from a national survey of developmental education practices.* https://postsecondaryreadiness.org/wp-content/uploads/2018/02/early-findings-national-survey-developmental-education.pdf

Clark, B. R. (1960). The "cooling-out" function in higher education. *The American Journal of Sociology, 65*(6), 569–576.

Clark, B. R. (1980). The "cooling out" function revisited. *Questioning the Community College Role. New Directions for Community Colleges, Number 32, 8*(4), 15–32.

Conchas, G., & Acevedo, N. (2020). *The Chicana/o/x dream: Hope, resistance, and educational success.* Harvard Education Press.

Conrad, C., & Gasman, M. (2015). *Educating a diverse nation: Lessons from Minority-Serving Institutions.* Harvard University Press.

Contreras, F. (2019). *Becoming "Latinx responsive:" Raising institutional and systemic consciousness in California's HSIs.* American Council on Education. https://1xfsu31b52d33idlp13twtos-wpengine.netdna-ssl.com/wp-content/uploads/2019/12/Conteras-Essay_FINAL.pdf

Contreras, F., & Contreras, G. J. (2015). Raising the bar for Hispanic Serving Institutions: An analysis of college completion and success rates. *Journal of Hispanic Higher Education, 14*(2), 151–170. https://doi.org/10.1177/1538192715572892

Contreras-Garcia, N. (2023). Healing and sealing the cracks: Understanding and supporting Latina/o/x transfer student pathways. In J. R. Del Real Viramontes & M.C. Vasquez (Eds.), *Community college and beyond: Understanding the transfer pipeline for Latina/o/x students* (pp. 3–17). Information Age Publishing.

Creswell, J. W. (2013). *Qualitative inquiry & research design: Choosing among five approaches* (3rd ed.). Sage.

Cuellar, M., Garcia, G., Nuñez Martinez, M., & Bencomo Garcia, A. (2023). *Building capacity for equity and servingness across California's Hispanic-Serving community colleges.* College Futures Foundation.

Del Real Viramontes, J.R., & Vasquez, M.C. (Eds.). (2023). *Community college and beyond: Understanding the transfer pipeline for Latina/o/x students.* Information Age Publishing.

Felix, E. R., & Fernandez Castro, M. (2018). Planning as strategy for improving Black and Latinx student equity: Lessons from nine California community colleges. *Education Policy AnalysisArchives, 26*(56). http://dx.doi.org/10.14507/epaa.26.3223

Fisk, G. M., & Friesen, J. P. (2012). Perceptions of leader emotion regulation and LMX as predictors of followers' job satisfaction and organizational citizenship behaviors. *The Leadership Quarterly, 23*(1), 1–12. https://doi.org/10.1016/j.leaqua.2011.11.001

Foundation for California Community Colleges. (2017). *Vision for success.* https://foundationccc.org/Portals/0/Documents/Vision/VisionForSuccess_web.pdf

Garcia, G. A. (2019). *Defining "servingness" at Hispanic-Serving Institutions (HSIs): Practical implications for HSI leaders.* American Council on Education. https://www.equityinhighered.org/resources/ideas-and-insights/defining-servingness-at-hispanic-serving-institutions-hsis-practical-implications-for-hsi-leaders/

Gonzales, L. D., & Rincones, R. (2013). Using participatory action research and photo methods to explore higher education administration as an emotional endeavor. *The Qualitative Report, 18*(32), 1–17. http://nsuworks.nova.edu/tqr/vol18/iss32/2

Gonzales, L. D., Kanhai, D., & Hall, K. (2018). Reimagining organizational theory for the critical study of higher education. In M. Paulsen (Ed.), *Higher education: Handbook of theory and research: Vol. 33.* (pp. 505–559). https://doi.org/10.1007/978-3-319-72490-4_11

Henson, L., & Hern, K. (2014, November/December). *Let them in: Increasing access, completion, and equity in college English.* The RP Group. https://rpgroup.org/LinkClick.aspx?fileticket=KZy1UoQuHrg%3d&portalid=0&timestamp=1477600054350

Hern, K., Snell, M., & Henson, L. (2020). *Still getting there: How California's AB 705 is (and is not) transforming remediation and what needs to come next.* Public Advocates. https://accelerationproject.org/Portals/0/Documents/Still_Getting_There_Final.pdf

Hochschild, A. (1983). *The managed heart: Commercialization of human feeling.* University of California Press.

Hodara, M., Jaggars, S., & Karp, M. (2012). *Improving developmental education assessment and placement: Lessons from community colleges across the country.* Community College Research Center, Teacher's College, Columbia University. https://ccrc.tc.columbia.edu/media/k2/attachments/developmental-education-assessment-placement-scan.pdf

Hope, L. L., & Bruno, J. (2017, December 6). *AB 705 implementation and timeline.* Modesto Junior College. https://www.mjc.edu/governance/curriculum/documents/ab705_implemetation_memo.pdf

Hurtado, S., & Ruiz Alvarado, A. (2015). Realizing the potential of Hispanic-Serving Institutions: Multiple dimensions of organizational transformation. In A. M. Núñez, S. Hurtado, & E. Calderon Galdeano (Eds.), *Hispanic serving institutions: Advancing research and transformative practice* (pp. 25–46). Routledge.

Jones, T. (2013). *Addressing a historical mission in a performance driven system: A case study of public historically Black university engaged in the equity scorecard process* (Publication No. 3609916) [Doctoral dissertation, University of Southern California]. ProQuest Dissertations and Theses.

Jones, T., & Assalone, A. (2016). *Not just faster: Equity and learning centered developmental education strategies.* Southern Education Foundation. http://www.

southerneducation.org/getattachment/c33a8962-f5a5-4112-989a-0199b59bd85f/Not-Just-Faster-Equity-Learning-Centered-Developme.aspx

Kezar, A. (2014). *How colleges change: Understanding, leading, and enacting change.* Routledge.

Malcom-Piqueux, L. E., & Bensimon, E. M. (2015, Spring). Design principles for equity and excellence at Hispanic-Serving Institutions. *Perspectivas: Issues in Higher Education Practice and Policy, 3*, 1–16.

Merriam, S. B., & Tisdell, E. J. (2016). *Qualitative research: A guide to design and implementation* (4th ed.). Jossey-Bass.

Miller, K. (2001). The experience of emotion in the workplace: Professing in the midst of tragedy. *Management Communication Quarterly, 15*, 571–600. https://doi.org/10.1177/0893318902154003

Núñez, A. M., Crisp, G., & Elizondo, D. (2015). Hispanic-Serving community colleges and their role in Hispanic transfer. In A. M. Núñez, S. Hurtado, & E. Calderón Galdeano (Eds.), *Hispanic-Serving Institutions: Advancing research and transformative practice* (pp. 47–64). Routledge.

Osei-Kofi, N., & Rendon, L. (2005). Latinos, higher education, and the "needs" of the market. *Latino Studies, 3*, 249–260. https://doi.org/10.1057/palgrave.lst.8600135

Pérez Huber, L., Malagon, M. C, Ramirez, B. R., Gonzalez, L. C., Jimenez, A., & Velez, V. N. (November 2015). *Still falling through the cracks: Revisiting the Latina/o education pipeline.* UCLA Chicano Studies Research Center. https://files.eric.ed.gov/fulltext/ED574691.pdf

Public Policy Institute of California. (2016). *Higher education in California.* http://www.ppic.org/content/pubs/report/R_0416HEBKR.pdf.

Rodríguez, O. (2014). *Increasing access to college-level math: Early outcomes using the Virginia placement test.* (Brief No. 58). Community College Research Center, Teacher's College, Columbia University. https://ccrc.tc.columbia.edu/media/k2/attachments/increasing-access-to-college-level-math.pdf

Rodríguez, O., Cuellar Mejia, M., & Johnson, H. (2018, August). *Remedial education reforms at California's Community Colleges: Early evidence on placement and curricular reforms.* Public Policy Institute of California. http://www.ppic.org/wp-content/uploads/remedial-education-reforms-at-californias-community-colleges-august-2018.pdf

Salas, S. (2014). *Pipeline dreams: Latina/o community college students pushed out of the transfer path* (Publication No. 3708287) [Doctoral dissertation, California State University, San Bernardino]. ProQuest Dissertations & Theses Global.

Saldaña, J. (2016). *The coding manual for qualitative researchers* (3rd ed.). Sage.

Scott-Clayton, J., Crosta, P., & Belfield, C. (2014). Improving the targeting of treatment: Evidence from college remediation. *Educational Evaluation and Policy Analysis, 36*(3), 371–393. https://doi.org/10.3102/0162373713517935

Stake, R. E. (1995). *The art of case study research.* Sage.

Suárez-Orozco, C., Casanova, S., Martin, M., Katsiaficas, D., Cuellar, V., Smith, N. A., & Dias, S. I. (2015). Toxic rain in class: Classroom interpersonal microaggressions. *Educational Researcher, 44*(3), 151–161. https://doi.org/10.3102/0013189X15580314

U.S. Department of Education. (2023). *Hispanic-Serving Institutions (HSIS) | White House Initiative on advancing educational equity, excellence, and Economic Opportunity for Hispanics*. https://sites.ed.gov/hispanic-initiative/hispanic-serving-institutions-hsis/

Wood, L., & Harris, F. (2017). *Supporting men of color in the community college: A guidebook*. Montezuma Publishing.

Yin, R. K. (2009). *Case study research: Design and method* (4th ed.). Sage.

**CHAPTER 7**

# "Unapologetically and Proudly … A Young Mexican American": Capturing the Hope and Resistance of Chicana/o/x Students through *Testimonios*[1]

*Gilberto Q. Conchas and Victor DeAlba*

> Having suffered so much as a child, because of a lack of economic resources, my father was determined to change that for his own family … Knowing the fact that mainstream America expected me to fall into a path of crime, and of failure, pushed me to perform as best as I could in any given aspect. At my job, I strived to be the best. I knew that I was not only representing myself, but my family and my community as well … Looking at my parents, and what I have accomplished thus far in life, have only drove me to, unapologetically and proudly, flaunt that I am a young Mexican American.
>
> —Rafael

> I recognize that every privilege that I have is because of my parents and every obstacle they have faced I have internalized to help me finish college. Though I have had to work harder than other people I would not trade my life for anyone else's because I have learned to understand people and their struggles.
>
> —Ximena

## Introduction

THERE IS SIGNIFICANT scholarship that discusses the educational challenges that students of color enrolled in higher education encounter and overcome throughout their educational journeys. While there are some similarities across different groups of historically excluded populations, the experiences of first-generation Chicana/o/x[2] college students have unique characteristics that have shaped how they navigate educational systems within the United States. As highlighted in the first quote, Chicana/o/x students often utilize the support of their family and peers to break through the barriers that are created and exacerbated by deficit-based perspectives and colonial mechanisms. They also continue to hold onto their identity and the roots of their parents and ancestors to unapologetically embrace their *Chicanidad,* despite the stereotypes that are often placed on them in certain educational spaces. These firsthand experiences help us understand how Chicana/o/x students navigate systems of inequity within educational institutions and how they utilize the group-level support systems that aid them through this process. By acknowledging the multitude of factors that contribute to Chicana/o/x students' perception of inequity and how Chicana/o/x students describe the interactions of systems of marginalization in regard to their ethnicity, gender, and citizenship status, we are able to see how these students enact *la facultad,* or critical consciousness, to shaping their educational opportunities and experiences. As emphasized in the second quote, Chicana/o/x students acknowledge these struggles and often use the support of their families, peers, and communities as assets to counter educational disparities.

In this chapter, we present a historical overview of Chicana/o/x students' schooling experiences and how their experiences vary due to different forms of marginality. We build on the award-winning book, *The Chicana/o/x Dream,* and the Framework of *Atravesada/o/xs Nepantleando* (FAN), which highlights how Chicana/o/x students navigate intersectional systems of oppression and access opportunities in higher education (Conchas & Acevedo, 2020). Among the tools that Chicana/o/x students use to navigate and create opportunities, the support and knowledge they gain from their family, peers, and community serve as vital assets. Through an asset-based lens, we aim to emphasize the importance of schools, families, and communities in assisting Chicana/o/

xs to pursue the *Chicana/o/x Dream* and to counter longstanding deficit-based perspectives, colonial mechanisms, and systems of oppression within the education borderlands. Using interview data and *testimonios,* we center Chicana/o/x voices to provide a unique perspective that can help educational researchers, policymakers, and practitioners to better understand the experiences of these students.

## Historical Overview of Chicana/o/x Schooling Experience

Chicana/o/x students account for the largest percentage of the school-age Latina/o/x population in the United States (Conchas & Acevedo, 2020). Although many Chicana/o/xs are currently enrolled in primary, secondary, and postsecondary educational institutions, only about 10% of Chicana/o/xs that are age 25 and older have at least a bachelor's degree, compared to 14% among all U.S. Latina/o/xs and 30% of the entire U.S. population (Lopéz, 2015). Even though studies have found similar levels of educational aspiration among Chicana/o/x students as other students of color (Kao & Thompson, 2003; Kao & Tienda, 1998), Chicana/o/xs, educational and schooling experiences have unique characteristics that have shaped contemporary education. In this section, we aim to provide a brief historical overview of the schooling experiences of Chicana/o/x students to help readers understand the root of existing educational inequities, including systems of oppression that may have impacted their parents and families.

Early forms of schooling for Chicana/o/x[3] students came after the signing of the 1848 Treaty of Guadalupe Hidalgo and were attempts by Catholic and Protestant churches to strengthen their religious tenets (San Miguel & Valencia, 1998). The Catholic Church began to build schools throughout New Mexico, California, and Texas shortly after the Mexican American War. The Protestant Church began its schooling efforts after the U.S. Civil War. These schooling practices became a way to "Americanize" Chicana/o/x students and other students of color through the erasure of their history, culture, and language.

The schooling efforts made by these religious institutions served as a foundation of what became U.S. public schooling at the start of the 20th century. The erasure fueled by deficit-based perspectives and colonial mechanisms, such as biological determinism, claimed that the history, culture, and language of Chicana/o/x students and other Black, Indigenous, People of Color (BIPOC) contributed to their inability to learn at the same level as white students (Gonzalez, 1996). This led to forced assimilation, which has been historically used against BIPOC by early religious institutions and the U.S. government. These deficit-based perspectives resulted in the type of segregation that was not necessarily codified in law but still treated Chicana/o/x students as "others" through local policies and administrative violence enacted by school administrators. Many, if not all, of these segregated schools for Chicana/o/x students were not intended for them to achieve social mobility but rather a way to funnel them into fieldwork and the service industry.

The influx of people from Mexico or of Mexican descent between the 1930s and 1960s led to the expansion of Chicana/o/x communities across the Southwest region of the United States. This created a nativist sentiment among white people, which contributed to increased segregation and inequities within the U.S. schooling system (Valencia et al., 2002). Chicana/o/x students were given a white racial designation as a way to strip them of their identities. For this reason, there weren't laws that legally separated them from their white peers. This created significant legal barriers when Chicana/o/x students attempted to challenge segregation (Donato & Hanson, 2012). Despite this, Chicana/o/x students continued to resist these oppressive systems of schooling with little to no recognition from mainstream media. The communal and socially cohesive nature of Chicana/o/x communities aided their resistance efforts. An example of Chicana/o/x student resistance that many people are often unfamiliar with is the 1946 *Mendez v. Westminster School District* federal court ruling. The ruling specified that "separate but equal" schools for Chicana/o/x students in Orange County, California were unconstitutional, ultimately influencing the landmark 1954 *Brown v. Board of Education* decision (Aguirre, 2005).

The resistance of Chicana/o/x students did not end there. Scholars describe the mid-1960s through the mid-1970s as the militant and reformist era. Unified by their common or shared identity, Chicana/o/x students continued to make their presence known through mass demonstrations and calls for transformative change in education and schooling (Gonzalez, 2013). For example, the 1968 East Los Angeles Walkouts or Blowouts, which was a call to action by Chicana/o/x students for equitable education access. During this time, Chicana/o/x students experienced a 60% dropout rate and were being funneled into vocational programs. As a result, Chicana/o/x students collectively organized a mass walkout of more than 15,000 students, which still represents one of the largest student protests in U.S. history (Library of Congress, n.d.). This section highlights the historical significance of the Chicana/o/x student experience, their continuous struggle to achieve equity, and their persistence in resisting and navigating through the U.S. education and schooling system. These students made successful strides by maintaining group-level systems of support, with their families, peers, and communities playing a significant role. Their shared identity and cultural traditions and their persistence to gain recognition for the contributions of their ancestors led to effective organizing strategies of Chicana/o/xs that we read about and learn from today. The historical and current Chicana/o/x experiences are the basis for Conchas and Acevedo's (2020) FAN.

## The Framework of *Atravesada/o/xs Nepantleando* as an Asset-Based Conceptualization

FAN acknowledges that the exclusion and oppression of Chicana/o/xs are rooted in the colonial foundation of the United States and that schooling practices have served as a way of reinforcing those systems of oppression. The deficit-based and marginalizing practices, policies, and ideologies that exist in the U.S. education and schooling system cause Chicana/o/x students to feel "othered," thus leading them to be framed as *atravesada/o/xs* (Conchas & Acevedo, 2020). Through this constant othering and treatment as undeserving *atravesada/o/xs,* Chicana/o/x students have to find ways to navigate the spaces and institutions that were built to exclude them.

FAN is influenced by Anzaldúa's theories that help explain how historically excluded groups of students understand their marginalization within educational institutions and society. These spaces where multiple cultures collide can be characterized as the education borderlands. In these spaces, Chicana/o/x students enact *la facultad de los atravesada/o/xs,* which is defined by Anzaldúa (1987) as:

> the capacity to see in surface phenomena the meaning of deeper realities, to see the deep structure below the surface. It is an instant "sensing," a quick perception arrived at without conscious reasoning. It is an acute awareness mediated by the part of the psyche that does not speak, that communicates in images and symbols which are the faces of feelings, that is, behind which feelings reside/hide. The one possessing this sensitivity is excruciatingly alive to the world. (p. 38)

*La facultad* is about how Chicana/o/x students identify and understand the inequities they face and how they resist the barriers, navigate the spaces, and access or build bridges to opportunities in these education borderlands. Through the enactment of *la facultad,* Chicana/o/x students are able to become *nepantlera/o/xs.* The word "*nepantla*" originates from the Indigenous language of Mexico known as Nahuatl. The word *nepantla* represents the in-between space of multiple and overlapping worlds, which resembles the space of the education borderlands. Anzaldúa (2002) theorized that "living between cultures results in 'seeing' double, first from the perspective of one culture, then from the perspective of another. Seeing from two or more perspectives simultaneously renders those cultures as transparent" (p. 549). Thus, when in *nepantla,* a *nepantlera/o/x* has the ability to see multiple cultures in their overlapping, complementing, or conflicting relationships. *Nepantlera/o/xs* "are threshold people, agents of change, spiritual activists who employ liminal states of consciousness and ways of thinking as they enact their visions" (Keating, 2005, p. 7). Nevertheless, a *nepantlera/o/x* aims to transform perspectives and possibilities. In being able to see multiple perspectives and identify with multiple cultures, *nepantlera/o/xs* also aim to build bridges between these worlds.

What makes this contribution unique is how we expand FAN to examine how it is activated through the resources within schools, familial contexts, and community-based institutions of first-generation Chicana/o/x college students. The students in this section describe their experiences of being labeled as *atravesada/o/xs* early in their educational journeys, and the systems of support that help enable the activation of FAN. As highlighted in the historical overview section, the Chicana/o/x student experience is rooted in how people view and try to change the cultural differences of these students. Chicana/o/x students and other BIPOC students have almost always had their cultural differences categorized as deficiencies or inferiorities by white Americans and those in positions of power. As a result, some school officials and scholars have adopted deficit-based perspectives, which have impacted and continue to impact the approaches and development of scholarship within the field of education. FAN aims to counter these deficit-based perspectives by acknowledging that cultural differences are assets instead of deficiencies.

We adopt an asset-based lens because it aligns with FAN. Chicana/o/x students, as *atravesada/o/xs,* develop and utilize social and cultural assets by enacting *la facultad.* These skills and forms of knowledge are rooted in the experiential and historical knowledge of their families, peers, and communities. While scholars may have different conceptualizations of what an asset is, Yosso's (2005) seminal work on community cultural wealth has guided how we use it throughout this chapter. Yosso's (2005) idea of community cultural wealth challenges the traditional interpretations of Bourdieuean theory of cultural capital by recognizing the assets of BIPOC communities as forms of wealth or capital. Existing scholarship has primarily focused on the use of asset-based approaches or pedagogy within educational practice, but it is equally important to understand its role within research and information dissemination. The use of FAN in educational research can help us reveal the ways in which Chicana/o/x students apply the knowledge and assets they've accumulated from their experiences as well as families, peers, and communities to navigate their educational journeys and overcome the inequities within the education borderlands. We now turn to the student voices to elucidate how they navigate the unequal education borderlands.

## Uncovering Student Voices

### *Chicana/o/x Student Perceptions of Inequalities Through Interviews*

While an asset-based framework aims to focus on students' assets, as opposed to the deficits, we feel it is important to emphasize the way Chicana/o/x students perceive the inequities they face. These inequities are structural and not a result of deficits of the students, but rather a result of deficit-based approaches that only serve to widen the achievement gap. For this reason, we look at Chicana/o/x student perceptions to better understand how they make meaning of these inequities and how they utilize group-level systems of support to navigate these systems of oppression through the enactment of *la facultad*.

In this section, we draw on data from interviews with 54 Chicana/o/x first-generation college students from a California Hispanic-Serving Institution (HSI) with a Carnegie Classification as a public 4-year university with very high research activity. Considering that Chicana/o/x students face various sociocultural obstacles in their educational experiences that often complicate their actual socioeconomic outlooks and trajectories, it is important and necessary to turn to their perspectives in the higher education borderlands. As shown in Figure 7.1, Chicana/o/x students perceive various contributing factors of U.S. inequality, ranging from cultural to structural factors. The most prominent contributing factors to inequality identified across genders were racism and socioeconomic status (SES) (53% for Chicanas and 46% for Chicanos). This was followed by educational opportunities, with 32% among Chicanas and 30% among Chicanos. There were some gendered differences in how Chicanas and Chicanos perceived the other factors of social inequality, also shown in Figure 7.1. Unsurprisingly, Chicanas were more acutely aware of gender inequalities than Chicanos, as it was the third most frequently mentioned factor of inequality among Chicanas (28%). On the other hand, Chicanos listed stereotypes as the third most prominent contributing factor to social inequality (26%).

These findings further elucidate the perceptions of Chicana/o/x students on their structural and cultural experiences with social inequalities. Scholars who focus on intersectionality have supported that multiple forms of inequality simultaneously impact individuals' experiences and perceptions. Likewise, *Chicana*/o/x students have a unique experience within society, as a number of different but intersecting factors contribute to their marginalization and oppression. They are the subject of stereotypes and deficit-based thinking in the larger American society as minoritized people and immigrants or children of immigrants. Additionally, factors such as being a woman, a sexual minority, and/or coming from a disadvantaged social background contribute to further subjugation. However, these different forms of marginalization do not necessarily apply to Chicana/o/x individuals uniformly. As Patricia Hill Collins (1990) has argued in her conceptualization of the matrix of domination, systems of oppression exist and intersect, influencing the penalties and privileges that individuals experience based on their identities.

**Figure 7.1**
*Perceptions of existing inequalities by Chicana/o/x students*

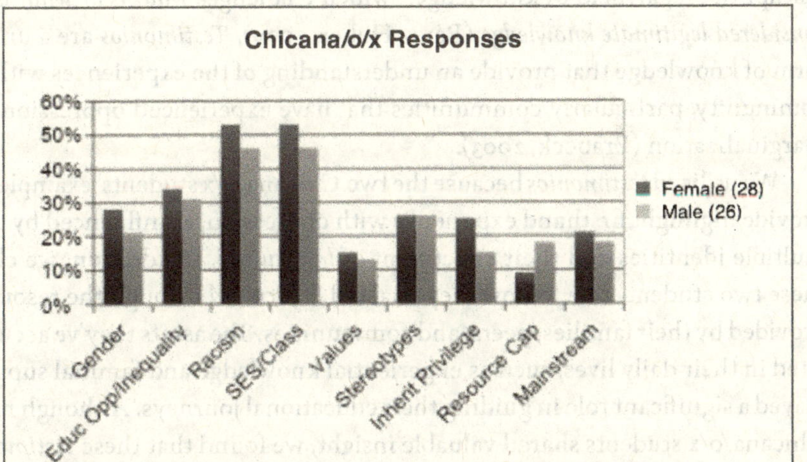


Overall, both Chicanos and Chicanas were aware of the structural factors as perpetuating social inequalities in contemporary U.S. society. The responses of Chicana/o/x students show us that they are cognizant of the structural inequalities that they regularly face as well as the cultural dimensions of inequality, such as stereotypes, values, and those characteristics considered out of the mainstream, such as immigrant status, skin color, and language skills. Now, we turn to two *testimonios* to further explore how first-generation Chicana/o/x students navigate these social inequalities.

## *Testimonios* as Method and Methodological Tool

*Testimonios* have a history dating back to the 1970s, with their roots and origins tied to Latin American and Chicana/o/x social movements (Delgado Bernal et al., 2012). More recently, *testimonios* have gained attention in educational research, as they can be a powerful tool for revealing how oppression operates in the lives of Chicana/o/x students, and they also serve as a way for students to reject the labels that are often placed on them while they create their own narratives (Delgado Bernal et al., 2009; Pérez Huber & Cueva, 2012). *Testimonios* can be described as a method and methodological tool that aim to disrupt the "apartheid of knowledge," which challenges *what is or what is not considered legitimate knowledge* (Pérez Huber, 2009). *Testimonios* are a unique form of knowledge that provide an understanding of the experiences within a community, particularly communities that have experienced oppression and marginalization (Brabeck, 2003).

We utilized *testimonios* because the two Chicana/o/x students' examples we provide highlight firsthand experience with oppression, as influenced by their multiple identities and their enactment of *la facultad*. In addition, we chose these two students due to how they enacted *la facultad* through the resources provided by their families, peers, and communities. The assets they've accumulated in their daily lives, such as experiential knowledge and familial support, played a significant role in guiding their educational journeys. Although many Chicana/o/x students shared valuable insight, we found that these *testimonios* help us understand how Chicana/o/x students identify, perceive, and overcome barriers within higher educational borderlands utilizing those group-level support systems. Lastly, *testimonios* as a method operate with the intention to bring about justice and social change within educational policy, practice, and research (Blackmer Reyes & Curry Rodriguez, 2012; Delgado Bernal et al., 2012). The two Chicana/o/x students in this chapter provide compelling statements geared towards social justice, describing the utilization of experiential and historical knowledge as assets to navigate their educational journeys and to give back to others within their communities.

The interviews and *testimonios* in this chapter, coupled with FAN and an asset-based lens, reflect the memories and experiences of Chicana/o/x students as they relate to oppressive conditions (capitalism, racism, patriarchy, nativism, heteronormativity, and ableism) and opportunity (healing, empowerment, educational engagement, and agency for social justice) in education and society. We specifically examine the *testimonios* of two Chicana/o/x students[4] to further explore how Chicana/o/x students perceive their experiences with marginalization, how they enact *la facultad*, and how they describe the systems of support that they identify as critical for helping them through their educational journey.

### Rafael's Story: Proudly, Unapologetically Mexican American

Rafael is a first-generation college student who is about to graduate from the University of California. Like many other Chicana/o/x first-generation college students, Rafael is an American-born son of Mexican immigrants. More specifically, Rafael grew up with a single mom who immigrated to the United States as a teenager with her parents under the *Bracero Program* and worked odd jobs all her life to make ends meet and raise a child on her own. However, Rafael's father was not completely absent from his life. On the contrary, Rafael thinks very highly of his father, who crossed the border from Mexico without proper documentation to pursue and achieve his American Dream. As Rafael explained, his father's struggles and eventual success as an immigrant greatly motivated his own educational success and enactment of *la facultad*. However, his parents' tireless efforts to provide a better future for their sons did not stop Rafael from experiencing marginalization and oppression in the U.S. Rafael stated,

> Working with the fact that I was a young Mexican American expected to not amount to much, like a vast majority of my peers that came from my same community ... As I grew older, I started to notice the different treatment that I received, from simply being followed at a store to the different tone me and my family would be "greeted" at different restaurants. The extent of this reality [of being a minority and a child of immigrants] did not set in until I was in high school, when we competed in [sports] against a predominantly white high school. From the time that we got there to the time that we left, racial remarks were screamed from around the track ... these types of remarks only became more common with time. As I expressed to different [people] my intent to go to college, people were automatically surprised, granted, there were many students that did not care about school, but that was not the case for all of us, and it was not fair for people to make that assumption.

The negative interactions Rafael had in predominantly white settings reveal the ways in which Chicanos are labeled *atravesados*. Not only do people assume deficit-based stereotypes and criminality in minoritized men like Rafael, but they also make it known that minoritized students like Rafael are not welcome in the educational domain—whether it's high school athletics or college campuses. Even though Rafael had been a determined and motivated student all his life, these experiences of being labeled as an *atravesado* instilled fear in Rafael. At the center of his fears was internalized doubt due to his marginalization and *atravesado* status as a second-generation Chicano.

After receiving constant messages that he did not belong in higher education, he recalled the time he received his acceptance letter from the University of California and immediately started doubting himself and his own potential:

> As the day got closer to deciding what school I was going to transfer to, I explained to my father my fears of accepting the offer. This was a top university; how would this second-generation Mexican American kid be able to hold his own at this great school?

Fortunately, Rafael's parents did not share his apprehension. On the contrary, his parents provided encouragement, emotional support, and aspirational capital in each of their own ways. Rafael's mother, resenting that she could not pursue formal education, always pushed Rafael to prioritize his education before anything. She constantly encouraged him, "*le tienes que echar ganas, mijo!* (you have to give it your all, son!)." All throughout his high school years, she stayed awake late into the night, trying her best to help him finish his homework. When Rafael expressed his concerns regarding family finances prior to his decision to apply to the University of California schools, Rafael's mother sternly stated that they would make it work and that Rafael's educational pursuit was more important than immediate financial troubles. In the end, as Rafael put it, "they found a way to make it happen."

Similarly, Rafael's father, even though he did not make financial contributions to the household, provided assurance and encouragement. Not only did his encouraging words motivate Rafael to try his best in everything, but his life experiences also provided Rafael with much-needed guidance on how to persevere when faced with adversities. More specifically, Rafael's father's experiences of marginalization as a Mexican immigrant *atravesado* and his eventual accomplishment and success showed Rafael that his marginalized position in society did not stop him. He shared:

> Having suffered so much as a child, because of a lack of economic resources, my father was determined to change that for his own family ... Knowing the fact that mainstream America expected me to fall into a path of crime, and of failure, pushed me to perform as best as I could in any given aspect. At my job, I strived to be the best. I knew that I was not only representing myself, but my family and my community as well ... Looking at my parents, and what I have accomplished thus far in life, have only drove me to, unapologetically and proudly, flaunt that I am a young Mexican American.

In other words, Rafael enacted *la facultad* through the support and encouragement of his parents, which helped him look beyond the surface reality and resist the colonial oppressive system that expected him to fail. He pushed back against those deficit-based perspectives that only served to limit his potential and was encouraged by the radical love provided by his parents.

Rafael's educational experiences at the University of California further assisted his enactment of *la facultad*. The knowledge he acquired in his classrooms, coupled with the lived experience he accrued from growing up as an *atravesado*, a Chicano who is expected to fail, who does not belong in the mainstream domain, allowed him to understand that the larger society is structured to perpetuate inequalities through coloniality, limiting potentials of many BIPOC. The knowledge and resources he accessed by being a student at a prestigious educational institution like the University of California led to the awakening of a deeper consciousness to resist unequal and oppressive social structures and discourses. Additionally, the support he received from his parents, along with the experiential knowledge they shared, and that he experienced, served as assets that contributed to his success at the university. Rafael shares,

> I think back at all of my peers that I went to school with, that were so much more intelligent than I was, but due to circumstances in life, and most importantly, to the lack of social capital, they were not able to

> thrive. I know that I could have, very easily, fallen into that very same predicament. That knowledge now fuels my future aspirations in academia and in my future career goals.

Influenced by the existence of institutional inequities, Rafael aspires to be an educator. Rafael wants to teach at under-resourced high schools, where predominantly minoritized students attend, to provide the social, cultural, and aspirational capital that such schools often block from students. Both from his personal experiences and from his college education, Rafael understands that the educational system is not designed to embrace and accommodate poor BIPOC students but designed with deficit-based perspectives that perpetuate the larger societal inequities that limit their academic success. In this sense, Rafael's aspiration was motivated by his desire to become a *nepantlero*, one who could see the intersecting worlds of marginalized minoritized people and the marginalizing mainstream and bridge the two worlds while empowering the marginalized minoritized people to pursue success and resist coloniality using their assets. As Rafael argued, "the color of [my] skin or the language are no indicators of what I can accomplish;" he wishes to instill this sense of empowerment and resistance in the future generation of Chicana/o/x students who may otherwise not be able to tap into their power in the marginalizing and colonial educational system.

### *Ximena's Story: A Proud Chicana With Undocumented Parents*

Ximena is a 19-year-old second-generation and first-generation college student whose parents were undocumented at one point in her life. Like many other Mexican immigrants, Ximena's parents decided to immigrate to the United States to pursue better economic opportunities and provide a better future for their unborn children. Even though they both obtained college degrees in Mexico, Ximena's parents experienced downward mobility upon their arrival in the United States. Ximena's father worked at a dairy farm, and Ximena's mother at a McDonald's. Despite all the hardships, Ximena's mother managed to attend an adult language school and obtain the necessary certificates to become a dental assistant aide, while Ximena's father continued working as an undocumented immigrant laborer. Being a U.S.-born child, Ximena was largely unaware of the uncertainties and fears undocumented immigrants and their family members experienced until her father was deported. Fortunately for Ximena's family, Ximena's mother quickly hired a lawyer to resolve the issue, and ultimately, Ximena's father was able to obtain a residence permit to come back to the United States to be with his family. However, this experience left a lasting impression on Ximena; she realized that her own U.S. citizenship does not necessarily shield her from the *atravesada* experiences of immigrant families.

> I believe that the lives of children whose parents are immigrants is complicated by their immigration status, whether they are undocumented, legal residents, or naturalized citizens. This statement is proven to be true through personal experiences and experiences my friends have faced as well. The fact that my dad was unable to attain his legal residency prevented him from giving his family the assurance of financial stability. I don't think it's fair for any family to be living under constant fear of deportation, especially if the family's intentions are to stay and work. It's baffling to think that many of these immigrants are stimulating the economy and even giving back to corporate America, but because they don't have documentation, it allows the American government to separate them from their families. It becomes complicated because the children of these immigrants have to endure hardship and are still expected to go through school. It becomes more complicated because even if they have the resources to go to school, they still lack the support system that they would otherwise have if their parents were not deported.

This framing of Mexican immigrants and their children as *atravesadas* further affected Ximena's relationship with her parents. Even though her parents provided tremendous emotional, familial, and social support and capital for Ximena to succeed—by supporting not only her main educational curricula but also her extracurricular involvements in sports, arts, and volunteering programs and building a rapport with teachers—Ximena's parents were strict on Ximena's social life, especially with regards to dating during her adolescence. Ximena recalls the tension during her high school days:

> Eighth grade was when I began to come out of my shell a lot more than previous years, and my extroversion resulted in a bad relationship with my dad. I had my first boyfriend in the beginning of eighth grade, and my parents were not happy about that. At the time, I didn't know I was too young to have a boyfriend, so as a result, I ignored what my parents had to say and continued to have several boyfriends. I would always talk back to my dad, and eventually there would not be a day when we would not fight, literally. Did they not understand that I just wanted to have fun and live my life? Well, the answer is yes but they also worried about me. It wasn't until college that I realized that they wanted to shield me from opportunities that would potentially lead me to drugs, sex, or death.
>
> My high school's nickname was "Prego High," which indicated that many of our girls got pregnant. Unfortunately, this was true. Many girls, beginning from their freshman year, would get pregnant and drop out of school. In the Latino culture, girls are supposed to have many children and become housewives while the men work. Girls are not pushed to obtain an education because, in the traditional culture, girls are only created to have kids and do household chores. My parents did not want to carry that tradition over and have worked hard to make sure I pursue an education before anything else. My dad was always angry at me for having boyfriends because he was afraid I would end up pregnant and without an education. I knew better than to engage in that kind of activity, but I realize now that he was just doing his job as a dad who wanted a better future for his daughter.

As shown in Ximena's accounts, gendered and racialized socialization of Chicanas labels them as *atravesadas* who do not belong in the mainstream educational domain but in the domestic sphere as future mothers and wives. Rather than highlighting their potential as students, Chicanas and Latinas, especially if they are from under-resourced and heavily minoritized school districts and residential areas, are treated as if they are not pursuing or serious about educational opportunities and, therefore, do not deserve such opportunities.

Fortunately for Ximena, her parents were well aware of such stereotypes and the adversities Ximena may be subjected to and instead instilled in her the idea that education is important for Chicanas, just like it is for anyone else. As a result of her parents' tireless support, Ximena enrolled in GATE and AP courses throughout high school and became the president of a couple of student organizations. Moreover, Ximena's mother formed friend-like relationships with her students to ensure that "their children received the best education possible." During these years, Ximena was able to accrue important assets and knowledge, such as social, emotional, and aspirational capital, via her parents, teachers, peers, and the communities in which she is embedded.

However, Ximena herself was not aware of how the resources and opportunities she was able to access were not universally available for other minoritized individuals and their communities. This realization came once she started attending college and shaped her career aspiration:

> I did know one thing, and that was that I didn't want to be a teacher, especially because they were not paid enough. Fast forward a couple months later, and I'm taking a sociology course, and I was astonished at how corrupt our education system really is. I was appalled at the inequity of the system and how it has failed so many, especially those who are disadvantaged ... I also learned that students were constantly being pushed out of the education system. Since many students were undocumented in my high school, they were more prone to the school-to-deportation pipeline. This is a result from the lack of college-going culture present in schools, and the lack of important places for these students. Students who come from different countries throughout the year are more likely to face bullying, discrimination, and lack of peer support. These are just some problems that they could potentially face apart from problems at home. Ultimately, these struggles pose a threat to their opportunities in the United States because as they are pushed out of the education system, they are pushed into a sphere of criminalization and eventually deportation. It was during this class that I vowed to be a teacher and I vowed to make a difference in my community. It was no longer about what I was going to get paid or the benefits I was going to receive, it was now about the lives that I was going to change for the better.

The sociology courses she took allowed Ximena to see the inequality in the larger educational system that alienates many socioeconomic and ethnoracial minoritized students as *atravesadas* and further made her realize that her own success was a result of the assets that her parents provided rather than strategic approaches to her early educational experiences. This realization, coupled with the inevitable feelings of loneliness as one of the few minority students on campus, brought Ximena and her parents closer together. Her parents provided crucial emotional support for Ximena even when she went through her first adult breakup during her sophomore year.

In addition to emotional support, Ximena's parents' emphasis on extracurricular involvement during her adolescence inspired her to take on a leadership position at an international youth program during her college career. She was able to widen her social network, access social capital, and tap into community support outside of her immediate family, peer group, and college campus through this experience. This leadership experience further drives Ximena's enactment of *la facultad*. She was able to see beyond social inequities that adversely impact poor, undocumented, ethnoracially minoritized students and create a support system, access resources and opportunities that may not have been available to her immediately, and successfully adapt to academically as well as psychologically demanding college curricula and environments.

> Deportation due to undocumentation is inhumane, especially when the person who is being deported has a family to maintain. When it comes to the cases that deport people without due process, I think that it's due to underlying racism and discrimination. I am a proud Chicana with undocumented parents! ... My first two years of college were a wild ride, but if it wasn't for my struggles, I would not be the same person I am today. I recognize that every privilege that I have is because of my parents and every obstacle they have faced I have internalized to help me finish college. Though I have had to work harder than other people I would not trade my life for anyone else's because I have learned to understand people and their struggles. Through these experiences and identities, I have been able to undergo a personal metamorphosis that always encourages me to become a better person than I was the day before. I am a proud Chicana!

Informed and inspired by her father's experiences of being undocumented and deportation, Ximena aspires to become a teacher who is not only aware of the issues facing undocumented immigrant families and communities but also the culturally sensitive educator with an asset-based perspective who could help students subvert their *atravesada* experiences to become successful despite systematic inequity that robs minoritized people of equitable opportunities, such as the school-to-prison or school-to-deportation pipeline. Ximena's ability to see beyond systems of inequity to become a *nepantlera,* moving within and among multiple, often conflicting, worlds, transforming perspectives and possibilities not only for herself but for others as well. In other words, Ximena and her family's experiences of being *atravesadas* as a child of immigrant and undocumented immigrants allow Ximena to see issues of immigration, economic justice, and criminal justice as interconnected. Her aspirations to become a teacher further reflect her capacities as a *nepantlera* who shares this knowledge of the intersecting and conflicting realities as assets that guide other individuals to reject the coloniality inherent in the American educational system and the larger society.

## We are Children of the Corn/Somos Hija/o/xs del Maíz: Husks of Hope, Resistance, and Latina/o/x Educational Success

For many people, *maíz* (corn) is just one of many globally mass-produced crops, but for Chicana/o/xs and many other Latina/o/x and Indigenous cultures, *maíz* is sacred and deeply symbolic of who they are, where they come from, and what they are made of (Rodriguez, 2014). Because *maíz* is not a natural crop and does not grow in the wild, many people, including scientists, were confused about where it came from. There has since been a consensus that *maíz* was domesticated by the Indigenous peoples of what is now Mexico nearly 9000 years ago and would not have developed into the crop it is today if it weren't for the ingenuity and care of Indigenous cultivators (Smithsonian Institution, 2020). *Maíz* is a central part of the ancestral history of Chicana/o/xs and continues to be a staple and inspiration in food, architecture, music, art, and much more. *Maíz* is representative of the connection that Chicana/o/xs have with their Indigenous ancestors as well as Mother Earth herself.

This idea of being *Hija/o/xs del Maíz* is linked to the Framework of *Atravesada/o/xs Nepantleando,* as *maíz* represents the commitment to resist and counter coloniality by preserving indigeneity. Just as Indigenous peoples have had their culture stripped away from them and their contributions often go unnoticed, Chicana/o/xs continue to experience similar patterns of exclusion as they are labeled as *atravesada/o/xs.* By reconnecting with their roots and rediscovering the many ways that their Indigenous ancestors contributed to society and paved the way before them, they develop *la facultad* necessary to become *nepantlera/o/xs.* In this section, we build on the notion that Chicana/o/xs are *Los Hija/o/xs del Maíz* (Children of the Corn) due to how they enact *la facultad* through resources from their family, school, and community.

Additionally, they utilize experiential knowledge based on cultural traditions and experiences that are passed down from their parents, grandparents, ancestors, and overall communities. We focus on the role of family, school, and out-of-school spaces that serve as assets to guide them through the education borderlands. We highlight how this generational knowledge not only helps to shape their experiences at home and in their neighborhoods but also to help them overcome adversity and form the identity of *Los Hija/o/xs del Maíz* (The Children of the Corn).

### *Familial and Peer Support*

As we examine the experiences of Chicana/o/x students, it is important to understand the role of family and peers in helping Chicana/o/xs enact *la facultad* and tap into resources and support that serve as assets to overcome inequalities that are deeply engrained within the educational system. The *testimonios* of Rafael and Ximena demonstrate the importance of family and peer support for navigating their educational journeys. Rafael shares how differential treatment based on deficit-based stereotypes was placed on him and how that contributed to internalized doubt and a feeling of being an undeserving *atravesado.* His mother's encouragement and emotional support served as assets that helped him enact *la facultad* to navigate difficult situations. Rios-Ellis et al. (2015) explained that "family unity or *familismo* is a core characteristic among Latinos ... Latino students experience many opportunities to maintain healthy relationships, communicate with others, and build connections with their resources. In this regard, familial capital provides them with many relational skills that can be helpful along their academic path" (p. 39). The familial and aspirational capital and experiential knowledge that Rafael gained from his father also served as an asset for overcoming barriers within the education borderlands. Similarly, Ximena acknowledged the emotional, familial, and social support and capital that her parents provided for her through her academic journey as well as her involvement in extracurricular activities. Essentially, their parents were the husks who supported them through the difficult times and provided them with the necessary resources to eventually become independent.

### *Community/Out-of-School Contexts*

In addition to the deficit-based stereotypes that Chicana/o/x students face within educational spaces, they also navigate environments outside of school while being labeled as *atravesada/o/xs*. These students have found ways to counter these perspectives by enacting *la facultad* and becoming *nepantlera/o/xs* through the resources provided by their communities. Ordoñez-Jasis and Jasis (2004), in their study on the impact of community programs on Chicana/o/x students, share that these community resources "have the strength and the purpose to identify and problem-solve the educational needs of their own children" (p. 63). As Ximena's experience showcases, although she was U.S.-born, the community she was born in played a significant role in deciding her educational aspirations. Just as her parents and community helped her overcome barriers through their support and motivation, Ximena's experience in environments that didn't necessarily value educational attainment influenced her decision to want to enact *la facultad* and become a *nepantlera* to assist her family and friends to overcome the barriers that were placed on them due to their immigration status. The radical love that is provided by communities serves as an important and necessary asset for supporting these students to overcome inequalities within educational spaces.

## Conclusion

We contribute to the literature by centering our analyses of the interviews and the *testimonios* of Chicana/o/x students to examine how they tap into the resources provided by their families and communities to respond to and subvert systems of coloniality and oppression in the U.S. educational system to achieve success. Rafael and Ximena's *testimonios* provide valuable insights into how different forms of marginality shape students' experiences in the mainstream educational realm and the significance they place on the role of group-level support systems.

Rafael's *testimonio* captures the hardships faced by his parents because of socioeconomic barriers. At the same time, those barriers provided him with a deep-rooted motivation to create a better life for himself and his family. His *testimonio* underscores a distinct characteristic amongst those labeled as *atravesada/o/xs*—the use of adversity as a driving force for creating opportunity and success for themselves, their family, and the community. Ximena's *testimonio* highlights her appreciation for the sacrifices and struggles of her parents, acknowledging that her existing privileges are a result of her parents' determination. Her *testimonio* shows that Chicana/o/x students develop a unique perspective through their experience to strengthen their abilities to empathize with the struggles of others.

The *testimonios* demonstrate that deficit-based stereotypes placed on Chicana/o/x students have not deterred their ambition to excel. Using an asset-based lens, we can see that the two Chicana/o/x students utilized knowledge/assets from their familial and community support systems to make sense of their marginalized positions and empower themselves by turning adversities into opportunities in their pursuits of academic achievement and success. Thus, their accounts provide powerful vernacular forms for individuals subjected to coloniality moving beyond realities surrounding them to perceive positivity, potential, and success in their present and future selves despite institutional and cultural barriers and precariousness. Their stories shine a light on how Chicana/o/x students embark on this collective journey towards resilience, achievement, and a cultural identity that is unapologetic and proud to be Chicana/o/x.

## Endnotes

[1] Portions of this chapter appeared in Conchas, Lee, Cambero, and Acevedo-Gil (2019) and Conchas and Acevedo (2020).

[2] Throughout this article, the authors intentionally employ the term Chicana/o/x to support the inclusivity of all Mexican ethnic-identified peoples regardless of gender identity or expression.

[3] San Miguel and Valencia (1998) use Mexican American when referring to students of Mexican descent. For the purpose of consistency, we use Chicana/o/x in place of Mexican American.

[4] Pseudonyms are used to protect the confidentiality of the respondent.

## References

Aguirre, F. P. (2005). *Mendez v. Westminster School District*: How it affected *Brown v. Board of Education. Journal of Hispanic Higher Education, 4*(4), 321-332.

Anzaldúa & A. Keating (Eds.), *This bridge we call home: radical visions for transformation* (pp. 540–578). Routledge.

Anzaldúa , G.(1987). *Borderlands/La Frontera: The New Mestiza*. Aunt Lute.

Anzaldúa, G. (2002) Now let us shift ... the path of conocimiento ... inner work, public acts. In G.Anzaldúa, G., & Moraga, C. (1983). *This bridge called my back writings by radical women of color.* SUNY Press.

Blackmer Reyes, K., & Curry Rodríguez, J. E. (2012). Testimonio: Origins, terms, and resources. *Equity & Excellence in Education, 45*(3), 525-538.

Brabeck, K. (2003). IV. Testimonio: A strategy for collective resistance, cultural survival and building solidarity. *Feminism & Psychology, 13*(2), 252-258.

Collins, P. H. (1990). Black feminist thought in the matrix of domination. *Black feminist thought: Knowledge, consciousness, and the politics of empowerment, 138*(1990), 221–238.

Conchas, G. Q. (2006). *The color of success: Race and high-achieving urban youth*. Teachers College Press.

Conchas, G. Q., & Acevedo, N. (2020). *The Chicana/o/x Dream: Hope, Resistance and Educational Success*. Harvard Education Press.

Conchas, G. Q., Lee, J., Cambero, S., & Acevedo-Gil, N. (2019). The Chicana/o/x promise: Testimonios of educational empowerment through the enactment of la facultad among first-generation college students. *Journal for Leadership, Equity, and Research, 5*(1–2).

Delgado Bernal, D., Alemán Jr., E., & Garavito, A. (2009). Latina/o undergraduate students mentoring Latina/o elementary students: A borderlands analysis of shifting identities and first-year experiences. *Harvard Educational Review, 79*(4), 560–586.

Delgado Bernal, D., Burciaga, R., & Flores Carmona, J. (2012). Chicana/Latina Testimonios: Mapping the methodological, pedagogical, and political. *Equity & excellence in education, 45*(3), 363-372.

Donato, R., & Hanson, J. (2012). Legally white, socially "Mexican": The politics of de jure and de facto school segregation in the American Southwest. *Harvard Educational Review, 82*(2), 202-225.

Gonzalez, G. G. (1996). Chicano educational history: A legacy of inequality. *Humboldt Journal of Social Relations*, 43-56.

Gonzalez, G. G. (2013). *Chicano education in the era of segregation* (No. 7). University of North Texas Press.

Kao, G., & Thompson, J. S. (2003). Racial and ethnic stratification in educational achievement and attainment. *Annual Review of Sociology, 29*(1), 417–442.

Kao, G., & Tienda, M. (1998). Educational aspirations of minority youth. *American Journal of Education, 106*(3), 349–384.

Keating, A. (2005). Introduction shifting worlds, una entrada. In *EntreMundos/AmongWorlds: New Perspectives on Gloria E. Anzaldúa* (pp. 1-12). New York: Palgrave Macmillan US.

Library of Congress. (n.d.). *Research Guides: A Latinx Resource Guide: Civil Rights Cases and Events in the United States: 1968: East Los Angeles Walkouts*. https://guides.loc.gov/latinx-civil-rights/east-la-walkouts

López, G. (2015). *Hispanics of Mexican origin in the United States, 2013: Statistical profile*. Pew Research Center.

Ordoñez-Jasis, R., & Jasis, P. (2004). Rising with de colores: Tapping into the resources of la comunidad to assist under-performing Chicano-Latino students. *Journal of Latinos and Education, 3*(1), 53–64.

Pérez Huber, L. (2009). Disrupting apartheid of knowledge: *Testimonio* as methodology in Latina/o critical race research in education. *International Journal of Qualitative Studies in Education, 22*(6), 639–654.

Pérez Huber, L., & Cueva, B. M. (2012). Chicana/Latina *Testimonios* on effects and responses to microaggressions. *Equity & Excellence in Education, 45*(3), 392–410. https://doi.org/10.1080/10665684.2012.698193

Reyes, K. B., & Curry Rodríguez, J. E. (2012). Testimonio: Origins, terms, and resources. *Equity & Excellence in Education, 45*(3), 525-538.

Rios-Ellis, B., Rascón, M., Galvez, G., Inzunza-Franco, G., Bellamy, L., & Torres, A. (2015). Creating a model of Latino peer education: Weaving cultural capital into the fabric of academic services in an urban university setting. *Education and Urban Society, 47*(1), 33-55.

Rodríguez, R. C. (2014). *Our sacred maíz is our mother: Indigeneity and belonging in the Americas*. University of Arizona Press.

San Miguel, Jr., G., & Valencia, R. (1998). From the Treaty of Guadalupe Hidalgo to Hopwood: The educational plight and struggle of Mexican Americans in the Southwest. *Harvard Educational Review, 68*(3), 353–413.

Smithsonian Institution. (2020). *Ancient DNA continues to rewrite corn's 9,000-year society-shaping.* https://www.si.edu/newsdesk/releases/ancient-dna-continues-rewrite-corns-9000-year-society-shaping-history

Valencia, R. R., Menchaca, M., & Donato, R. (2002). Segregation, desegregation, and integration of Chicano students: Old and new realities. *Chicano school failure and success: Past, present, and future*, 70-113.

Yosso, T. J. (2005). Whose culture has capital? A critical race theory discussion of community cultural wealth. *Race Ethnicity and Education, 8*(1), 69–91.

CHAPTER 8

# Cosechando Éxito:
## Growing Academic Familias That Facilitate Student and Institutional Transformation

*Arlene Cano Matute, Alexis Meza, Elizabeth Claassen Thrush, and Louie F. Rodriguez*

> Forming a group of peers ... was very beneficial. It gave me a sense of community and support from a diverse group of students ... influential to my academic success was seeing other Chicana/o/x/Latina/o/x students graduating and succeeding.
>
> —Chicana/o/x/Latina/o/x participant

## Introduction

THE QUOTE ABOVE, along with the voices of other successful Chicana/o/x and Latina/o/x[1] students shared in this chapter, helps to define the concept of "Academic Familia"[2] utilized to tell a story of resilience, persistence, and transformation. Within higher education and in the Hispanic-Serving Institution (HSI) context, this chapter is a story of Chicana/o/xs and Latina/o/xs who are thriving and the institutional practices, processes, and commitments that facilitate their success. We argue that the success of Chicana/o/xs and Latina/o/xs in higher education is a harvest, or "cosecha," realized through a collection of institutional agents, culturally validating practices and structures, and intentionally created university pathways that foster Academic Familias for students.

### *Institutional History and Context*

At Highland University,[3] a group of Chicana/o/x students, staff, and faculty came together to form a close-knit community that functioned as a family in 1968 (Cano Matute, 2023). This community was purposeful, aligning with the local, statewide, and national movements for Chicana/o/x liberation at the time. The leaders of this community were activists, organizing beyond the boundaries of the ivory tower and traditional academic disciplines. They were committed to creating a pathway for higher education and used the university as a tool for change. Their mission was to create a more inclusive and equitable higher education system for Chicana/o/x students, as outlined in *El Plan de Santa Barbara: A Chicano Plan for Higher Education* (CCCHE, 1969).

The Chicana/o/x leaders at Highland University worked tirelessly for a Chicana/o/x and Latina/o/x-serving identity at Highland University "prior to the creation of the federal designation" (Doran & Medina, 2017, p. 45). Thus, Highland University is considered a grassroots HSI with a culture of "servingness," established as early as the 1960s by a small critical mass of Chicana/o/x leaders who created institutionalized structures of serving that continue to stand today. These leaders created the Mexican American Studies program, establishing the first courses on campus centering on Chicana/o/x and Latina/o/x identities. Through their continued engagement, the program transitioned into a robust Chicana/o/x Studies major where many staff, students, and faculty established a community that carved a co-curricular counterspace, the Chicana/o/x Cultural Center[4] in 1972, that provided academic, social, and culturally affirming campus events (Cano Matute, 2023). These initial structures fostered a shared ethos, and those involved, the colibrís, understood the significance of forming an Academic Familia. The colibrís, the institutional change agents, were individuals not related by blood but provided significant social and institutional support (Stanton-Salazar, 2011) to create a nurturing environment that felt like home. Together, they planted a semilla (seed), and throughout five decades, it has been nurtured, sustained, and continues to thrive.

***Present-Day Context and Introduction***

This semilla, based on the aforementioned history at Highland University, established an Academic Familia and community over the last several decades that led to a cosecha of student success—the focus of this chapter. Situated within this rich history, we focus on the voices and experiences of academically successful Chicana/o/x and Latina/o/x students, and we argue that HSIs have the potential to harvest belonging and servingness (Garcia et al., 2019). Our work suggests that Academic Familias help plant seeds of transformation that nurture student development before and after graduation whereby students become *nepantlera/o/xs* (Conchas & Acevedo, 2020) and contribute to institutional change.

First, we contextualize our chapter within the context of the relevant literature on academic homeplaces, validation theory, and the framework for "servingness" at HSIs. This knowledge provides a constructive approach to comprehend students' experiences throughout their university journey or camino. By utilizing this information, we can shift toward institutional transformation that enables students to thrive in their academic and nonacademic pursuits. We define la cosecha as twofold: a student's self-advocacy, where they achieve individual success, and it can also be community advocacy, where they plant future seeds, instilling reciprocity for a future harvest. Following the literature, we describe our methods and data analysis and explore implications for other institutions and the institutional change agents, or colibrís, who strive to serve Chicana/o/x/Latina/o/x students, not only for academic success, but to become change agents themselves or, within the theoretical framework of this book, *nepantlera/o/xs*.

## Literature Review and Conceptual Frameworks

To understand Chicana/o/x and Latina/o/x students' transition and success in university life, we build on the literature of belonging and familia in academia. While many university students of color will highlight numerous spaces that negatively impact their university experience, resulting in feeling like *atravesada/o/xs*, some students find positive spaces on campus that help them resist and heal from a negative campus racial climate (Comeaux et al., 2021; Garcia et al., 2019). Serrano (2022) introduced the concept of "academic homeplaces," inspired by the writings of bell hooks, describing communities to resist a negative campus racial climate. Homeplaces are spaces that provide more than service but also affirmation and healing of many of the wounds caused by racial domination (hooks, 1990, as cited in Serrano, 2022).

The presence of homeplaces has relevance not only for students of color generally but in the context of this book chapter, for Chicana/o/xs and Latina/o/xs specifically, and within an HSI context. For example, students who have faced racial oppression at their HSI find these homeplaces through interactions with faculty, participating in cultural organizations, engaging with cultural centers, and taking courses through Ethnic Studies departments, which all become homeplaces that are necessary for growth, development, and nourishment of their spirit (Serrano, 2022). Homeplaces become the sites where the struggle for identity, support, and justice are affirmed, cultivated, and supported, producing the conditions to build communities of *nepantlera/o/xs*.

Academically successful Chicana/o/x and Latina/o/x students seek and experience community in the multiple spaces they navigate—primarily spaces that cultivate feelings of family. This is supported by the literature where scholars emphasize the importance of "familia" (Segura-Herrera, 2006), familial capital (Yosso, 2005), and familismo (Calzada et al., 2012; Leidy et al., 2012; Piña-Watson et al., 2013) as key to the academic success of Latina/o/x students. Here we explore how and why familia, as one type of homeplace, cultivates the academic success of Chicana/o/x and Latina/o/x students.

### *Validating Practices*

Laura Rendón's (1994) seminal work on validation theory considers the implications of validating students on college campuses. Her focus group, which included 132 first-year students from four regionally diverse institutions, including 2-year and 4-year institutions, revealed that validation can transform underserved and underrepresented students into powerful learners. As a pedagogical practice, validation theory has been utilized as a tool to improve teaching and learning (Linares & Muñoz , 2011). Faculty can play a crucial role in creating validating environments within the classroom or what Rendón (2011) defines as the curricular space, the formal academic space within the institution.

Chicana/o/x and Latina/o/x students demonstrate remarkable resilience when they receive validation. Peers, staff, and faculty validation significantly influence Chicana/o/x and Latina/o/x students' navigation of the campus climate and sense of belonging. Chicana/o/x and Latina/o/x students experience a sense of capability and competence, especially when their identity and culture are acknowledged (Hurtado & Carter, 1997; Hurtado & Ponjuan, 2005; Rendón, 1994; Yosso, 2005; Yosso et al., 2009). For example, Quiñonez and Olivas (2020) surveyed participants in 10 first-year literacy courses led by Academic Librarians at an HSI in Southern California. A total of 233 students were surveyed throughout three semesters, and most students identified as Latina/o/x. Of the 10 courses, 6 were taught using the traditional curriculum and 4 were taught using a culturally validating curriculum that included the work of Latina/o/x scholars. Quiñonez and Olivas (2020) found that all participants gained practical skills; however, the students enrolled in the culturally validating course expressed a stronger sense of connection and established a sense of familia. These findings indicate that agents such as faculty or staff can foster meaningful connections that allow Chicana/o/x and Latina/o/x students to be seen and valued.

### *Servingness Counters Deservingness*

The act of questioning the legitimacy of a student's place in higher education is used as a tool to reinforce coloniality, perpetuating dominance. This practice is often carried out in higher education by those who hold privileged positions within academia and can have significant implications for students from marginalized communities. According to Patel (2015, p. 12), "deservingness" reinforces the exclusion of marginalized communities, as it calls into question their right to be present or whether they deserve this right. Conchas and Acevedo (2020) use deservingness to understand the conditions of Chicana/o/x students along the educational pipeline. Their findings illustrate that Chicana/o/x students are historically and presently subjected to illegitimacy and thus have a perception that they do not deserve to be in higher education, which leads to their exclusion, or push out, from the education system (Conchas

& Acevedo, 2020). In contrast, our study argues that "servingness" counters deservingness within a Hispanic-Serving Institutional context because it values Chicana/o/x and Latina/o/x students as scholars who deserve a quality education. The concept of "servingness" refers to an institution's capacity to foster a culture that prioritizes the enrollment, development, validation, and graduation of Chicana/o/x and Latina/o/x students (Cano Matute, 2023; Garcia et al. 2019; Malcom-Piqueux & Bensimon, 2015).

To achieve success, it is essential to acknowledge and embrace the cultural strengths of Chicana/o/x and Latina/o/x students. According to Yosso (2005), students of color possess a wealth of strengths derived from their family and community, which she refers to as community cultural wealth. Yosso (2005) views community cultural wealth as a concept that counters the deficit mindset by recognizing the powerful assets of communities of color that are rooted in social justice. These forms of capital build on the experiences and knowledge of Chicana/o/x and Latina/o/x students. Similarly, Delgado Bernal (2001) finds strength in the home of Chicana/o/x and Latina/o/x students, recognizing the family's role in the student's higher education journey. Delgado Bernal (2001) argues pedagogies of the home extend Chicana feminist pedagogies that elevate Chicana ways of knowing that identify the home as a source of knowledge for students. For Chicanas, the familia, whether in the household or the community, plays an important role in providing valuable lessons that aid students in navigating their academic journeys. Furthermore, a student's home space can also serve as a place to acquire knowledge and develop skills.

The literature on homeplaces, validation, and asset-driven perspectives in education, such as community cultural wealth and servingness, are not only important to acknowledge because of their theoretical significance for Chicana/o/x and Latina/o/x students, but these perspectives matter within the institutional context.

### *Framework of Atravesada/o/xs Nepantleando*

The Framework of *Atravesada/o/xs Nepantleando* (FAN) provides a comprehensive perspective to understand complex social and cultural issues, especially within marginalized communities. FAN offers a tool for scholars and activists who aim to dismantle oppressive systems and promote social justice.

FAN is grounded in the narratives of students. The authors build upon Anzaldúa's (1987) concept of borderlands, which refers to the spaces where different cultures meet and clash, to examine how U.S. educational structures create such borderlands. Conchas and Acevedo (2020) use the idea of borderlands to investigate the experiences of Chicana/o/x students in higher education institutions, which have been shaped by their colonial foundation and a history of exclusion, what they identify as education borderlands. They find that these structures often position Chicana/o/x students as transgressors within the educational system. However, Chicana/o/x students navigate the education borderlands as *atravesada/o/xs*, resist by engaging their facultad, and maintain hope in dehumanizing and marginalizing spaces to become *nepantlera/o/xs*.

Embracing *la facultad* as a potent source of knowledge can be effectively leveraged with tools like community cultural wealth to develop growth and transformation. This empowers Chicana/o/x students to overcome challenges and thrive academically. By cultivating a sixth sense of awareness and embracing an asset-based lens, Chicana/o/x students can unlock their full potential within the education borderlands. With this approach, students recognize their wealth of knowledge and skills, paving the way for success along their educational journey. The authors' analysis explains the systemic issues that perpetuate inequality and marginalization in education, particularly for students from historically underrepresented and marginalized communities.

## Methods: Buscando La Cosecha

### *Institutional Context*

The current study explores servingness at a Hispanic-Serving Research Institution (HSRI), defined as HSIs classified as R1 or doctoral-granting institutions with high research activity (Marin & Pereschica, 2017). The institution has been recognized with the "Seal of *Excelencia*" for its efforts to effectively serve Chicana/o/x and Latina/o/x students, as marked by a 74.8% Chicana/o/x and Latina/o/x 6-year graduation rate and numerous successful student support programs. While Highland University (pseudonym) became an HSI over 15 years ago, it now serves nearly 40% Chicana/o/x and Latina/o/x students and recognizes that there is still work to do to better support undergraduate and graduate students at this HSRI.

### *Study Design*

This qualitative study explores the process of students becoming *nepantler-a/o/xs* through key entradas into the university and the *camino* that cultivates *Academic Familias*. The data analyzed were part of a larger survey designed to gather both quantitative and qualitative data on Chicana/o/x and Latina/o/x student experiences at a research institution from students at the point of graduation. This design allows for the analysis of the experiences of students who have achieved academic success to better understand the experiences that shaped their success. The study has completed three waves of data collection, including a pilot study in 2021 and two additional rounds of data collection in 2022 and 2023. The rationale and instrument for the pilot study were initially developed based largely on the Seal of *Excelencia* framework, particularly the emphasis on student retention and institutional culture. The HSI committee that developed the study prioritized student voices to better understand the student experience. Subsequent iterations have included questions based on the multidimensional framework for servingness, with particular attention to questions about belonging, research, and leadership.

### *Participants*

The survey instrument was sent in May 2021 to the 327 graduating seniors who indicated they wished to participate in the cultural graduation ceremony for Chicana/o/x and Latina/o/x students. This population was selected because these students all identify as Chicana/o/x and Latina/o/x and have all achieved a measure of academic success since they were graduating from a four-year institution. The survey was conducted in English and yielded 42 responses. The 2022 survey was sent to 437 students (all graduating Chicana/o/x and Latina/o/x students) and received 51 responses. The 2023 survey was sent to 434 students (again, all graduating Chicana/o/x and Latina/o/x students) and received 48 responses.

We analyzed responses from 141 graduating Chicana/o/x and Latina/o/x students between the three waves. Among the respondents, 43% identified as transfer students and 88% as first-generation college graduates.

### *Analytical Frameworks*

In analyzing the first round of responses, our research team (the authors of this chapter) became particularly interested in the qualitative responses from students, describing the on-campus experiences that led to their academic success. This led to a deeper qualitative analysis using the Multidimensional Conceptual Framework for Understanding Servingness (Garcia et al., 2019). We coded the participants' responses based on validating experiences, racialized experiences, and nonacademic outcomes.

Since many of the responses did not fit neatly into the categories of validating experiences in the framework, the group then approached the data for another round of analysis using a more emic approach to allow new categories to emerge from their descriptions (Creswell, 2007). The researchers identified themes of university entrance points, or entradas, to illuminate how validation informed their experiences (see Figure 8.1).

**Figure 8.1** *Conceptual model for "entradas" within the multidimensional framework for understanding "servingness" in Hispanic Serving Institutions*

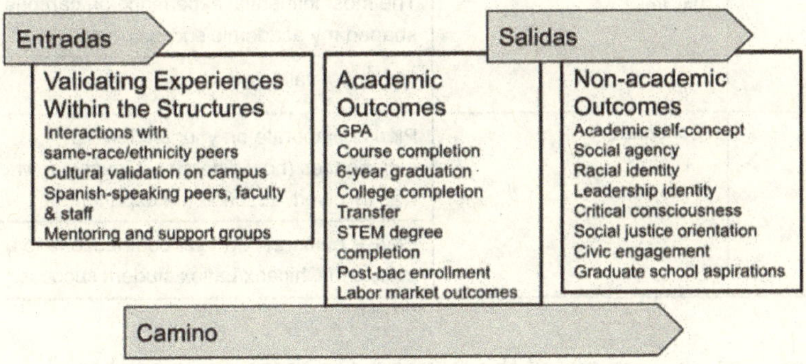


*Note.* Adapted from the multidimensional conceptual framework for servingness at HSIs (Garcia et al., 2019). Used with permission.

We approached the data with three specific tools: coding the qualitative responses, creating a heat map, and using art as a mechanism to visualize the emerging themes.

*Coding Qualitative Responses.*

As a result of our analysis from the first two waves of data, the 2023 survey was updated to include questions more specifically about how students define their Academic Familia. The current analysis for this study focuses on the qualitative responses to the following questions (a subset of the larger survey) across the 2021, 2022, and 2023 data waves. The table (Table 8.1) organizes these questions according to the emerging framework of entradas, caminos, and salidas:

**Table 8.1** *Connections between the "entradas" model, the "cosecha," and the survey question analysis*

| Model Categories | Related words and images to the "cosecha" | Survey questions highlighted for this study |
|---|---|---|
| Entradas | Semillas | What was the first experience you had of feeling at home at Highland University? |
| Camino | Colibrís<br>Flores | Who is your academic familia (a community of people on or off campus who had an impact on your academic success)? |
| | Jardín | The most influential experience on campus that shaped my academic success was ... |
| | | I felt most validated when ... |
| Salidas | Cosechas | Please elaborate on your leadership experiences (how did you get involved, who was involved, describe the experience). |
| | | Please elaborate on your contributions to a culture of Chicanx/Latinx student success. |

The research team coded the responses to these questions based on both the servingness framework as well as the emerging framework of entradas (entry points to validating experiences —specific times students identified as key to establishing a sense of belonging and beginning to navigate academia), caminos, and salidas. Within the caminos, we further coded the responses based on change agents, culturally validating practices, and validating structures. Within the salidas, the analysis included both self-advocacy and community advocacy.

*Mapping the Camino (Heat Map).*

As part of the survey, we asked two questions that included a campus map. The questions read:

- Please click on the top three physical spaces on campus in the map below that were the most significant to your academic success. For example, students may highlight the place where they took a formative class, the office of an advisor, an important study space, etc.
- Please click on the top three physical spaces on campus in the map below that were the most significant to your sense of belonging. For example, students may highlight the places where they connected with friends, participated in clubs, etc.

These responses in the aggregate show a color scale of "heat" where on-campus students feel the greatest sense of academic support (Figure 8.4) and belonging (Figure 8.5).

*Artivism Approach.*

In Anzaldúa's (1990) *Haciendo Caras, un entrada,* she reminds us that the hand is both a symbol and vehicle of communication. When tongue and hand work together, they unite art and politics, attacking the dominant ideology (Anzaldúa, 1990). In this chapter, we utilize art as a research mechanism to capture and disseminate the story and *camino* of Chicana/o/x Latina/o/x students within Hispanic Serving Institutions. The central image (Figure 8.6) here is one example. Created by Alexis Meza, artist, and co-author of the chapter, he captures his *camino* including his *familia,* Academic Familia, and the institutional agents that helped create a meaningful pathway to his success. By utilizing art as a form of research, we can visually capture the nuances, culture, and story of Chicana/o/x and Latina/o/x students' journeys in a way that is accessible, comprehensible, and intentional. Artivism allows us to de-academize theory and connect the community to the academy. By sending our voices, visuals, and visions outward, we alter the walls and make them a framework for new windows of possibilities (Anzaldúa, 1990). Our findings below describe how the qualitative data, heat map data, and artivism help us better understand how Chicana/o/x and Latina/o/x students experience Academic Familias and, for some, become *nepantlera/o/xs*

## Findings: Encontrando La Cosecha

The qualitative analysis of student responses through coding, mapping, and art led us to a deeper understanding of the *entradas* that helped students find an initial sense of home and belonging. These validating experiences along the *camino* guided students to their *salidas,* where some emerged as *nepantlera/o/xs.*

### *Entradas: Finding Home*

Chicana/o/x and Latina/o/x students in our study were asked about their first encounter with "feeling at home." The strongest factor (49% of the students in our sample) that facilitated feelings of home were peers and spaces that promoted peer engagement, such as the dorms or orientation, followed by the Chicana/o/x Cultural Center[5] (CCC) and other ethnic and gender programs on campus. A student's academic home department also facilitated feelings of home. Similarly, students also spoke about the significance of their advisors and the important role that the library played for them, especially during the pandemic.

About one-third of the respondents identified the Chicana/o/x Cultural Center, related student organizations such as programming and support for undocumented students, or academic areas such as the "Chicano department" as the first places that made participants feel at home. Specifically, one student shared:

> I started feeling at home at Highland University when I arrived at the Chicano Cultural Center. The student staff were very polite and welcoming. The students in the recreational area where inviting and courteous. Soon, I became a reoccurring student coming in and out of the center as well as offering volunteer services in support of their events that they coordinate.

The people in the Chicana/o/x Cultural Center—student workers, peers, and staff members—were welcoming, which provided a feeling of home for new students to campus or students who encountered the space for the first time. Some participants noticed the food and items available to students and the pride others exuded throughout the CCC space.

Participants also referenced other campus structures that helped cultivate feelings of home. These included peer connections and the development of friendships through the dorms and participants' academic engagement with learning communities, classes, and professors. One student shared: "Creating friendships in the dorms and becoming familiar with my community" were instrumental in cultivating feelings of home. Another student shared the important role of learning communities:

> The first experience of where I felt at home was when I got to meet my learning community. When I first came to Highland University, I felt all alone and a little scared of the large campus. Once I got to meet them and learn about them, I didn't feel so lonely anymore.

While Highland University still has a long way to go to hire and retain more faculty of color and more Chicana/o/x and Latina/o/x faculty specifically, it does have the highest number of Chicana/o/x and Latina/o/x faculty in the entire system of universities. A student recognized how the presence of Chicana/o/x and Latina/o/x helped create that feeling of home for them: "Meeting professor such as Prof. X and Prof. Y who made me realize I was not so alone."

### *Caminos: People, Practices, and Structures on the journey*

After a student establishes the foundation of an Academic Familia through the various university entradas, we have observed that a student's camino, or pathway, is also vital to their experience. Our findings support the significance of validation (Rendón, 1994) and help to further define the ways this validation occurs along the academic camino (journey) for students, specifically through people, practices, and structures.

### *People: Los Colibrís*

**Figure 8.2** *Los colibrís, symbolizing the institutional change agents.*

Through the qualitative responses, illuminated in the visual (Figure 8.2) included in this chapter, the colibrí are the people, or institutional agents, who cultivate the success of Chicana/o/x and Latina/o/x students on campus. These change agents were largely from within the institution, though there are poignant examples of family or community members serving as important academic mentors. The effect of peers and peer mentors also came through strongly in the responses.

When specifically asked about their Academic Familia—defined as the community of people on or off campus who had an impact on their academic success—nearly all respondents mentioned their peers or fellow students first. Several participants included their biological family, a few mentioned faculty, and there were some examples of mentors or supporters from work (on and off campus) or student organizations.

When discussing the most influential experiences shaping their academic success, students included a wider array of people contributing to these experiences, including advisors, specific student organizations, and staff in ethnic and gender program offices. For example, one student described a pivotal moment in academic success: "I told my advisor that I was giving up, but he sent me an email that stated I was enough and that there were other options."

In some examples of significant academic experiences, change agents played a background facilitating role, such as staff in the CCC providing "resources, advocacy, programming, etc. for students to succeed." At other points, they may start a chain reaction of introducing students to other people and networks that expand their social capital. For example, one student referred to a conference trip organized by CCC staff:

> There, I networked with medical students and staff, found essential resources for studying for the MCAT, learned about their Latino medical program they offer to incoming medical students, and understood the medical school application process.

The emphasis in the responses shifted when students were specifically asked about validating experiences. Here, students described faculty as the key people providing validating experiences. One student spoke about a faculty member's recognition of the moment and its importance to them:

> Professors knew that students were struggling because of world events, were struggling with lack of information on assignments, and were struggling with the amount of time given to complete assignments. ... [it] made it feel as if it wasn't just me.

Another student pointed to the importance of facultyspecifically acknowledging the work and challenges of Latina/o/x students:

> When professors acknowledged the lack of diversity in their classes, it helped validate my own experience. They spoke about how important it is to have Chicanx/Latinx and people of color represented in STEM fields and reached out to the class to know how to help encourage more

> diversity in their classes. They were also sure to reassure me that my work was just as valuable as my non-poc[6] classmates and encouraged us to reach out to them for more support and advice.

The data above provide an overview of how the people, or *colibrí*, were instrumental in shaping the *camino*, or pathway, for Chicana/o/x and Latina/o/x students at Highland University. The following section focuses on the practices that helped cultivate Academic *Familias* for students in this study.

## *Practices: Las Flores*

**Figure 8.3**

*Las flores, the flowers symbolize the programs and services offered to students*

In their responses to the three questions about Academic *Familia*, academic success experiences, and validating experiences, students pointed to several practices that specifically supported their success. These practices—including actions, resources, programs, and opportunities—are represented artistically by the flores, which are nurtured and specifically spread through the actions of the change agents (colibrí).

The strongest contributor to one's Academic *Familia* was the role that student organizations played. In fact, 23 of the 39 students, or 59% of respondents, referenced a student organization associated with various ethnic and gender programs or academically related organizations such as the learning community structure in their respective major, an academic organization related to engineering or pre-med students, or the humanities, arts, and social sciences. For example, one student spoke about their major-associated peers, in addition to peers outside of their major:

> On campus, my biochemistry peers helped with all of my classes. A lot of the time, subject material was dense or hard to understand, and when our brains worked together, it made comprehension easier. Off campus, I had friends from [social sciences, humanities, and arts] and school of business that I've known since freshman year to hang out with and talk about life.

Students not only described the impact of student organizations generally but also the impact of Latina/o/x student organizations, specifically. Nearly half of the student respondents to the question about Academic Familia included some reference to a Latina/o/x-specific campus organization or student organization that helped to shape their sense of family.

In the responses to all three questions, they describe studying together, mentoring and being mentored, participating in and planning events together, and providing a sense of being "heard" and "seen." This occurred inside and outside the classroom. One student summarized the importance of this community within a class, where "a majority of us could connect because we were children of immigrants and therefore could understand certain topics in the course better together."

Participants also regularly described the importance of emotional support. This support is often used specifically during difficult situations. For example, one student describes their Academic Familia as "helping each other through tough times," while another participant said they "encouraged me when things were tough," and another recalled that they "cried and built community."

Participants also described the importance of research, service, and leadership opportunities that became important practices for their success and in their journey of becoming *nepantlera/o/xs*. For example, one student described beginning with mentored research in the community and eventually becoming a manager. This student describes the *promotoras* as "Academic Familia" through this process:

> *Unidas por salud*, a group of community health educators (*promotoras*) that I have worked with within research with my mentor but also through being clinic manager at the Free Clinic.

Since faculty were a key source of validating experiences, discussing some of the practices they employed to provide this validation is important. In the section above, we reference the importance of faculty acknowledging students' challenges and assets within the classroom. Students also referred to the validation of receiving praise from faculty members or experiencing faculty devoting time to out-of-class communication. One representative quote came from a student who felt most validated when "faculty engaged in one-on-one conversations or took a genuine interest in their students." A student who received support for research and graduate school gave a specific example of the help received:

> He took the time to meet with me and was patient as I asked his thoughts about my research interests. As I started feeling discouraged and unsure about the status of my grad school applications, Dr. Hernandez reassured me of my potential and validated my research interests.

### *Structures*

The institutional structures that validate the Chicana/o/x and Latina/o/x student experiences are represented artistically by the overall jardín[7] (garden), or the ecosystem, in which the colibrí and flores can flourish. The artistic representation of the corazón (heart) flows from the heat map analysis (Figures 8.4 & 8.5), which provides a visual of students' sense of belonging in the corazón of campus. These heat maps became an important data piece here to complement the student responses because we can visually see where the physical and programmatic structures are concentrated on the campus and where Academic Familias were developed and cultivated, per the student responses.

In response to the question about the physical spaces most important to their academic success, there was a strong concentration around the CCC, with significant heat around the two campus libraries. Some students also noted the importance of the student recreation centers and the residence halls for their academic success.

**Figure 8.4**
*Heat map of physical spaces on campus most significant to academic success.*

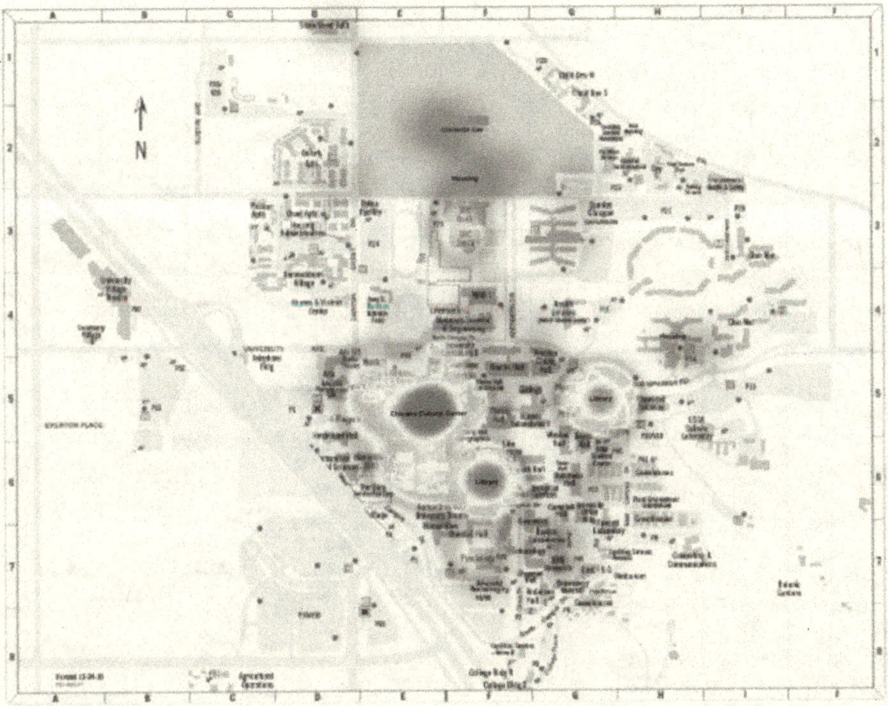


In the responses to the question about physical spaces most important to their sense of belonging, the heat is more strongly centered around the CCC, forming a clearer visual of the corazón. Students also had concentrated responses around the student recreation centers, which are sites for exercising and community-building, and the location of the Chicana/o/x/Latina/o/x graduation ceremony. The libraries and residence halls were also sites selected by some students as providing a sense of belonging.

**Figure 8.5**
*Heat map of physical spaces on campus most significant to a sense of belonging.*

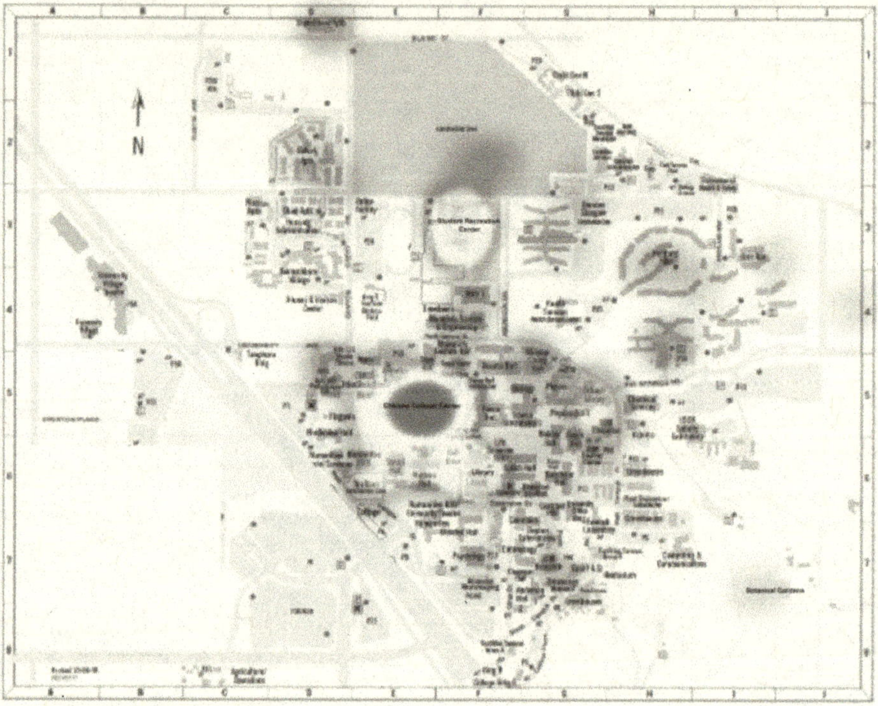


These visual heat maps corroborate the students' emphasis in their responses on the importance of the Chicana/o/x Cultural Center and the various student organizations it supports, as well as their references to institutional structures such as learning communities, transfer support pipelines, academic resources, graduation ceremonies, and the library.

### *Salidas: La Cosecha to Nepantlera/o/xs*

*Salidas* are the final point in our analytical framework that captures the outcomes, aspirations, or exit points from the university, particularly in our analysis of Chicana/o/x and Latina/o/x students in our study. We are evolving our framing of *salidas as la cosecha.* While "salida" could sound like a disconnection from community, "*cosecha*" connotes an ongoing fruitfulness that characterizes the lives of these *nepanlera/o/x* students and graduates.

We categorized responses as two types of *cosechas*: self-advocacy (students achieving individual success) and community advocacy (planting future leadership seeds and service with and for the community). Many students described their experiences of academic success as attaining high grades, preparing for graduate school, experience with research, gaining independence, weathering challenging experiences, participating in student organizations, and ultimately graduating. These are important *cosechas*.

Some of these same students, plus an additional group of students, described experiences of academic success that demonstrated an additional layer of leadership and contribution to their communities: planting future seeds. We categorized these as more "nepantlera/o/x" experiences, including participating in committees to plan for events, serving as a mentor or tutor, or doing community research or service. For example, one student noted that their most influential experience on campus shaping their academic success was "my involvement with projects and events that directly and directly attributed success, access, and advocacy for social justice and equity for Chicano/Latinos and BIPOC/QTPOC populations."

Peer mentoring was one of the primary ways that student respondents defined their leadership and contributions. There is a strong culture of peer mentoring at Highland University. In this study, we found that more than one-third of the students in our sample served as a peer mentor. Students describe their involvement and leadership as being active and mutual. For example, one student described the mutual benefits of peer mentoring in this way: "as a community, my mentor and mentees gave each of us the opportunity to grow and learn from each other."

This mutual sharing and encouragement ties back into the similarities with family—both academic and biological. Whether it is participating in a family event, cultural celebration, or helping one's family around the house, each member is a vital member and participates in the process. We found that academically successful Chicana/o/x and Latina/o/x students contribute to their Academic Familia through mentoring and leadership, among other experiences. We also see students' contributions to the familia as a strong reflection of their agency. One student described this link from Academic Familia back to biological familia when they helped their mother transfer and finish her education, in response to the question about their contributions to a culture of Chicana/o/x and Latina/o/x success:

> I guess attending the Raza grad and being Chicana myself, attending Highland University in general. Also, pushing my mom to continue her education in school and helping her transfer ... and guiding her along the way as well.

We believe that one of the ultimate goals of cultivating Academic *Familias* within the university and HSI context is to specifically produce graduates who have the consciousness, clarity, and will to advocate not only for themselves as individuals but for their communities as well. We are framing these students as *nepantlera/o/xs* and will expand upon this in the discussion section.

**Figure 8.6** *Nepantleando la Universidad*

## Discussion: *Cosechando Nepantlera/o/x*

This chapter has demonstrated, directly from the voices and experiences of academically successful Chicana/o/x and Latina/o/x students, that cultivating Academic Familias is vital to facilitating student success and articulating *how* and *why* such outcomes are created in a thriving HSI context. The literature on home places, validation and belonging, and community cultural wealth provide a language that both substantiates and legitimizes the experiences that Chicana/o/x and Latina/o/x realize within the university and HSI context specifically.

We articulated in this chapter that university entradas, caminos, and salidas are important ways to understand the Chicana/o/x and Latina/o/x student experience. As we developed our analysis for this chapter, we found that university entradas like the CCC, peer connections, learning community structures through students' academic departments, and professors were all vital to both welcoming and affirming students in the new university context, but for Chicana/o/x and Latina/o/x students specifically, creating home places that fostered validation and belonging, and recognize the community cultural wealth that Chicana/o/x and Latina/o/x students bring to the university and HSI context (hooks, 1990; Rendón, 1994; Yosso, 2005).

When examining the importance of the university camino, we elevated the concept of the colibrí, or institutional agents, and their role in helping establish Academic Familias for Chicana/o/x and Latina/o/x students at Highland University. Students in our study sometimes referenced their biological families as part of their Academic Familias but spoke at length about the role that cultural organizations and academic departments played in shaping students' caminos in our study. Here, the colibrí are the institutional agents who act in ways that shape the experiences of Chicana/o/x and Latina/o/x students and model how to promote self- and community advocacy.

In many ways, the colibrí are the people who help build and shape the power of home places (hooks, 1990). The colibrí are the people who realize Rendón's notion of validation and foster a sense of belonging for students within the institutional context. Finally, the colibrí are the people who enact the practices (flores) within the university structures that serve students. That is, programs, offices, or organizations alone do not foster Academic Familias;

rather, the colibrí are the facilitators of validation, belonging, and change that is required to serve Chicana/o/x and Latina/o/x students within the university and HSI context specifically.

Finally, our exploration of the salidas or cosecha is the realization that academic success is one of many important intentions within a thriving HSI context. Students in our study have demonstrated that becoming a self- and community advocate is an important outcome when Academic Familias are intentionally cultivated for Chicana/o/x and Latina/o/x students. These observations suggest that home places (hooks, 1990) become sites that not only foster validation and belonging (Garcia, 2019; Rendón, 1994) but help Chicana/o/x and Latina/o/x develop their critical consciousness (Yosso, 2005).

The effect of cultivating Academic Familias was illuminated visually in two ways. Chicana/o/x and Latina/o/x students in our study identified on the campus maps where their academic success and sense of belonging were most pronounced. On both questions, the CCC was the strongest place, or homeplace (hooks, 1990), followed by the two university libraries and the athletic facilities, which is likely a place that fosters peer engagement.

The second place where the ultimate visualization of the power of Academic Familias emerged was through our artivism approach (Anzaldúa, 1990), which is beautifully captured artwork by chapter co-author Alexis Meza. In fact, the artwork helps articulate the entrada-camino-salida framework, highlights the power of the colibrí and flores, and the cosecha that is the ultimate result of Academic *Familias*. Here, we would like to elevate a new way of understanding the purpose of Academic *Familias*—the emergence of *nepantlera/o/xs.*

*Nepantleanda/o/x*, as a verb, is the in-between place of the institution where a commitment rooted in love for the *familia* and *comunidad* exists. Chicana/o/x and Latina/o/x students' *facultad* has allowed them to see their degrees are a collective *cosecha,* shared with their *familia* and *comunidad.* Some students strive beyond graduation and transition to *Nepantla,* where they become a *colibrí* enacting reciprocity that nurtures the next *cosecha.* For many first-generation Chicana/o/x students, the path toward degree completion is not linear nor clearly defined. However, Highland University has historically created the conditions and structures necessary for a culture of Academic Familia, support, and empowerment to flourish (Cano Matute, 2023). Along their university camino, we continuously see the presence of the colibrí: faculty, peer-mentors (both formal and informal), student affairs staff members, advisors, and familia (both chosen and biological) that guide them throughout their *camino universitario* (university journey). These *colibrís* (people) are also action-oriented, providing resources, leadership development, graduate school preparation, and mentorship, represented in the illustration as *las flores*.

As these *nepantlera/o/xs* navigate the education borderlands, utilizing their facultad, they are guided by *los colibrí* (people), nourished by *las flores* (practices), and thrive in a *jardín* (institutional structures or environment) of validation, servingness, and Academic Familia. Upon their salida, they decide how they want to give back, continuing this collective cosecha, harvesting new *flores*[8] that will guide the next generation of Chicana/o/x and Latina/o/x students that enter this thriving HSI. *Nepantleando la Universidad*[9] (Figure 8.6) is the image included in this chapter that was originally designed in full color but had to be redacted in black and white for publishing purposes.

## Conclusions: Harvesting New Flores

As we think about the implications of our work for other universities, HSIs, and emerging HSIs, it is important to suggest what this means for other colibrí who are interested in cultivating Academic Familias on their respective campuses. Listening to student voices on each campus can help to illuminate where the people (*colibrí*), practices (*flores*), and structures (*jardín*) may exist currently or in the future. Utilizing multiple tools, including traditional qualitative data collection, along with mapping and art, helps campuses envision the next steps for nurturing *nepantleando en la universidad*.

As we strive to achieve this, we are reminded of the words of one of our study participants. Reflecting on their contributions and connecting the themes of the generations of Academic *Familias*, the student reflected: "It takes a village to raise a child, and soon enough, those children will be the next generation to show what success is like as a Latino. Redefining Latino success is the Highland University way."

In many ways, the student quote above captures the historical and intergenerational implications of our study's findings. Highland University has been fostering Academic Familias for over 50 years, and programs like the CCC and academic structures like the university libraries, Chicana/o/x Studies, and departmental learning communities are following suit by realizing the importance of home places, validation, belonging, servingness, and the cultivation of critical consciousness.

Collectively, our qualitative data, the heat maps, and the artwork included in this chapter point us to the power of the university's *corazón*[10]—a collection of university places, practices, and people that intentionally work to cultivate Academic Familias. This corazón, when fully realized, produces the cosecha. Together, they are nepanteleando la universidad, transforming the institution from the seed to the harvest.

University colibrí, leaders, policymakers, and staff can ask themselves the following questions: How are Academic Familias nurtured in the various campus spaces such as academic departments? Where is the corazón for Chicana/o/x and Latina/o/x students on your campus? Where and in what ways are *nepantlera/o/xs* nurtured at your university? While the relevance of such questions will be based on the unique institutional context of the reader, they are intended to be both practical and aspirational.

## Endnotes

1 We honor the students and alumni in the particular context of this institution, which has a proud heritage of Chicano scholarship in our region and scholarship from those with ties to Latin America. The use of "a/o/x" acknowledges the importance of intersectionality in regards to gender identity while also advocating for greater diversity and inclusiveness. In this chapter, we also build on scholars' ideas and use their terminology when citing them directly.

2 We use Spanish to acknowledge the language used by Chicana/o/x/Latina/o/x scholars in our region and utilize the culturally rooted and affirming terms "entrada," "camino," and "salida" to expand their use within the HSI context. We intend to connect with Chicana/o/x/Latina/o/x scholars and their families by utilizing language and familiar terms. We recognize that not all individuals within the Chicana/o/x/Latina/o/x diaspora speak Spanish and that the relationship with the language can be complicated. We have decided to utilize it as a critical touchpoint in the journey of these scholars. In doing so, we hope to make our work accessible and normalize the use of Spanish by not italicizing it. This way, language can become a tool for connection and inclusivity for the audiences we work alongside.

[3] Pseudonym
[4] Pseudonym
[5] Pseudonym
[6] People of Color, abbreviated by participant.
[7] The translation of jardín, is garden; in this chapter we utilize jardín to define the institutional structures or environment.
[8] Italicized for emphasis.
[9] Italicized for emphasis.
[10] Italicized for emphasis.

## Reference

Anzaldúa, G. (1987). *Borderlands/la frontera: The new mestiza*. Aunt Lute Books.

Anzaldúa, G. (1990). *Making face, making soul / Hacienda caras: Creative and critical perspectives by women of color*. Aunt Lute Books.

Calzada, E., Tamis-LeMonda, C., & Yoshikawa, H. (2012). Familismo in Mexican and Dominican families from low-income, urban communities. *Journal of Family Issues*, *34*(12), 1696–1724. https://doi.org/10.1177/0192513X12460218

Cano Matute, A. (2023). *Lo que nace del corazón, siempre crece: The origins of serving at a Hispanic Serving Research Institution the University of California, Riverside* (Publication No. 30639338) [Doctoral dissertation, University of California, Riverside]. ProQuest Dissertations & Theses Global.

CCCHE (Chicano Coordinating Council on Higher Education). (1969). *El Plan de Santa Barbara*. La Causa Publications.

Comeaux, E., Mireles, D., & Acha, A. (2021). Dis/abled student campusmaking: Sites of new possibility. *Education Sciences*, *11*(11), 745.

Conchas, G. Q., & Acevedo, N. (2020). *The Chicana/o/x Dream: Hope, resistance, and educational success*. Harvard Education Press.

Creswell, J. W. (2007). *Qualitative inquiry and research design: Choosing among five approaches* (2nd ed.). Sage Publications, Inc.

Delgado Bernal, D. (2001). Learning and living pedagogies of the home: The mestiza consciousness of Chicana students. *International Journal of Qualitative Studies in Education*, *14*, 623–639. 10.1080/09518390110059838.

Doran, E., & Medina, Ø. (2017). The intentional and the grassroots Hispanic-Serving Institutions: A critical history of two universities. *Association of Mexican American Educators Journal*, *11*(3), 29–49. https://doi.org/10.24974/amae.11.3.360

Garcia, G. A. (2019). *Defining "servingness" at Hispanic-serving institutions (HSIs): Practical implications for HSI leaders*. American Council on Education.

Garcia, G. A., Núñez, A.-M., & Sansone, V. A. (2019). Toward a multidimensional conceptual framework for understanding "servingness" in Hispanic-serving institutions: A synthesis of the research. *Review of Educational Research, 89*(5).

hooks, b. (1990). *Yearning: Race, gender, and cultural politics*. South End Press.

Hurtado, S., & Carter, D. (1997). Effects of college transition and perceptions of the campus racial climate on Latino college students' sense of belonging. *Sociology of Education, 70*(4), 324–345. https://doi.org/10.2307/2673270

Hurtado, S., & Ponjuan, L. (2005). Latino educational outcomes and the campus climate. *Journal of Hispanic Higher Education, 4*, 235–251.

Leidy, M., Guerra, N., & Toro, R. (2012). Positive parenting, family cohesion, and child social competence among immigrant Latino families. *Journal of Latina/o Psychology, 1*(S), 3–13. https://doi.org/10.1037/a0019407

Linares, L. R., & Muñoz, S. M. (2011). Revisiting validation theory: Theoretical foundations, applications, and extensions. *Enrollment Management Journal, 2*(1), 12-33.

Malcom-Piqueux, L. E., & Bensimon, E. (2015). Design principles for equity and excellence at Hispanic-serving institutions. *Perspectivas: Issues in Higher Education Policy and Practice.*

Marin, P., & Pereschica, P. (2017). Becoming an Hispanic-serving research institution: Involving graduate students in organizational change. *AMAE Journal, 11*(3).

Patel, L. (2015). Deservingness: Challenging coloniality in education and migration scholarship. *AMAE Journal, 9*(3).

Piña-Watson, B., Ojeda, L., Castellon, N. E., & Dornheker, M. (2013). Familismo, ethnic identity, and bicultural stress as predictors of Mexican American adolescents' positive psychological functioning. *Journal of Latina/o Psychology, 1*(4), 204–217. https://doi.org/10.1037/lat0000006

Quiñonez, T., & Olivas, A. (2020). Validation theory and culturally relevant curriculum in the information literacy classroom. *Urban Library Journal, 26*(1). https://academicworks.cuny.edu/ulj/vol26/iss1/2

Rendón, L. (1994). Validating culturally diverse students: Toward a new model of learning and student development. *Innovative Higher Education, 19*(1), 33–51.

Segura-Herrera, T. (2006). Querer es poder: Maintaining and creating familia as a doctoral student. In J. Castellanos, A. M. Gloria, & M. Kamimura (Eds.), *The Latina/o pathway to the PhD.: abriendo caminos* (pp. 221-232). Stylus. 10.4324/9781003447894-17.

Serrano, U. (2022). 'Finding home': Campus racial microclimates and academic homeplaces at a Hispanic-Serving Institution. *Race, Ethnicity and Education, 25*(6), 815–834. https://doi.org/10.1080/13613324.2020.1718086

Stanton-Salazar, R. D. (2011). A social capital framework for the study of institutional agents and their role in the empowerment of low-status students and youth. *Youth & Society, 43*(3), 1066–1109.

Yosso, T. (2005). Whose culture has capital? A critical race theory discussion of community cultural wealth. *Race, Ethnicity and Education, 8*(1), 69–91.

Yosso, T., Smith, W., Ceja, M., & Solorzano, D. (2009). Critical race theory, racial microaggressions, and campus racial climate for Latina/o undergraduates. *Harvard Educational Review, 79*, 659–691. 10.17763/haer.79.4.m6867014157m707l.

CHAPTER 9

# "This Space Is Not Open to All": Nepantleando in McNair Undergraduate Research Programs to Nurture College Completion

*Samantha Prado Robledo*

## Introduction

TIME AND TIME again, underrepresented minoritized students have obtained low graduating rates and lesser completion of higher education in the United States (Estepp et al., 2016; Sólorzano et al., 2005). In the United States, a society with a meritocratic belief system where hard work and effort are meant to make dreams come true, significant disparities persist in college-going rates by racial/ethnic group (Strayhorn, 2010). However, the disparate graduation rates and college success vary among underrepresented groups, which results from racism and deficit-based stereotypes that portray Chicana/o/x and Latina/o/x students as intellectually inferior. Achieving a higher education is a dream that fades away for many students from marginalized backgrounds early in life as a result of inaccessibility and inequity in the educational system. For this reason, although Latina/o/xs comprise the largest ethnically minoritized group in the United States (Noboa-Ríos, 2019), they compose 5% of graduate degree recipients (The Education Trust, 2017), the number being even lower when disaggregated by gender. Through the Framework of *Atravesada/o/xs Nepantleando* (FAN), this chapter seeks to challenge traditional undergraduate program structures and modalities that bring challenge to Chicana/o/x/Latina/o/x students pursuing a higher education. This chapter examines: (1) How does an *atravesada* look like in higher education and (2) How do *nepantleras* create bridges between higher education and their communities?

## Literature Review

Among the multiple factors that impede Latina/o/x student success are first-generation college status (Prado Robledo, 2023), immigration factors (Abrego, 2018), racism (Sólorzano et al., 2005), and the challenges of racist nativism in educational institutional settings (Ramirez, 2021). Because Latina/o/x students may originate from countries with lesser educational opportunities, rural regions, and lower socioeconomic statuses, it is harder for them to possess U.S.-based college-going knowledge and higher education experiences. Students who might be first-generation immigrants may face the challenges of acculturating into the new society and learning to navigate unfamiliar institutional settings. Similarly, students who may be 1.5-generation immigrants, meaning they arrived in the United States underage along with their parents, may face similar issues to those of their parents, including holding a complicated legal status. Also, students who may be members of mixed-status families, where there may be members with legal, undocumented, or unresolved legal statuses, may face psychological and financial challenges resulting from their family's unstable situation, including fears of deportation or assisting family by joining the labor market prematurely (Abrego, 2018). Xenophobia may be fueled by racist nativist beliefs to exclude Latina/o/x students from educational opportunities, which may improve their lives and those of their families (Perez Huber et al., 2015). Although ancestors to Latina/o/x populations were responsible for great innovations, ongoing prejudice of viewing Latina/o/xs as incompetent and suited for service work thrives in the United States, placing marginalized labels on them. This harsh reality presents itself to Latina/o/x students early in life. For example, even when tracked for college-ready courses in 10th grade, Latina/o/x students are less likely to have completed college-ready coursework upon high school graduation (Gates et al., 2011) because "minority students more frequently than their White peers endure lower levels of expectations and less affirmation from teachers" (Young, 2005, p. 208).

Throughout U.S. history, schools were utilized as a means of assimilation, where some of the strategies employed to accomplish this were the removal of the Spanish language and Mexican culture from the curriculum, transforming into a Eurocentric narrative (Conchas & Acevedo, 2020; Noboa-Ríos, 2019). Understanding the role that education plays as an institution in exacerbating one hegemonic narrative is crucial to understanding how this can impact underrepresented students' feelings of belonging and encouragement to persevere in the classroom.

Some opportunities have emerged to disrupt these unequal educational outcomes, such as policies and programs. Scholars have examined how participating in undergraduate research programs affects students' intentions of enrolling in graduate or professional programs, comparing Latina/o/x and white student populations (Eagan et al., 2013), program impact on building scientist identity and pursuing careers in hard science among Latina/o/x students (Camacho et al., 2021), and whether undergraduate research experiences (UREs) influence underrepresented minoritized students' (URM) likelihood of pursuing careers in hard science (Daniels et al., 2016).

Because students from underrepresented backgrounds have been found to be less likely to engage in high-impact practices such as undergraduate research experiences and programs, a solution was reached in the 1980s through the development of the McNair Scholars Program, a federally funded grant undergraduate research program found at 4-year institutions aimed at preparing racially and socioeconomically underrepresented students in pursuing graduate education studies with the end goal of a professoriate (Clayton et al., 2023). All of the literature aforementioned has had a heavy focus on Science, Technology, Engineering, and Math (STEM). Given the extensive focus on STEM fields, the purpose of this chapter is to shed more light on experiences in the underexamined areas of humanities, arts, and social and behavioral sciences.

## Theoretical Framework

Critical race theory (CRT) is most fitting as the theoretical framework because it highlights five principles, which are: (1) placing race and racism at the center of discourse; (2) centering the knowledge of people of color; (3)

challenging dominant ideologies; (4) employing interdisciplinary lenses; and (5) committing to social justice (Sólorzano et al., 2005). The first pillar of CRT is present in this chapter as race continues to be a central component of educational inequity in the United States, and this chapter examines the experiences of racially underrepresented college students. Given that we seek to gain knowledge and a better understanding of Chicana/Latina students in McNair, which traditional undergraduate research program research has hardly included, focusing on traditional student populations and general program evaluation, this chapter also honors the second principle of CRT. The analysis of these *platicas* hopes to bring knowledge that will provide traditionally underacknowledged knowledge and experience from Chicana/Latina students and their journeys as *atravesada/o/xs* in higher education, honoring the third pillar. Fourth, this chapter brings in a multidisciplinary approach to best understand higher education and the experience of underrepresented student groups. Lastly, the findings of this chapter wish to bring about social change in education by examining an area of understudy and exposing the inequities that exist involving undergraduate research programs, allowing for opportunities for improvement and inviting solutions. Through employing a critical race theory framework in education, this chapter acknowledges the challenges students of color face in their educational trajectories as they navigate higher education (Conchas & Acevedo, 2020).

This chapter also employs FAN. The FAN arises from the need to examine the intersectionality of systems of oppression that shape the experiences of Chicana/o/x and Latina/o/x students throughout their higher education trajectories (Conchas & Acevedo, 2020). Throughout the piece, different forms of intersectionality of systems of oppression such as race, ethnicity, gender identity, and low-income status are discussed, as well as commonly unacknowledged intersectionality of systems of oppression in higher education including community college student identity, transfer student potential, sexuality-questioning identities, and art and humanities backgrounds as fields of importance. These forms of the intersectionality of systems of oppression operate as education borderlands, which Conchas and Acevedo (2020) define as "the nexus of deficit and marginalizing practices, policies, and ideologies present in the education system that Chicana/o/x students confront" (p. 23).

FAN arises from Anzaldúan theory. Gloria Anzaldúa framed *atravesados* as those who did not belong in U.S. society and live within the borderlands. Hence, Conchas and Acevedo's (2020) framing of Chicanx/o/x students "as *atravesadxs* who navigate colonial structures, which were not established for their academic success" (p. 27). In this chapter, both collaborators reveal their *atravesada* identity given that they are Chicana/Latina, low-income, and first-generation college students, which are groups that have been traditionally held back from quality education throughout U.S. history (Noboa-Ríos, 2019). In addition to these stigmas, they are double *atravesadas* by entering the McNair program as a transfer student from a community college and as a junior, respectively, both statuses closer to graduation than traditional McNair recipients who begin the program in their first year of college. Not only that, but the collaborators in this chapter also came into the program majoring in fields of arts, humanities, and social sciences, going against the majority STEM focus.

## Methods

This chapter centers the experiences of two Chicana/Latina graduate students pursuing their respective degrees at Borderlands University and the role of McNair undergraduate research experiences. Trust had been built between the collaborators and the researcher prior to the birth of this project. Given its focus on underrepresented communities, *platicas* methodology was chosen as the method of investigation. *Platicas* methodology consists of five principles: (1) viewing the collaborator as a co-constructor of knowledge; (2) incorporating everyday lived experiences as part of the research inquiry; (3) drawing heavily from Chicana feminist theory; (4) honoring a two-directional approach where the researcher provides vulnerability, reflexivity, and reciprocity; and (5) allowing for potential healing for both collaborator and researcher (Fierros & Delgado Bernal, 2016).

The following are the ways in which the *platicas* methodology principles are honored in this research: First, this research places great value in the experiences and suggestions brought up by the collaborators throughout the *platicas,* recognizing that they are experts based on their experiences and knowledge. Second, these *platicas* arose from earlier encounters and informal conversations that led to the topic of undergraduate research programs, highlighting the experiences, thoughts, and centrality of the collaborators within this context. Third, since the *platica* methodology draws from Chicana feminist theory, it centers the experiences of women of color who have been historically denied a voice in research and academia and whose experiences drastically differ from traditional students. Fourth, both collaborator and researcher develop the creation of knowledge, having the collaborator share her experiences and thoughts as they connect to the topics. Lastly, the process of the *platicas* and reflection on both the collaborator and researcher are given much importance in this setting, with the collaborator sharing her experiences and knowledge gained through these and the researcher gaining greater awareness of her educational trajectory.

The author held *platicas* with the collaborators that lasted 1 hour and 11 minutes and 1 hour and 35 minutes, respectively. One *platica* took place over Zoom and was recorded to the Cloud, producing audio transcripts. The other *platica* took place in person over coffee and *pan dulce* and was recorded with a handheld recording device and then transcribed via the Microsoft Word Dictate function. Both videos and transcripts were kept safe under a password. The identities of the collaborators are protected using pseudonyms to maintain their anonymity. Given that communities of color have historically been devalued and exploited, each collaborator was compensated with a $75 gift card for their time and knowledge shared (Abrego, 2023). Following suit of other Chicana/o/x feminist pieces, this one insists on the value of understanding Chicana/Latina students as knowledge creators (Conchas & Acevedo, 2020).

### *Collaborators*

Through FAN, this chapter examines how two Chicana/Latina graduate students reflected on their experiences of participating in the Ronald E. McNair scholars undergraduate research program at their respective undergraduate institutions. Their identities and majors of study led them to be *atravesadas nepantleando* at the university and sparked a greater interest in them to pursue social justice and community building as a result. Both collaborators' Chicana/Latina backgrounds were crucial to this chapter, as statistics demonstrate that the Latina/o/x community is the largest ethnically minoritized group in the

United States and is greatly composed of Latina/o/xs of Mexican background (Conchas & Acevedo, 2020).

Elena is a 33-year-old second-generation Chicana whose parents migrated to the United States in search of a better life. Her mother earned a living as a cook and her father as a gardener. Her mother holds elementary school education training and her father had no formal education. She attended community college and transferred to Borderlands University where she joined the McNair program immediately as a junior, completing her undergraduate studies in sociology and an international immigration minor. Elena then joined a master's degree program in education at a nearby state university and shortly after returned to Borderlands University to pursue her doctoral degree in education.

Patty is a 24-year-old second-generation Chicana from her father's side and third-generation from her mother's side. Her mother is a procurement officer at a local community college and her father works in landscape. Although her mother completed some college, and her father holds a high school education, Patty is the first in her family to graduate college, having attended the University of San Junipero where she joined McNair shortly before completing her bachelor's degree studies. Soon after, she joined a master's program in Studies of Latin America at the Borderlands University.

Both Elena and Patty had been highly qualified students throughout their educational journey. During the *platica,* Elena revealed she had completed quite a few accomplishments while in high school and had also excelled while in community college. On a previous informal *platica,* Patty had revealed that through the strategic use of the community college, she completed lower division coursework and was able to graduate from the 4-year university in a fast track, within 3 years. Both collaborators completed their undergraduate studies in an Emerging Hispanic-Serving Institution (EHSI) and an HSI respectively. The rising HSI designation refers to institutions that hold 15% to 24% Latina/o/x students, whereas HSI designation belongs to institutions that house 25% or greater Latina/o/x student populations (Contreras et al., 2022). During the time these *platicas* took place, both collaborators were finalizing their doctoral and master's degrees at Borderlands University.

### *Researcher Positionality*

Although I share similarities in background with the collaborators, as I am also a low-income Chicana, daughter of immigrants, and first-generation college student, I did not participate in undergraduate research programs during my educational trajectory. Due to problems too common in our community, my family faced housing insecurity that led me to drop out of school upon completing my ninth grade in Barrio Logan. I never stepped foot in high school, and I never learned about any program that would assist me in pursuing college. In my late teens, I obtained my GED and entered community college, then transferred to a 4-year state university. I navigated my higher education without the knowledge of undergraduate research programs (URPs). Understanding the capital these URPs provide has fueled my interest in understanding how they can best prepare communities of color to succeed in higher education and how these can be transformed to create bridges with marginalized communities. This research has enabled me to further construct a picture of traditional educational processes and how these impact Chicana/o/x and Latina/o/x students. Given my positionality and the experiences of these brave women, I can better understand how U.S. education systems operate for underrepresented students. The following are key findings in this chapter resulting from the *platicas* with two McNair alumni.

## Findings

Understanding the experiences of both Elena and Patty is crucial to understanding the future of higher education. Although Latina/o/xs are the largest ethnically minoritized group, they only compose 14% of those holding a bachelor's degree in the United States (Conchas & Acevedo, 2022). The following are findings resulting from the *platicas* held with two *atravesadas nepantleras*.

### *Finding Validating Allies While Nepantleando*

Both Elena and Patty were very grateful to their McNair mentors for their strong support throughout the program. Elena had been supported by Joseph, an administrator who held a PhD and who shared a Chicana/o/x background with her and served as an advisor to all other Chicana/o/x and Latina/o/x McNair students. Elena felt uplifted and reminded of who she was and why she was doing the work she did. The following passage speaks of the way he impacted her views towards research:

> When I think about my experience in the McNair program, it is very much defined by my interactions with Joseph. He made that program worth it for me, and I think he opened up doors for me and ways that I didn't expect ... what I'm saying is that he really challenged me to think about what research is and what is the purpose of research.

Elena's relationship with research and her approach to it was cultivated by her experience with her McNair mentor. Unlike the traditional research approach she described as Eurocentric, his approach invited her to think about how her research could be transformative and how it would impact her community.

Patty also spoke very fondly about her two mentors, who also shared Chicana/o/x background with her although they came from different disciplines:

> I actually had two professors for McNair that helped guide me: two Chicana, queer [faculty] ... and they both taught at the U of J; one was in Women Studies and the other was in history and every time I went with them they reaffirmed me where McNair brought me down.

In the quote above, Patty explained that while the program was Eurocentric and left no opportunities for criticality, she could always find that support and validation in her femtors. In terms of positive program outcomes for them, a positive outlook to research, and community building, both *platicas* revealed that mentorship was very crucial to their development and ability to navigate their McNair experience. Not only were reoccurring meetings, dedication, and research interest similarities important, but also similarities in background and lived experience.

Although it is important to refrain from glorifying mentors, she stated the importance of honoring these principles and the importance for the programs and their stakeholders to understand this to be most effective and help underrepresented students. As seen below in Elena's comment:

> I don't think there was a conscious understanding of how difficult it was to get ... [a mentor that] ... not only aligned with your perspectives, your beliefs, [and] the research but who really understood it because they lived through it, too, and so I think that they [McNair] did kind of fracture my relation, not fracture ... but I think I just kept my distance.

The two faculty would continuously encourage Patty to follow her dreams and to approach her discipline and research through decolonized lenses.

### *Building Bridges Between La Facultad and Comunidad*

Elena reflects on her experiences learning research practices throughout her educational trajectory, highlighting a very important point about how systemic inequities can be diminished:

> I think it is important to be able to teach children, like, we can do this in fields beyond the hard sciences. ... I would argue that in the years to come we are gonna need scholars who are able to ... find the bridging between the hard science and the social sciences, because that's exactly what is missing right? Especially when we think about like medical inequalities around African American women and the death rates. Right? There is racism occurring like in all these things.

Elena enacted *la facultad* by supporting a change in the educational system where we encourage research experience in grade school. In addition to that, providing research experiences that not only connect with STEM, but with arts, humanities, and behavioral and social sciences in ways in which these can resolve systemic problems that currently exist and have been underexamined.

### *Diversifying Undergraduate Research Program Stakeholders*

In the case of diversifying the age group of stakeholders that took part in McNair, Patty had the following recommendation:

> ... in the context of when I was in ... [McNair] ... the leadership there were older, the TAs and the director was a professor but they're older ... the TAs were probably like 32-34 and the director was like 56 and I don't want to get into ageism but you need a range of TAs who have just had the experience of entering graduate school, I think you need a range of timelines represented in these people

Patty encouraged the diversification of the McNair staff and administrators. In addition to diverse identities, she also encouraged that these people's experiences would be able to identify with the students who participate in McNair. Prior research has explained the importance of mentor or stakeholder similarity in background such as race, ethnicity, and having experienced similar events to be able to effectively relate to and understand challenges faced by students (Garrett, 2006).

### *Identifying Sources of Additional Gatekeeping*

Throughout the *platicas* with Elena and Patty, themes of deservingness and normativity arose. Eurocentric teachings, hegemonic research practices, STEM as ideal fields, and competitiveness were common examples of how, although marginalized, students could reach respect and be accepted in a system that was not built for them. As found in Elena's excerpt, the notion of deservingness becomes a recurring theme in associating students who are part of McNair and who are accepted into the program. As stated by Conchas and Acevedo (2020), "deservingness is used by the state to legitimize existence and define who belongs and who does not belong in the U.S. Deservingness justifies who does and does not deserve to benefit from a quality education" (p. 25). Although in Elena's experience, her McNair program was efficient at providing evaluation methods for continuous improvement, this was not the case for Patty, who encourages better forms of program evaluation which will best guide the program evaluation process and bring about solutions to student participant needs. Both Elena and Patty spoke about the need for program institution openness to bring in diverse program participants as well as program stakeholders. Patty explained thoroughly an issue with that:

> ... all of them did their undergrad and the professor did his PhD at the U of J, so [the program], it's very like U of J centered and I think getting graduate TAs in that institution that did their work in other institutions is also important

Patty explained the importance of hiring diverse individuals who come with different experiences to prevent group-think and toxic in-group dynamics. She proposed that inviting new ways of thinking and inviting change promote student success.

### *Educational Majors and Late Starts as Means of Atravesadas*

Elena highlighted what traditionally has been theorized in higher education regarding rejecting community colleges as a place of empowerment and learning (Conchas & Acevedo, 2020; Prado Robledo, 2023). These systemic environments lead Chicana/Latina students to feel as *atravesadas* who do not fit into the education system (Conchas & Acevedo, 2020). Elena's experience also speaks to the lack of support and focus on non-STEM fields in the McNair program. She explained how bleak the numbers were:

> I think only two people of the humanities and social sciences got accepted that year. Everybody else was hard STEM ... It was three of us ... It was my first year as a transfer student, so I was a junior.

Elena explained that although the university is home to thousands of undergraduates, only a small number of students in the arts, humanities, and social sciences were chosen to be part of the McNair program. To best support minoritized students to succeed in higher education, it is crucial that we listen to their needs and provide the necessary tools for them to achieve their goals. Transfer student participation in undergraduate research programs should be further explored, given that prior literature has found the greater academic success of this group compared to their nontransfer student counterparts who attend 4-year institutions from the start (Jackson et al., 2013).

## Implications

Most of the existing literature on undergraduate research programs employs psychological theories (Byars-Winson et al., 2016; Morales et al., 2016), sociologically inclined frameworks (Eagan et al., 2013; Estrada et al., 2018), or none at all (Asher & Alexander, 2006; Daniels et al., 2016; Foertsch, 2020); it is important to develop research that employs critical theoretical frameworks such as FAN to better understand the experiences of students of color and how these programs shape their educational success. The application of FAN allows for a transparent intersectional analysis of systems of oppression that shape the experiences of Chicana/o/x and Latina/o/x students as they navigate their higher education. The majority of research on undergraduate research programs examines general undergraduate student populations and do not tend to disaggregate by racial/ethnic group; more research on specific underrepresented groups such as Latina/o/x, African American, and Native American must be conducted to better understand how these programs impact their retention and success. Additionally, qualitative research such as this humanizes participants and provides suggestions for program improvement and evaluation by providing input otherwise missed given that most research on undergraduate research programs apply quantitative research methods.

## Recommendations

As a component of the FAN, Conchas and Acevedo (2020):

> propose that while the educational borderlands prepare students to view the world from a deficit Eurocentric perspective, their experiences living on the margins of society and navigating the physical and psychological borderlands allow them to enact *la facultad* and see the underlying U.S. structures of inequality. (p. 28)

The following section provides recommendations for future research.

### *Supporting Students' Sense of Belonging*

For Chicana/o/x and Latina/o/x students to succeed in higher education, they must feel a sense of belonging and acceptance of their identities and communities. Being aware of the constant pressure for students to adjust to university values rather than accepting what students have to offer, Patty was aware of hegemony being internalized by McNair students and program stakeholders. Patty urged the need for educational institutions to confront and change the process:

> ... the institution needs to reevaluate itself of how it's allocated efforts for diversity, equity, and inclusion ... they create these programs that are supposed to help organize but it's definitely internalized some of those hegemonic features of like, who's being helped, who's getting the priority, and I do understand like helping ... marginalized people in the STEM—let's face it, this then brings in money for the universities

Patty further expressed that marginalized students pursuing STEM may be perceived as valued over marginalized students who may be majoring in fields that are perceived to have less value.

### *Rethink New Ways of Teaching, Knowing, and Developing Curriculum*

Being in *Nepantla,* a place of in-betweenness, allowed both collaborators to understand clearly various issues faced in educational systems and envision ways in which these could be resolved. Both Elena and Patty possess great knowledge of how to improve the educational system. Elena brought an example of how preparing students for research in the arts, humanities, and social sciences can assist in resolving social problems:

> I don't think we provide those skills in the humanities and the social sciences early enough for students to apply and for it to be a competitive application as opposed to the hard science ... We're taught as children to conduct research on the hard sciences ... We do research projects since we're in elementary ... that is so ingrained in us ... as opposed to

> if we were to go to any ... undergrad class, and be [told] like, 'develop a research project rooted in humanities and social sciences.' I am willing to bet you more than half of ... [the class] ... are not gonna be able to produce anything that's quality, right?

Elena urged the shift in the culture and educational practices to include research training in humanities and social sciences. Both collaborators provided instances where they enacted *la facultad,* "this ability to see beyond surface phenomena into the meaning of deeper realities as a strategy to persist when faced with adversities and proactively begin to assert their belongingness in the educational system" (Conchas & Acevedo, 2020, p. 18).

### Fostering Students' Critical Thinking

The following excerpt of the *platica* highlighted Elena's reflection, identifying a disconnect between the educational system she was a part of and her community:

> I knew there was something wrong. I saw it every day ... I knew it was in my community and I didn't like it ... I took a psychology class ... I hated it ... I didn't know it then, but knowing now, reflecting on the content ... it was very Eurocentric. It was very racist. It was very like, traditional psychological perspectives that I don't think for me helped explain anything and then when I took that sociology class and they're like, we're gonna talk about race, gender, social-economic status, and immigration, it opened up these doors for me that I'm like, these are the conversations I wanna have, these are the things I wanna focus on and I think I'll give credit to my high school teacher, who, like, was very intentional and saying, like, this is a field for research, and this is how we do research ... I didn't know I was analyzing. I didn't know that I was, like constructing a critical perspective It was just something fun to do with my friends, and we got kicked out of Target and we have a fun story to share ... that's all it meant at that time, right? But I think it had deeper, a deeper impact than what I realized at that time.

Elena explained her first exposure to research in a high school sociology class and that it fostered her critical mindset. Similarly, Patty's thoughts aligned with what "studies have shown that the contemporary U.S. educational system is built upon coloniality and does not adequately capture or even accommodate the histories and lived experiences of minoritized groups" (Conchas & Acevedo, 2020, p. 18). Patty shared her observations of internalization among underrepresented students and faculty:

> I definitely saw them like internalizing some of the systems and programs ... like "It's going to be shitty ... you're gonna have difficult PIs and all you could do is like push through a way that works within the system so you can't be pushing it away [in a way] that is counterhegemonic because that just won't work within the system."

Patty reflected on the ways in which stakeholders in her McNair program invested in hegemonic knowledge. It is important to also highlight that Patty came from a state where multiple racist and xenophobic laws have led to prohibiting multicultural education and inviting racial profiling, perhaps further influencing the Eurocentric state of her McNair program experience. Above are examples of Chicana students using "their *facultad* to resist marginalization and transform into *nepantleras* by tapping into various institutional resources to navigate college" (Conchas & Acevedo, 2020, p. 22).

The *platicas* with both Elena and Patty were illuminating problems in the educational system that claims to bring about equity. Both collaborators' successful transition from *atravesadas* to *nepantleras* led them to envision better programs and solutions for how to reduce inequities faced by marginalized students in a system that claims to already be creating opportunities for such.

## Conclusion

This chapter explores how *la facultad* entails the ability to see beyond the superficial, allowing individuals to see beyond the surface and operate as a sixth sense of consciousness (Conchas & Acevedo, 2020). The developers of FAN state that being on the margins of society allows for the development of *la facultad,* particularly when feeling oppressed, as expressed by Elena's judgment as a transfer student or Patty's pain experienced through her McNair experience where she faced attacks toward her field of study and writing practices, and even resource allocation during her current graduate program.

As a researcher and educator, something that stays with me the most is this newly gained awareness of the importance of finding ways to provide underrepresented students with research skills. Honoring the *platica* principle that allows for healing, I am better able to understand the ways in which the research skill attainment gap remains. Nevertheless, we must find ways to capacitate our students with these so that they can be most likely to succeed in completing their goals and dreams. If we all get on board with teaching our underrepresented students how to conduct research in the arts, humanities, and social sciences, marginalized students may be able to solve future and ongoing social justice problems as pointed out by Elena. Pushing beyond, these students may secure future job opportunities in fields where traditionally bachelor's degrees have not been enough for competitive-pay employment.

Although Elena and Patty have stories of success, we must remember that they comprise the mere approximately 23% of Latina/o/x students who have earned an associate degree or higher (Conchas & Acevedo, 2020), and we must continue to find effective solutions to assist underrepresented college students to achieve their dreams. Not only that, but bringing an awareness of research to marginalized students may serve as a method to find solutions to existing social problems.

## Reference

Abrego, L. (2023). Research as accompaniment: Reflections on objectivity, ethics, and emotions. In l. Chua & M. Massoud (Eds.), *Out of place: Power, person, and difference in socio-legal research* (pp. 1-18). https://escholarship.org/uc/item/34v2g837

Abrego, L. J. (2018). Renewed optimism and spatial mobility: Legal consciousness of Latino deferred action for childhood arrivals recipients and their families in Los Angeles. *Ethnicities, 18*(2), 192–207. https://doi.org/10.1177/1468796817752563

Asher, C., & Alexander, J. O. (2006). The library internship and Expo as a pathway to diversity: A case study. *Journal of Education for Library and Information Science, 47*(1), 17–26. https://doi.org/10.2307/40324334

Byars-Winston, A., Rogers, J., Branchaw, J., Pribbenow, C., Hanke, R., & Pfund, C. (2016). New measures assessing predictors of academic persistence for historically underrepresented racial/ethnic undergraduates in science. *CBE – Life Sciences Education, 15*(3), 1–11. https://doi.org/10.1187/cbe/16-01-0030

Camacho, T. C., Vasquez-Salgado, Y., Chavira, G., Boyns, D., Appelrouth, S., Saetermoe, C., & Khachikian, C. (2021). Science identity among Latinx students in the biomedical sciences: The role of a critical race theory–informed undergraduate research experience. *CBE—Life Sciences Education, 20*(2), 1–10. https://doi.org/10.1187/cbe.19-06-0124

Clayton, A. B., Breeden, R. L., & Davis, T. J. (2023). "My entire support system for graduate school": Black students' experiences in a McNair scholars program. *Journal of College Student Retention: Research, Theory & Practice.* https://doi.org/10.1177/15210251231182683

Conchas, G. O., & Acevedo, N. (2020). *The Chicana/o/x dream: Hope, resistance, and educational success.* Harvard Education Press

Contreras, F., Prado Robledo, S., & Gomez, V. (2022). Cultivating the Chicano/Latina/o/x faculty pipeline across HSI systems: The role of RHSIs in transforming the professoriate. *Journal of Leadership, Equity, and Research, 8*(2). https://journals.sfu.ca/cvj/index.php/cvj/article/view/215.

Daniels, H., Grineski, S. E., Collins, T. W., Morales, D. X., Morera, O., & Echegoyen, L. (2016). Factors influencing student gains from undergraduate research experiences at a Hispanic-Serving Institution. *CBE—Life Sciences Education, 15*(3), 1–12. https://doi.org/10.1187/cbe.15-07-0163

Eagan, M. K., Hurtado, S., Chang, M. J., Garcia, G. A., Herrera, F. A., & Garibay, J. C. (2013). Making a difference in science education. *American Educational Research Journal, 50*(4), 683–713. doi:10.3102/0002831213482038

The Education Trust. (2017). *Degree attainment for Latino adults: National and state trends.* https://edtrust.org/wp-content/uploads/2014/09/Latino-Degree-Attainment_FINAL_4-1.pdf

Estepp, C. M., Velasco, J. G., Culbertson, A. L., & Conner, N. W. (2016). An investigation into mentoring practices of faculty who mentor undergraduate researchers at a Hispanic serving Institution. *Journal of Hispanic Higher Education, 16*(4), 338–358. https://doi.org/10.1177/1538192716661906

Estrada, M., Hernandez, P. R., & Schultz, P. W. (2018). A longitudinal study on how quality mentorship and research experience integrate underrepresented minorities into stem careers. *CBE-Life Sciences Education, 17*(1), 1–13. https://doi.org/10.1187/cbe.17-04-0066.

Fierros, C. O., & Delgado Bernal, D. (2016). Vamos a platicar: The contours of pláticas as Chicana/Latina feminist methodology. *Journal of Chicana/Latina Studies, 15*(2), 98–121. https://thisbridgecalledcyberspace.net/FILES/3943.pdf

Foertsch, J. (2020). Impacts of undergraduate research programs focused on underrepresented minorities: Twenty years of gradual progress and practices that contributed to it. *Council on Undergraduate Research Quarterly, 3*(2), 31–37. https://doi.org/10.18833/spur/3/2/2

Garrett, R. U. (2006). Effects of mentoring on the quality of the doctoral experience at Historically Black Colleges and Universities: Results of ground investigation. *Race, Gender & Class, 13*(3), 311–327.

Gates, A. Q., Hug, S., Thiry, H., Aló, R., Beheshti, M., Fernandez, J., & Adjouadi, M. (2011). The computing alliance of Hispanic-Serving Institutions. *ACM Transactions on Computing Education, 11*(3), 1–21. https://doi.org/10.1145/2037276.2037280

Jackson, D. L., Starobin, S.S., & Laanan, F. S. (2013). The shared experiences: Facilitating successful transfer of women and underrepresented minorities in STEM fields. *New Directions for Higher Education, 2013*(162), 69–76. Retrieved from https://doi.org/10.1002/he.20058

Morales, D. X., Grineski, S. E., & Collins, T. W. (2016). Influences on faculty willingness to mentor undergraduate students from another university as part of an interinstitutional research training program. *CBE-Life Sciences Education, 15*(3), 1–15. https://doi.org/10.1187/cbe.16-01-0039.

Noboa-Ríos, A. (2019). *The story of Latinos and education in American history.* Peter Lang Publishing Inc.

Perez Huber, L., Malagon, M. C., Ramirez, B. R., Gonzalez, L. C., Jimenez, A., & Velez, V. N. (2015). *Still falling through the cracks: Revisiting the Latina/o educational pipeline.* CSRC Research Report, UCLA Chicano Studies Research Center. https://www.chicano.ucla.edu/files/RR19.pdf

Prado Robledo, S. (2023) Instilling the capacity for critical empathy in the classroom. *New Directions for Student Leadership,* 23–31. https://doi.org/10.1002/yd.20538

Ramirez, B. R. (2021). Racist nativism in the college access experiences of undocumented Latinx students. *Journal of College Access, 6*(2), 65–79. https://scholarworks.wmich.edu/jca/vol6/iss2/6

Sólorzano, D. G., Villalpando, O., & Oseguera, L. (2005). Educational inequities and Latina/o undergraduate students in the United States: A critical race analysis of their educational progress. *Journal of Hispanic Higher Education, 4*(3), 272–294. https://doi.org/10.1177/1538192705276550

Strayhorn, T. L. (2010). Bridging the pipeline: Increasing underrepresented students' preparation for college through a summer bridge program. *American Behavioral Scientist, 55*(2), 142–159. https://doi.org/10.1177/0002764210381871

Young, H. (2005). Secondary education systemic issues: Addressing possible contributors to a leak in the science education pipeline and potential solutions. *Journal of Science Education and Technology, 14*(2), 205–216.

**CHAPTER 10**

# Empowering Latina/o/x Youth by Reconnecting to Our Ancestral and Indigenous Roots

*Nancy Acevedo, Gilberto Q. Conchas, and Victor DeAlba*

> The Indigenous peoples of the Americas have always known that maíz is sacred. For de-Indigenized people, reconnecting to maíz brings us back to the sacred sustenance of our roots. It is not our traditions that are lost, but us. And we have the power within to find and reclaim ancestral memory by reconnecting with the land and the gifts that she offers.
>
> —Suzy González, 2023

## Introduction

Corn is rooted in the term *maize,* which comes from the Caribbean Taíno word, *mahis* (McClung Museum of Natural History & Culture, 2022). *Mahis* translates to life-giving seed. We centered Latina/o/x students as children of the corn because participants in this book embodied histories of Mexico, El Salvador, Guatemala, Afro Latina/o/x, and Indigeneity. While the Latina/o/x identity is not a monolith, if we had adequate resources, we would highlight and honor the differences in the histories and intersectionality of the various contexts. As the quote above explains, this anthology is a way for us to reclaim and reconnect to our ancestral memory.

By centering the concept of Latina/o/x students as *maíz,* we aimed to align a central piece of the ancestral history of Latina/o/x participants in the book chapters. The foundational aspects of this anthology are represented by symbolism that the roots of the *maíz* are sprouted by seeds. The seeds in our book represent the dreams and aspirations that are passed down from generation to generation, dreams that are planted in the minds of Latina/o/x children. Thus, our first theme focused on "planting the seeds to foster college access;" we highlighted "pillars and resources of support that nurture college preparation" for Latina/o/x students. The programs in this section centered college *access* efforts that prepare students to make informed postsecondary decisions.

Considering the process of growing corn, a seed sprouts roots. The roots of the crop represent ancestors and cultural traditions that have been passed on from generation to generation, including the dreams for a better future. With appropriate soil and nutrients, the cornstalk grows strong, which represents the opportunity structures that allow for the dreams of Latina/o/x students to grow and thrive. Without adequate soil, the sprouted seed cannot grow into a strong stalk. As such, the second theme aimed to prepare the soil, represented as learning environments; "cultivating to foster college readiness" noted the "pillars and resources of support that nurture student development and college navigation." Studies in this theme included the importance of fostering college *readiness* among Latina/o/x students to reinforce academic and metacognitive skills that prepare students to navigate postsecondary education.

As the corn grows, husks are developed to protect the corn seeds growing on the ear of the plant. We note that institutional, familial, and community-based support systems represent the corn husks that protect and contribute to the Latina/o/x students as they navigate a college journey. These husks not only protect the *maíz* from varying environmental conditions as it grows with the sun, water, and soil nutrients. Once the *maíz* can withstand its environmental conditions, the husks open, thus allowing the *maíz* to flourish, mostly on its own. The *maíz* itself is representative of Latina/o/x students who are cultivated through this process that will then continue the cycle. The top of a corn plant is the tassel, which produces pollen to ensure proper growth and the husks opening. Like a student with their tassel on their cap, the third theme in our book was "harvesting for college completion." This section included "nurturing students for post-graduation" so they may be equipped to "plant future seeds."

The aim was to emphasize resources that fostered college *completion* and prepare students for post-graduation decisions.

The empirically-based chapters in this book engaged with the Framework of *Atravesada/o/xs Nepantleando* (FAN) developed by Conchas and Acevedo (2020) to discuss the various support systems of nurturing seeds of college aspirations, preparing the soil to ensure college transitions and a productive harvest as college completion. In line with critical race theory in education, which challenges the "American" notion of meritocracy and blaming an individual's culture or racial group for not meeting academic benchmarks, FAN begins with brokering moments to activate *la facultad*—the abilities to see beneath surface level justifications for inequitable and unequal outcomes. We acknowledge that *nepantlera/o/xs* build bridges between two conflicting spaces, such as the *familismo* within Latina/o/x communities (Calzada et al., 2013) and the individualistic notion of success in the American education system. Over the years, we have seen the development of bridges, from the Civil Rights Movement in the 1960s to the LGBTQIA+ movements that began in 1969. More recently, the Supreme Court eliminated affirmative action and overturned *Roe v. Wade*. Legislators in various states have outlawed critical race theory and the U.S. President has implemented numerous Executive Orders that eliminate diversity, equity, and inclusion policies and practices. It is within this context that local and state legislations and policies aimed to create educational opportunities to exist and resist. While California legislators require Ethnic Studies as a high school and college graduation requirement in public institutions, they now confront the national realities of a U.S. President that threatens to defund such efforts.

Therefore, we conclude this book by maintaining a critical race theory lens and centering racial realism—racism is permanent and endemic in the United States (Bell, 1992). As such, we acknowledge the need to continue equipping current and future Latina/o/x college students to navigate an unjust, inequitable, and white supremacist society. Doing so entails proactively continuing to foster college pathways for Chicana/o/x, Latina/o/x, Afro Latina/o/x, and Indigenous students. However, with the pendulum swinging toward white supremacist national restrictions, it will require educators to nurture the maíz seeds in direct resistance to the revamped efforts of marginalization.

## Cycle of Fostering College Pathways for Latina/o/x Students

Informed by findings from chapters in this book and with these questions in mind, we propose elements to consider for all three themes: planting seeds of college aspirations, equipping the soil and utilizing the husks to grow strong college-going pathways, and cultivating postgraduation efforts. We build on the Framework of *Atravesada/o/xs Nepantleando* to emphasize key elements found throughout the chapters of this book. As indicated in Figure 10.1, these elements represent the cycle to foster college pathways for Latina/o/x students.

**Figure 10.1**
*Cycle of fostering college pathways for Latina/o/x students.*

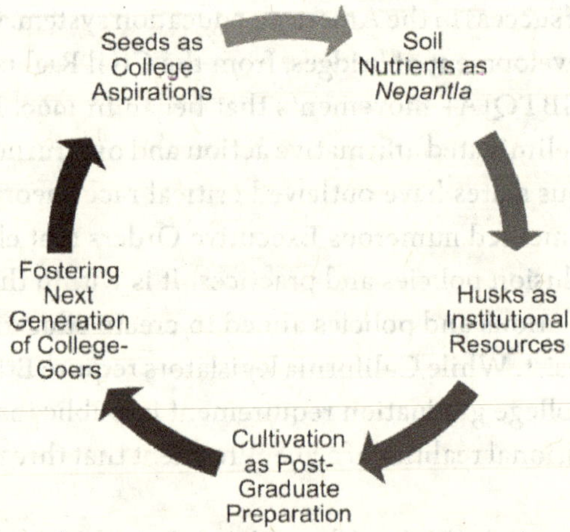


The process begins with planting seeds of college aspirations, which often occurs at home and is reinforced by schooling structures. The balance of soil nutrients represents the space of *nepantla*. The balanced soil allows for proper nourishment to grow the corn plants; in the space of *nepantla, la facultad* becomes possible and can be nurtured by educators. In Chapter 2, we see the role of planting seeds as Omar Davila Jr., Thalia Rodriguez, Mikaela Dacanay, Brianna Roberto, Donna Garcia, and Aaron Rivas examine a Grow-Your-Own (GYO) teacher pipeline program and the impact it has on Latina/o/x students and future educators. Through the examples in this anthology, we can underscore the systems of support that have existed for generations and have served to nurture Latina/o/x students as they navigate through the U.S. schooling system.

Once the college plant begins to grow, the husk protects the corn. Similarly, once the dream is established, institutional resources equip Latina/o/x students to navigate postsecondary pathways. Eventually, the corn is cultivated to collect the seeds. In this space, cultivation is aligned with adequate post–high school graduate preparation for Latina/o/x students. In Chapter 5, for instance, we see cultivations in practice as Brianna R. Ramirez provides insights from a summer bridge program that served to support student preparation for navigating institutionalized racism and marginalities in higher education.

Last, but certainly not least, we underscore the vital role of harvesting. This is the postgraduate preparation that includes engaging in life in ways to contribute to the next generation of Latina/o/x students. Institutional resources have been developed by building on the outcomes of previous successful programs. In Chapter 9, Samantha Prado Robledo investigates how two Chicana/Latina graduate students overcame limited institutional resources and built bridges as *nepantleras* in their respective undergraduate research programs. Based on the chapters, this anthology fundamentally emphasizes how, from planting to cultivating to harvesting, we must integrate school, family, and community to foster spaces that allow Latina/o/x youth to view themselves as capable and deserving of success, as opposed to accepting a state of *atravesada/o/xs*.

## Considerations for Practitioners and Researchers

We emphasize our original call for educators and scholars to be prepared to foster Latina/o/x student critical consciousness at both K-12 and higher education levels (Conchas & Acevedo, 2020). With both in mind, we pose the following considerations for educators, policymakers, and scholars who seek to utilize this book as a guide for their personal and professional growth.

### *Activating a Child's Facultad During Their Elementary School Years*

Although some scholars have begun to explore the impact of activating a child's *facultad,* there continues to be a gap in the literature that focuses on this activation in early schooling. Much of the existing research has focused on students in higher education institutions and the positive and long-lasting effects of the enactment of *la facultad.* Educators and scholars who aim to explore this impact should consider elementary education as a focal point and examine what types of curricula can be implemented to facilitate Latina/o/x student engagement, critical consciousness, and self-awareness. Research focused on culturally relevant pedagogy in early education has demonstrated the positive sociocultural impact of these practices (Durden et al., 2015). Among the central tenets of culturally relevant pedagogy is the rejection of deficit-based perspectives that often perpetuate oppressive stereotypes (Howard, 2003). These types of transformative practices require that educators and educational leaders be critically aware of their own positionality and its impact on students. For this to effectively support Latina/o/x students with enacting their *facultad,* critical reflection must be continuous and grounded in fostering social justice.

### *Equipping Latina/o/x Students to Navigate the Intersecting Systems of Oppression*

Scholars and practitioners should examine the power of equipping Latina/o/x students to navigate a world of racial microaggressions and intersectionality (Crenshaw, 1992). Existing scholarship has demonstrated the impact that those skillsets have on the life trajectory of Latina/o/xs and other students of color. Practitioners should consider introducing Ethnic Studies programs (including Indigenous methodologies) that have their foundations in developing the critical consciousness of Latina/o/x students. By engaging with Ethnic Studies, scholars and educators should not only seek to honor historical knowledge and traditions but also tools for assisting Latina/o/x students to navigate and resist existing systems of oppression with U.S. schools.

In addition, there is a need for scholars and practitioners to develop resources and support systems that serve the purpose of preventing deep wounds and unwanted detours in their schooling experience. One way to do this is by strengthening teacher-student relationships. As Li (2018) explains,

> Latino cultural values may play a significant role in teacher–student relationships for Latino youth. Failure to incorporate such values into practice may negatively impact teachers' relationships with Latino students. Teachers need to become familiar with the subtle nuances and explore how these values influence teacher–student relationships. (p. 404)

There is also a need for those working and doing research in the field of education to focus on the importance of community partnerships and the role of mentors for equipping Latina/o/x students with necessary tools to navigate their educational journeys. By strengthening these support systems and developing lifelong skills, Latina/o/x students can be more prepared to navigate the U.S. schooling system.

### *Preparing Latina/o/x Students to Interrupt and Transform Systems of Oppression*

As educators, educational leaders, and scholars seek to actively intervene on systems of marginalization that continue to marginalize Latina/o/x students, it is important and necessary to recognize the transformative approaches and traditions that have been passed on to us in the field of Ethnic Studies and through Indigenous epistemologies. Even through the historical marginalization of Indigenous knowledge and teachings, the symbolism of *maíz* has withstood the attempts of erasure and served as a central element of the cultural identity for Latina/o/xs. Despite the barriers that *maíz*-based philosophies have faced, scholars of color have continued to highlight the importance and impact of these teachings in academia.

Scholars and practitioners should be intentional in their approaches to intervene against oppressive systems that create barriers often faced by Latina/o/x students. Given that the U.S. schooling system continues to operate through colonial mechanisms (Conchas & Acevedo, 2020), it is necessary for educators to help dismantle the oppressive forces that impede Latina/o/x student college completion. Once understanding of the experiences of marginalized students and critically reflecting on their positionality is gained, educators and educational leaders can help facilitate the transformative action necessary for fracturing the marginalizing systems that persist in U.S. schools.

## Moving Forward

All the examples within this book are examined using transformative and Indigenous-centered approaches that attempt to build on existing literature in a manner that focuses on the experiences of Latina/o/x students at multiple levels of the educational system. Given that these Latina/o/x students are navigating their higher education journey as both *atravesada/o/xs* and *nepantlera/o/xs*, their perspectives provide valuable insights when seeking to reform and transform educational policy, practice, and research. As demonstrated throughout this anthology, these chapters highlight the need to continue to foster college access, readiness, and completion.

This book brings together scholars from across the United States who are actively contributing to the work of brokering structural power to foster Latina/o/x student success. The examples highlighted in this book underscore the critical role of educators, educational leaders, and scholars for supporting Latina/o/x students in an educational landscape that has historically treated them as outsiders. By illuminating the husks of hope, resistance, and success, we celebrate the pathways of knowledge and support created by our ancestors and passed down to our families and communities. As we reflect on the experiences of Latina/o/x students across the country, we can work to create new opportunities that allow these students to not only plant their seeds but to watch them bloom.

## Reference

Bell, D. (1992). Racial realism. *Connecticut Law Review, 24(2)*, 363–379.

Calzada, E. J., Tamis-LeMonda, C. S., & Yoshikawa, H. (2013). Familismo in Mexican and Dominican families from low-income, urban communities. *Journal of Family Issues, 34*(12), 1696–1724.

Conchas, G. Q., & Acevedo, N. (2020). *The Chicana/o/x dream: Hope, resistance and educational success*. Harvard Education Press.

Crenshaw, K. (1992). Race, gender, and sexual harassment. Southern Californian Law Review, *65*, 1476.

Durden, T. R., Escalante, E., & Blitch, K. (2015). Start with us! Culturally relevant pedagogy in the preschool classroom. *Early Childhood Education Journal, 43*, 223–232.

González, S. (2023). *Sacred maíz — Veggie mijas.* Veggie Mijas. https://www.veggiemijas.com/articles/sacred-maiz

Howard, T. C. (2003). Culturally relevant pedagogy: Ingredients for critical teacher reflection. *Theory into Practice, 42*(3), 195–202.

Li, Y. (2018). Teacher–student relationships, student engagement, and academic achievement for non-Latino and Latino youth. *Adolescent Research Review, 3*(4), 375–424.

McClung Museum of Natural History & Culture. (2022). *Plant of the month*: Corn. The University of Tennessee. https://mcclungmuseum.utk.edu/2022/08/31/plantofthemonth-corn/#:~:text=The%20term%20maize%20actually%20derives,as%20maize)%20is%20called%20Selu

## About the Authors

**Gilberto Q. Conchas** is the Wayne K. and Anita Woolfolk Hoy Endowed Chair of Education at the Pennsylvania State University. He received his PhD in sociology from the University of Michigan, Ann Arbor and his BA in sociology from the University of California, Berkeley. He is the author and coauthor of over a dozen books—including *The Color of Success, Streetsmart Schoolsmart, Cracks in the Schoolyard, Educational Policy Goes to School, The Complex Web of Inequality, The Chicana/o/x Dream, Race Frames in Education*, and *Repertoires of Racial Resistance.* Dr. Conchas has been a professor at the Harvard Graduate School of Education and the University of California at Irvine and visiting professor at the University of Southern California, San Francisco State University, University of Washington, University of Barcelona, and the University of California, Berkeley and Santa Barbara. He was also senior program officer for the Bill & Melinda Gates Foundation.

**Nancy Acevedo** is a professor in the Educational Leadership Doctoral Studies Program at California State University, San Bernardino. As an interdisciplinary scholar, she uses critical race theory and Chicana feminist theories to examine transitions along the higher education pipeline for Latina/o/x students. Dr. Acevedo's experience as a college advisor at under-resourced high schools inform her commitment to social justice; her research advocates for equitable opportunities to college preparation and aligning college access with college completion. A first-generation college student from a farmworker background, Nancy earned her B.A. from the University of California, Berkeley, her M.A. from San Jose State University, and her Ph.D. in Education with a focus on Race and Ethnic Studies at the University of California, Los Angeles.

**Victor DeAlba** is a Ph.D. candidate and graduate research assistant at the Pennsylvania State University. He was raised in the city of Lompoc, located on the Central Coast of California. He earned his A.A. in sociology from Allan Hancock College. He then transferred to UCLA where he earned his B.A. in sociology. His current research includes the power of transformative approaches and critical pedagogical spaces for amplifying Latina/o/x student voice, promoting educational opportunity for Latina/o/x students, and countering inequity in urban school systems.

**Eduardo Mosqueda** is an associate professor in the Education Department at the University of California, Santa Cruz. His research qualitatively examines the relationship between the English proficiency of ethnically and linguistically minoritized students, their access to rigorous mathematics courses, and their performance on standardized secondary school mathematics assessments. His research has implications for minoritized students' readiness and academic preparedness for college. Another area of his research examines mathematics teaching and learning in dual language education contexts to examine how students can develop mathematical proficiency across languages. Mosqueda is the co-principal investigator of the Mathematics and Language, Literacy Integration (MALLI) project, a U.S. Department of Education–funded grant to support research in math teaching and learning in dual language immersion classrooms. He has authored or co-authored articles in *Equity and Excellence in Education*, the *Journal of Urban Mathematics Education*, the *Journal of Science Teacher Education*, and *Review of Research in Education*.

**Raul Meneses Samperio** is a Ph.D. candidate in education at the University of California, Santa Cruz. His research interests lie at the intersection of education, sociology, and critical race and ethnic studies, where he engages in decolonial research methods to examine how race, class, gender, sexuality, and culture shape the experiences of undocumentized/illegalized students and teachers within educational institutions.

**Omar Davila Jr.** is assistant professor of Child Studies and director of the Future Teachers Project at Santa Clara University. He received his PhD in education from the University of California, Berkeley. Dr. Davila's research examines the nexus of education policy, political discourse, and the social construction of merit. Specifically, he investigates how social inequality is reproduced and resisted; how political ideologies shape academic contexts; and how to reimagine education to serve a transformative end. His research is published in peer-reviewed journals including *Race Ethnicity and Education, Teachers College Record,* and *Urban Education.*

**Thalia Rodriguez** is a Fellow in the Future Teachers Project at Santa Clara University. Her research interests include policies in bilingual education, child advocacy, and the importance of transformative dialogue within the classroom. Following her undergraduate experience, she plans to earn her Masters in Education, along with her teaching credentials for bilingual settings. She is co-author of a recent publication entitled *From "Teacher Shortage" to Resistance: A Critical Perspective on Political Discourse, Education, and Imagining Otherwise,* which was published in the *Teachers College Record.*

**Mikaela Dacanay** is a Fellow in the Future Teachers Project at Santa Clara University. Her research interests include emotionality, racialization, and the reproduction of unjust educational practices. As a future educator, Mikaela is passionate about educational equity and enacting holistic and transformative praxis in and out of the classroom. Most recently, she presented her work, "Transformative Possibilities: Emotionality, Resistance, and Teachers of Color," at the 2023 Critical Race Studies in Education Association Conference in Chicago, IL.

**Brianna Roberto** is a Fellow in the Future Teachers Project at Santa Clara University. Her research interests include early childhood and arts education. She was previously an assistant teacher and worked as an art tutor at St. Leo's Elementary School. Currently, Brianna serves as a camp teacher for Camp Captivate and works for Kids on Campus, the daycare center at SCU. After completing her graduate school training, Brianna plans to become an elementary school teacher.

**Donna Garcia** was a Summer Fellow in the Future Teachers Project at Santa Clara University. She is a rising senior at Sacred Heart Preparatory High School in Atherton, CA. Her research interests include racial disparities in education, students from marginalized communities, and self-advocacy among students. As a future teacher, she is passionate about challenging and redefining notions of academic success and is excited to build pathways for students from marginalized communities to thrive in our inequitable world.

**Aaron Rivas** was a Summer Fellow in the Future Teachers Project at Santa Clara University. He is a rising senior at William C. Overfelt High School in San Jose, CA. Becoming a Summer Fellow garnered interest in research on educational inequality, students of color, and public school systems. Aaron wishes to become a teacher and is passionate about finding ways to enact social change, support students of color, and dismantle structural inequality. It begins in the classroom, he argues.

**Jacey de la Torre,** a relative before all else, lives in Oakland with their wife and teaches middle school. In their free time they run, read, write, and spend time with their loved ones.

**Brianna R. Ramirez** received her Ph.D. in Education Studies with a specialization in Critical Gender Studies from UC San Diego. Her research draws from critical race feminista methodologies and pedagogies to challenge normative forms of knowledge construction in higher education and to explore the intersecting systems and structures of marginality that shape access and transition to college for Latinx students. She is currently a lecturer in the California State University (CSU) and University of California (UC) systems, teaching education, ethnic studies, and Chicanx studies courses.

**Luis M. Andrade** is a professor in the Communication & Media Studies Department at Santa Monica College located on the homelands of the Tongva and Chumash communities. Dr. Andrade's research centers on performance studies, educational equity, Latinx student education, rhetorical criticism, intercultural communication, and philosophy. Dr. Andrade's work has been featured in *Text & Performance Quarterly, Journal of Hispanic Higher Education, Journal of Diversity of Higher Education,* and in textbooks, including *This Bridge We Call Communication: Anzaldúan Approaches to Theory, Method, and Praxis,* and *Latina/o/x Communication Studies: Theories, Methods, and Practice.*

**Audrey Baca Lopez, EdD** is a first-generation scholar and servant-leader, who prioritizes student success throughout the educational pipeline. She engages with professional organizations dedicated to Latinx success, serving as a Puente mentor and holding active membership roles with the American Association of Hispanics in Higher Education (AAHHE) and California Community Colleges Organización de Latinx Empowerment, Guidance, Advocacy for Success (COLEGAS). She was a 2019 AAHHE Graduate Fellow and now serves as AAHHE's conference planning committee chair elect. Baca Lopez has over 20 years of educational experience in public and private organizations. She is a 2019 graduate of CSUSB Doctorate in Educational Leadership Program. Her dissertation research centered on critical organizational change related to California Assembly Bill 705 in a Hispanic Serving California Community College. In her previous roles, she worked as a program specialist facilitating pathways for doctoral scholar-practitioners and was an educational consultant and manager in various PK-12 school districts throughout California (specializing in literacy and language learner programs). Baca Lopez served also as an adjunct English professor for San Diego Miramar and Moreno Valley community colleges. In Fall 2022, she began teaching full-time as a tenure-track English professor for Mt. San Jacinto College.

**Arlene Cano-Matute, Ph.D.,** is the assistant director of Chicano Student Programs and co-chair of the Hispanic Serving Institution (HSI) Committee at the University of California, Riverside. As a scholar and practitioner, her work focuses on the historical and ongoing experiences of Chicana/o/x and Latina/o/x students at HSIs, participatory action research, collective memory and preservation, student affairs, and identity centers in higher education institutions.

**Alexis Meza** is a Ph.D. student in education and a UC Chancellor's Fellow at the University of California, Berkeley. His scholarship centers on the experiences/journeys of Chicanx/Latinx students at Hispanic Serving Research Institutions (HSRI) and how cultural centers facilitate student transformation at HSRIs, specifically, analyzing how these "third spaces" manifest, expand, and impact the broader university's HSRI organizational identity. He identifies as an artistic scholar who blurs the lines between artistry, research, and HSI scholarship. He has published in the *Encyclopedia of Mental Health*, *NYU Journal of Student Affairs*, and *The Journal of Hispanic Higher Education*.

**Elizabeth Claassen Thrush, Ph.D.**, is the director of Strategic Initiatives for the chancellor and provost at the University of California Riverside. Her research focuses on school-community partnerships, international comparative education, and Latina/o/x student engagement. Her professional experience spans K-12 and university teaching, international nonprofit work, and creating and scaling higher education initiatives.

**Louie F. Rodriguez** is a professor of education and the vice provost and dean of the Division of Undergraduate Education at the University of California Riverside. His research examines issues in Latina/o/x education, participatory action research, and educational equity. Dr. Rodriguez earned his doctorate from Harvard. He is the author of nearly 50 publications and 4 books, including *Intentional Excellence: The Pedagogy, Power, and Politics of Excellence in Latina/o Schools & Communities*. He has received numerous honors, including the AERA Hispanic Research Issues SIG Award for Research in Elementary, Secondary, and Postsecondary Education.

**Samantha Prado Robledo** is a first-generation college student and second-generation Mexican American. She attained a bachelor's and master's degree in sociology at California State University San Marcos and a Ph.D. in Education Studies with a Critical Gender Studies concentration at UC San Diego. Samantha has served the community in this past decade as an instructor countywide at continuing education programs as well as in community college and university as a sociology lecturer capacity. She has also engaged in research efforts that focus educational equity and underrepresented student access to higher education.

## Index